office
politics

office politics

How To Thrive In A World Of Lying,
Backstabbing and Dirty Tricks

Oliver James

Vermilion
LONDON

3 5 7 9 10 8 6 4 2

Published in 2013 by Vermilion, an imprint of Ebury Publishing
Ebury Publishing is a Random House Group company

Copyright © Oliver James 2013

Oliver James has asserted his right to be identified as the author of this Work
in accordance with the Copyright, Designs and Patents Act 1988

The Random House Group Limited Reg. No. 954009
Addresses for companies within the Random House Group can be found at
www.randomhouse.co.uk

A CIP catalogue record for this book is available from the British Library

The Random House Group Limited supports The Forest Stewardship
Council® (FSC®), the leading international forest-certification organisation.
Our books carrying the FSC label are printed on FSC®-certified paper.
FSC is the only forest-certification scheme supported by the leading
environmental organisations, including Greenpeace. Our
paper procurement policy can be found at
www.randomhouse.co.uk/environment

Printed and bound in Great Britain by Clays Ltd, St Ives PLC

Hardback ISBN: 9780091923945
Trade paperback ISBN: 9780091923952

Copies are available at special rates for bulk orders.
Contact the sales development team on 020 7840 8487 for more information.

To buy books by your favourite authors and register for offers,
visit www.randomhouse.co.uk

This book is a work of non-fiction. The names and identifying features of people
in the case studies have been changed to protect their privacy.

To John Cummins, Michael Jackson and David Macindoe (RIP),
whose thankless task it was to school me in office political skills

Contents

Introduction

Julle's boss is a nightmare. He is surly and liable to lose his temper if anything is not exactly as he wants. He frequently blames her for his mistakes.

John has two employees who are at each other's throats. He has tried to reconcile them by getting them together and having it out; he has tried talking to them individually. Nothing works.

Andrea wants a pay rise. Several others on the team do less work than her and bring less money into the business, yet they are paid more. When she points that out to her boss, he is not persuaded by her argument, and Andrea is left feeling resentful.

If you have similar everyday dilemmas, this book offers solutions. The first part explores what makes troublesome colleagues tick and suggests ways in which you can protect yourself against these types. The second part explains how office politics work and how to become better at them.

The expression 'office politics' has got a bad name. We think of them as something undesirable, unwholesome, toxic. But, as you will see, they are far from bad, just an inevitable part of professional life. They must be embraced with as much humour, self-conscious deliberation and wisdom as possible.

On a daily basis, it's absolutely unavoidable that people will find themselves in competition with one another. Interests at work frequently do not coincide. Resources, like the most stimulating tasks, the best shift hours or pots for bonuses, are finite. It is healthy for us to use our wiles to try and get the best of these for ourselves. At its simplest, that's all I mean by 'office politics': the normal wheezes everyone uses to advance their interests.

More precisely, researchers have identified four components of office political skill:

Astuteness: This is the foundation of being a good office politician: being able to read others, your organisation and yourself. If you cannot interpret the signals of people around you, there's little likelihood of you working out how to get your way. If you do not understand how your organisation works, you will be blundering about in the dark. If you are not clear what you want, how are you going to act in ways that will get it? You must try to be as astute as possible about others, your organisation and yourself.

Effectiveness: Having understood what is going on and made plans, you have to be skilled at executing them. That means knowing which combination of tactics to use, who to direct them at, choosing the right moment and performing the words and deeds effectively, always with some measure of actual thespianism – deliberate pretences and acting.

Networking: Carefully nurtured relationships, within and beyond your organisation, enable you to press the right buttons. They build your reputation, oil wheels and are vital for moving between jobs.

The appearance of sincerity: The closer the fit between who you really are and who you come across as, the better. But quite often, the inner and the outer must necessarily be different in order for you to achieve successful management of the impression you are creating. You need to be able to do this in ways that seem sincere. If your colleagues have lost faith in your honesty and integrity, it will be hard to progress.

Defined as these four skills, my suggestion to you is that there is nothing wrong with office political activity. In fact, my ambition is to help you to become much more self-aware about your use of it. If you are someone who wants to believe that you should never try to advance your interests at the expense of others using these skills, I would plead with you to think again. You are almost certainly deceiving yourself: like it or not, one in five communications we have with others contain a white lie. Many lies are said to protect others' feelings but some are necessary and healthy deceptions that advance our interests. If you can be more conscious of what you and others get up to, you will be much better able to do good for others, as well as yourself. Being shy or self-deceiving about this will only make you frustrated and resentful. You will be thwarted and outwitted by better operators. I am hoping to persuade you that there is nothing wrong with being a good office politician and improve your skills.

That does not mean I am advocating cold, selfish ruthlessness, far from it. I am not in favour of dog-eat-dog, self-preening career bestiality. Psychopaths, Machiavels and narcissists are rife in many sectors of the business world and it's in your best interests to be able to identify them and develop strategies to effectively deal with them. The first part of this book is devoted to the fascinating new evidence regarding those kinds of people. It has been proven they are the sort most likely to be making your life hell at work. There are three kinds, which overlap:

Psychopaths: Highly impulsive thrill-seekers who lack empathy for others. Think Stalin and Gordon Gekko from the film *Wall Street*. They are four times commoner* among senior executives than in the ordinary workforce.

Machiavels: Exceptionally calculating, they behave in a cold and manipulative fashion, ruthlessly pursuing their self-interest. Think Henry Kissinger and Peter Mandelson. People at or near the top* have this trait much more than those lower down the food chain.

Narcissists: Commonly perceived as vain, they are prone to grandiosity, a sense of entitlement, a desire for dominance and feelings of superiority. Think Madonna and Maradona. Senior managers are more likely* to be like this than ordinary people and, believe it or not, than mental hospital patients.

New evidence shows that people who have one of these tendencies are liable to possess the others. This Dark Triad of characteristics is very likely to be present in that person in your office who causes so much trouble.

The awful truth is that the number of such triadic people has greatly increased* in the last thirty years, how much depending on which country you live in. The reason is because the global economy increasingly demands elements of triadic behaviour in order to succeed. This is especially true of English-speaking nations, like Britain and America, but also in emerging nations, like China, India and Russia. Frankly, it's scary. Whether you work in the corporate sector, a small business or a public sector job, the system you are in is liable to reward ruthless, selfish manipulation. The likelihood of your daily working life being troubled by a person who is some mixture of psychopathic, Machiavellian and narcissistic is high. If you do not develop the skills to deal with them, they will eat you for breakfast.

In developed nations, the fundamental reason why such characters are able to thrive is the huge shift from manufacturing jobs to service sector ones. In Britain, for example, only 11 per cent of people now work in manufacturing. It is much easier to quantify what someone has produced when that object is able to be picked up or seen with your own eyes. However, determining how well or poorly a person in the social sector performs is subjective, and much more difficult to pin down. With that shift comes a crucial difference in how reward and promotion are decided.

If you work in a factory producing wooden dolls and are paid a set amount per doll, everyone knows where they stand: you either make 100 or 1,000 a day and will be paid accordingly. If you are a prodigious doll-producer, this merit may be rewarded with promotion.

Matters are completely different in the vast majority of service sector occupations. There are no objective metrics, no quantities of dolls, by which your contribution can be measured. A prime example of such a profession is television production, in which I worked, on and off, for twenty-five years. I once came upon an amusing admission of the way things work there when I saw the following sign pinned on the wall of a television production office:

THE SIX STAGES OF ANY TELEVISION PRODUCTION:
1. Enthusiasm
2. Disillusion
3. Panic
4. Hunt for the guilty
5. Punishment for the innocent
6. Reward for those who had nothing to do with it

Whether you work in television, public relations, financial services or as a nurse, it's extremely difficult to prove your achievements or for your boss to obtain hard evidence, positive or negative.

If the client is pleased by your public relations performance, your boss has little to go on objectively. The boss will be substantially influenced by what the client says about you and that often depends on whether you got on well with them. Your boss will also be heavily affected by your relationship with him or her. If they like you it will be much easier to persuade the boss that any adverse outcomes, like bad publicity, were due to someone else on the team, or to the difficultness of the subject; you can still emerge smelling of roses.

As an investment banker, you might have thought there would be objective criteria for measuring success, but it is largely not so. You can usually argue when things go wrong that it was not your fault, whilst taking credit for the positives, especially if the boss likes you. If you have a good relationship with clients, they will give positive feedback about you to your boss.

As a nurse, if many of your patients die, how can it be proven that this was your fault (assuming you are not a mass murderer)? So many other clinicians were involved in the case. As long as you are nice to patients, they will not complain about you. If you foster positive feelings in your matron, she is much less likely to blame you for mistakes, or to notice them.

In service industries, instead of objective measures, your relationship with your boss becomes critical to your appraisal, their subjective evaluation paramount. At its simplest, this is hugely influenced by whether they like you. Schmoozing works. You can use tactics like ingratiation (flattery, chameleonism – which is mirroring another person's mannerisms, way of speaking, style and ideas – and doing favours) to increase the likelihood of favourable assessment.

What others say about you behind your back, for good or ill, also affects your boss's perception. This reputation can also be manipulated by ingratiation. If you are skilled at covering your tracks whilst taking credit for what is not yours and shifting blame for your mistake on to others, so much the better for how your boss views your contributions.

Small wonder, then, that studies show that those social skills that make you likeable* and favourably appraised have become vastly more important in determining success in careers during the last thirty years in the UK: that was the period when service sector jobs replaced manufacturing.

But it is more specific than 'social skills', it is office political ones that are crucial. Studies of crude measures of personality* show that they hardly predict who will be successful. Just being outgoing or a Steady Eddy is not enough. Far, far more than the ability to do a job well or being a nice person, office political skill determines who gets to the top. To put it another way, what enables success in a great many professions is, more than any other, the ability to be an office political animal, rather than excelling at the jobs you do.

It is a pious, sacred wisdom of our age that we live in a meritocracy, or at the least, that we should do: that technical ability, hard work and intelligence enable career success. The reality is that huge surveys of all the evidence show that conventional measures of intelligence or general mental ability are very poor predictors of who will succeed. Whilst they may explain about one quarter, and therefore, yes of course being clever helps, the fact is that office political skill is much more important.

Nor does cleverness explain who is good at office politics. There is no link between how well you do on tests of intelligence and how good you are at office politics. Being clever at exams and tests does not mean you will be clever at politics. As you have probably already observed in your working life, some apparently not very bright people do extremely well, whilst many people with great educational qualifications and high IQ scores, do quite badly. The reason is varying degrees of political skill.

I am not saying that conscientiousness, integrity and ability play no part in who succeeds. The trouble is that they are not enough. In most modern occupations, the perception of your performance is more important than your actual contribution. Politics is the critical ingredient.

Into the shifting sands of this modern work environment slides the triadic person. An occupation that is an amoral desert is fertile soil for the triadic, in fact, it actively fosters it. A terrain in which it is almost impossible to objectively measure individual contributions to work outcomes makes it much easier for triadic people to succeed. The same is true if the environment is highly competitive and insecure. The boss's perception is crucial and the triadic know how to work a boss.

Being Machiavellian is extremely helpful if you want to manipulate your boss's perception of you. Being psychopathically cold and ruthless makes it far easier to shove others out of the way without guilt about the harm you may be doing or your lack of merit. Being narcissistic makes it only natural for you to 'big yourself up' and run down others. If the triadic manage to conceal these unattractive traits through skilled office politics, the triadic will thrive.

Of course, because triadic people have obnoxious attributes, they run the risk of being unpopular and gaining negative reputations. In most countries and organisations, unless they are skilled at concealing their unpleasantness and are adept at office politics, they will be held back. Indeed, a significant number of them do not succeed. But the ones who learn to conceal their unsavoury tendencies do very well.

In some societies, like America, the traits are actually rewarded. Studies show that Americans who are aggressive and rude* are more likely to get to the top. There is an epidemic of narcissism in America and Machiavellianism is celebrated by its culture. The same is increasingly true in Britain. By contrast, in most of the rest of the world, especially Asia, concealment is vital, especially of narcissism. But with skilful concealment, the triadic will thrive there too, and their national and organisational environments increasingly reward triadic behaviour. As John Lennon observed in one of his songs, we are always being told that anyone can get to the top, even working-class people, but you have to learn how to kill with a smile on your face in order to do so. To varying degrees, this applies to triadic people everywhere if they want to succeed.

This book offers you a chance to do more than survive an increasingly unpleasant world of work. In fact, you can thrive in it. Insecure employment laws, massive rewards for the undeserving and decreasing autonomy make for huge stress. It is caused by having to try ever harder to keep smiling when you feel like killing: the customer is being offensively rude but you must smile through gritted teeth. Known as 'emotional labour', having to be false in this way on a daily basis for years on end is proven to be very bad for your physical and mental health.

This book shows you how to develop the skills to cope in such a world and it explains the reasons for the shocking behaviour of your triadic colleagues. That knowledge is the spade for digging an oasis of sanity for yourself in your career. By creating a persona for coping with your work relationships, you can get as close a fit as possible between who you really are and the face you present to your colleagues. You can become savvy without becoming toxic to yourself and others. By becoming deliberate and poised in your performance, you can be more, rather than less, real. You are also more likely to end up in fulfilling occupations and in roles within them, and to contribute benignly to your family and society. Indeed, at the end of this book I conclude that office political skill is an important component of true emotional health.

Before we start, a brief account of the basis for the book. I interviewed more than fifty people from a wide variety of professions. I have gone to considerable lengths to ensure their anonymity, busily changing much more than their names. I have used these interviews extensively because I am hoping that reading the stories will help you to learn from experience. Hopefully, just hearing them is a way of having office political practice.

Interestingly, I have done interviews for previous books that covered intimate matters, like sex, money and relationships with parents, but it was often harder for the interviewees in this book to talk about their political activities than those subjects. Most people are reluctant to acknowledge to themselves what they get up to politically, let alone to others. For many it was an uncomfortable experience squeezing out the truth about their manipulations because they were only semi-aware of them. Once admitted to, they then had the unease of sharing these secrets, feeling shame or guilt in some cases.

The book is also based on the scientific evidence in this field. Only the most illuminating studies are described in any detail, mostly I have simply summarised the findings in a few sentences. Where I refer to a specific study or literature, I have provided an endnote as reference for that minority of readers who care to pursue the original research. When I have provided a reference, a * symbol appears in the text beside the relevant words, indicating that the endnotes will contain a reference relating to this page.

I have brought very little of my personal experience directly into this book, but it has helped me to understand the subject. My first career job was as a research fellow in a university that provided management consultancy services to health service professionals. Then I worked for six years as a clinical psychologist in a mental hospital before switching to television production, first a researcher, then producer, then presenter. I have also worked as a journalist for many years. These media jobs, along with some of the books I have written, have enabled me to observe a wide variety of professions from the inside.

Part One

Coping with Toxic Colleagues and Professions

Chapter 1

A Vicious Combination: Psychopathy, Machiavellianism and Narcissism

When I have mentioned that I am writing this book I have frequently received this reaction: 'Oh great, there is someone in my office who is just a nightmare. I would dearly love to know what makes them tick and how to deal with them.' Hopefully, this part of the book will be what you are looking for if you are dealing with snakes, hyenas and other dangerous office predators. Spotting over-promoted, malicious animals has become crucial for anyone hoping to survive the office jungle. Whilst most of us are usually unthreatening – the sheep, cows, pigs and other common livestock eking out a living as best we can – there are always some hungry predators above, alongside and below you, making your life a misery.

Most toxic people do not rise very far for the simple reason that they are disliked and frequently not very good at their work. However, a significant number learn to conceal their objectionable traits or manage to worm their way under the protection of a powerful patron. These people can go all the way to the very top, usually with lamentable consequences for their colleagues.

Luckily, there has been some good-quality research* done recently into their psychology. In the chapters that follow, you will gain a fresh understanding of how their minds work. Just this, in itself, should make it easier for you to cope with them. In most cases, there will be little you can do to actually beat them at their own game but at the least, having spotted them, you will have a better chance of keeping out of their way. Since the successful ones are often hard to identify, doing so is half the battle. If nothing else, by the time you have finished this part of the book, you are likely to pity as much as hate them.

The new evidence shows that the people who most cause you harm at work are likely to have three interlinked traits: psychopathy, Machiavellianism and narcissism. There is a simple test by which you can assess if someone is like that.

Picture the most problematic person you deal with at work. Now apply the following 12 statements to that person, scoring low (1) if you feel it does not apply much or at all, high if it applies quite a bit or a lot (5). Specifically, score it as follows:

A. If you 'strongly disagree' that the statement applies to them, score a 1.
B. If you 'disagree' that it applies, score 2.
C. If you feel it maybe applies sometimes but not much, score 3.
D. If you 'agree' it applies, score 4.
E. If you 'strongly agree' it applies, score 5.

Here are the statements, give each one a score for the person you have in mind.

1. They tend to exploit and trick others for self-advancement.
2. They have used lies and deception to get their way.
3. They have used ingratiation to get their way.

4. They tend to manipulate others for selfish reasons.
5. They tend not to feel regretful and apologetic after having done wrong.
6. They tend not to worry about whether their behaviour is ethical.
7. They tend to be lacking in empathy and crassly unaware of the distress they can cause others.
8. They tend to take a pretty dim view of humanity, attributing nasty motives and selfishness.
9. They tend to be hungry for admiration.
10. They tend to want to be the centre of attention.
11. They tend to aim for high statuses and signs of their importance.
12. They tend to take it for granted that other people will make extra efforts to help them.

If the person scored more than 25 out of the maximum possible of 60, this chapter will tell you a great deal about them. People scoring high on the test will be conspicuous for their disagreeableness, aggression and penchant for coercive, forceful behaviour. It means that, to a greater or lesser degree, they possess what is known as the Dark Triad of personality traits: the nearer their score to 60, the more so. (The three traits being psychopathy, Machiavellianism and narcissism.) And there is considerable overlap between the three types. To varying degrees, all tend to be socially malevolent characters with tendencies towards self-promotion, emotional coldness, duplicity and aggression. In situations where detection and punishment can be avoided, they adopt a short-term strategy that exploits others.

The discovery of the triad began with a study in 1998* that separately measured the degree of psychopathy and Machiavellianism in a large sample of people. It turned out that those with high scores on one test were very liable to score highly on the other. They were almost indistinguishable.

Machiavels have a great desire and capacity to seek power over others through deliberate manipulation. They lack emotional commitment and expression in their dealings with intimates. They reject conventional morality, being largely free of ideologies or ethical belief systems. They are plausible, they do not immediately appear to be grossly disturbed or otherwise conspicuously weird.

All these traits were also found in that significant proportion of psychopaths who live in the community. Of course, some psychopaths are in prison or display signs of mental illness, which lead to psychiatric treatment. But the great majority manage to remain at large, undetected.

The classic list of primary psychopathic traits is:

> Glibness and superficial charm
> Grandiosity
> Pathological lying
> Conning and manipulation
> Lack of remorse or guilt
> Superficial emotions
> Callous lack of empathy for others
> Failure to accept responsibility

In addition, psychopaths tend to have sex lives in which they treat people as objects and often their sexual relationships are separated from the rest of their social existence. If married, they are prone to divorce, remarriage and further divorces. If criminal, they show versatility, committing a wide variety of crimes.

In a series of further studies* after the first in 1998, it was shown again that Machiavels are just as likely to have these traits as psychopaths living in the community (sometimes called 'successful' or 'subclinical' psychopaths): both groups are antisocial people who nonetheless often manage to keep out of prison and mental hospital.

In 2002, narcissism was added to the mix*, providing hard evidence of the Dark Triad of personalities. In a normal sample of 245 students, there was considerable overlap between the three categories: if someone scored high on narcissism, they were also likely to do so on Machiavellianism and psychopathy. Each category was distinct, yet similar.

This finding was repeated in 2006*, with the interesting twist that there had been a significant increase in Machiavellianism in the previous twenty-five years: average scores on the Machiavel test were significantly higher when compared with results from studies using the same test twenty-five years ago. It was speculated that American society had become much more competitive and materialistic during those years (1980–2006), and that these traits might be necessary to succeed in this type of society. By implication, since psychopaths are so similar to Machiavels, it is likely there has been a significant growth in psychopathy too. There is also strong evidence from other studies that narcissism greatly increased during that period.

A further study explored the issue* of how such potentially unpopular people could thrive in civilised societies. After all, they are disagreeable, with exaggerated self-esteem, individualistic and competitive, and conspicuously lacking in altruism. Combined with their glib charm, the researchers suggested that they were reminiscent in many respects of the popular character James Bond. Whilst being like this carries costs, such as unpopularity and a bad reputation, they were sometimes able to extract what they wanted from their environment by being so ruthlessly self-serving.

In accord with the Bond image, it was proven that such people play fast and loose in their love lives. They are more likely to poach* partners from other couples and to be poached from themselves, so their relationships tend not to last. They are less likely to feel intimate connection with lovers*. Detailed examination of their romantic style* revealed game playing and a detached, cerebral attitude. They avoid getting too dependent, making promiscuity likelier. Loving with the head rather than heart reflected a limited capacity for empathy, although they are often desperate for love and confuse it with sex.

Their impatience and need for immediate gratification* also drives their sex lives, so that if they feel desire for someone, they have to act on it without regard for the consequences in other existing relationships. This greedy neediness means that, given the choice, triadic people prefer to take $100 today over $1,000 in a year's time and they are more prone to short-term hits from stimulants like alcohol, cigarettes and illegal drugs. Their lack of self-control means they are more prone to symptoms of adult Attention Deficit Hyperactivity Disorder (twitchy people with a short concentration span who find it hard to sit still). The psychopathic aspect of the triad explains many of these tendencies.

Yet, confusingly, because they are Machiavellian as well, they have a considerable capacity to anticipate the future. Despite being impulsive, 'buy now, pay later' people, they are also very skilled at planning ahead. It makes them proactive in trying to control their environment, adept at manipulating desired outcomes and better able to anticipate them. An ability to control others and predict circumstances is adaptive if pursuing an exploitative approach to the world. The triadic are, therefore, a strange combination of impulsiveness and manipulative calculation.

Allied to this, narcissism provides inflated self-confidence. This can rub off on others positively, at least in superficial relationships, so that their self-publicity is bought into, the razzle-dazzle of the con artist. Repeated experience of successful social exploitation makes them better at predicting what will happen next time. Their psychopathy attracts them to high-stakes, high-risk situations where being a colourful chancer and blagger is actually advantageous.

Humour can be one of their weapons*. Machiavels are prone to a negative style that puts others down or humiliates them in front of peers, using aggressively disparaging jests, or the threat thereof. Done skilfully it can undermine rivals and increase their status in the eyes of peers and bosses. Psychopaths are oblivious to the emotional impact their words have on others, sometimes providing a freedom and range to their jokes that can make them funnier. By contrast, narcissistic individuals may make more people-pleasing jokes, perhaps excelling at mimicry, heightening their self-esteem and increasing popularity. Their narcissism gives you a feeling that they are self-absorbed show-offs, yet you may not be able to help laughing at their entertaining jokes and personae, sometimes meaning that you give them the benefit of the doubt as 'lovable rogues'. Depending on the precise mixture of the triadic traits, through trial and error, they discover the style that is maximally self-serving to them.

Childhood maltreatment explains why some people are triadic and not others. Feeling deprived in infancy, neglected as a toddler and suffering abusive, traumatic care in childhood predisposes a person to be short term in thinking, impulsive, distrustful, manipulative and self-serving, and to need the exaggerated self-esteem of narcissism. They lack identity, having been let down by their parents, invisible to them and maltreated. This lack of identity gives them fluid, plastic personalities, which are able to adapt quickly to the situation they are in, and a heightened awareness of what others may be thinking or feeling for purposes of manipulation: so they can be cerebrally empathic even whilst they are emotionally unempathic. By contrast, having needs met in early life leads to a secure pattern of relationships with others, longer-term thinking and stable romantic partnerships.

Having one of the triadic traits makes you likely to have many of the traits of the others, but in most cases, one trait is predominant. I will present each one separately therefore, including analysis of how to cope with them. Of course, if the reader has recognised themselves as triadic, what I have to say will be of considerable interest too …

Chapter 2

Psychopaths

One per cent of the population are psychopaths, which translates into 600,000 Britons, and 3 million Americans. About one quarter of the British prison population fits the profile, but that is only 15,000 people. This means that the vast majority are at liberty, and in your lifetime you are likely to know one well. They are to be found everywhere, not just in films (Hannibal Lecter in *The Silence of the Lambs*), on TV (Tony Soprano from *The Sopranos*), psychological crime novels (Patricia Highsmith's Ripley) and romantic fiction (Jilly Cooper's Rupert Campbell-Black) but among your friends, colleagues and, if you are honest, they probably echo in some of your own behaviour.

Whilst not necessarily getting to the top*, many psychopaths manage to sustain careers that are reasonably successful, made all the easier by the rapidity with which people now move between companies and professions. For example, Rat was the nickname of an ambitious assistant director who worked in a large advertising film production company when I interviewed him. At that point he was twenty-five years old. He is enormous, both in stature and girth, his huge hands and feet making him seem like a giant.

From a young age he has suffered from such a severe skin problem that any contact with water is damaging. He has to apply cream all over his body, morning and evening, to avoid rashes and dryness. In some respects he resembles an enormous reptile and, just as chameleons change the colour of their skin, so does Rat's personality change in the presence of others. Like them, too, he sheds his skin, it literally flakes off him, but he also changes it according to his social environment. His affections are skin deep, you could say he is not comfortable in his skin, that you would not want to be in it. On Saturday nights he tends to get 'out of his skin', drinking enormous amounts of alcohol and taking illegal drugs.

Rat had an unresponsive and cold mother, a lawyer, and her relationship with her equally uncongenial, unempathic ex-husband is rocky. Rat was neglected to the point of abuse as a baby and toddler, and loathes both his parents.

His relationships with girlfriends are savage. Talking of his current one, he said, 'Hmm, yes, we did do something interesting in the park near Chelsea Bridge last week, very sexy. But something is going to have to be done about her, she is getting too serious.' He went on to say that he intends to 'sack' her. He speaks of 'my harem' when referring to the various women he has sexual encounters with from time to time.

Bill, the colleague of his who introduced Rat to me, discovered a mournfully angry postcard from one of his ex-girlfriends. It read: 'Rat: Don't bother to write. I think it is a pity that you seem unable to give much of yourself, in all ways, to anyone but yourself. It is a shame because I had thought a while ago that things boded well.'

Bill felt much the same after his period of working with Rat.

As the project producer, Bill was the boss but Rat paid no attention to their different statuses within the organisation. At their first meeting, Rat launched into a series of quick-fire questions. He asked about Bill's previous projects, about his personal preferences in a strange variety of domains ('Have you ever had a bisexual experience? Do you like slugs?'). The questions seemed a little crazy at times, given that they had just met and were only colleagues. He paused at one point to ask 'Do you mind my asking you these questions?' only to plunge on, apparently eager to test out how easy it would be to establish his dominance. He handed Bill his show reel and a creepy poem about a slug that he had written (one that was apparently about himself). He subsequently badgered Bill when he had not had time to look at them and once he had, closely questioned him on his reaction, as if he had set Bill some kind of test. The Machiavel was at work alongside the psychopath from the start.

His coldness was chilling. Their boss felt guilty about the recent suicide of his son, who, by a remarkable coincidence, had the nickname Rat as well. Rat said, 'I can't really miss with the boss, can I, given my name and what happened to his son?' There were no signs of empathy for the boss's loss, only a chance to exploit the tragedy for self-advancement. He presented himself to their boss as a vulnerable young person seeking to express himself, in need of help, a creative figure battling to produce real art in a commercial world, exactly the image the boss had of the industry. He pretended to be eager to learn from the 'Master', as he called the boss when in his presence, faking unlimited admiration for a man that he not very secretly despised, as he made clear whenever the boss was absent.

On the only occasion that Bill introduced me to him in person, I witnessed an exchange between Rat and a colleague in the company canteen that indicated how disturbed and disturbing he was. She was a woman he had known at university, Suzy, who was relatively junior to him in the hierarchy and who he had not seen for a few years. She wandered up and said hello. Rat turned to Bill and said by way of introduction, 'The last time I saw Suzy she was stark naked', a reference to a photographic project they had done together.

It seemed clear that Rat felt the need to say this because he was stripped bare by her presence, his emotional thin skin making him anxious but also, his fears that the psychopathy of his personality would be exposed. He feared she would reveal facts about his past sex life and relations with his parents. Feeling suddenly naked, he instantly passed the unease over to her by evoking her naked body among strangers.

Psychoanalysts label this kind of mental operation 'projection', the evacuation of an unwanted experience into someone else. The thought process entailed is: 'I feel dreadful. I do not like feeling this so I will use you as a dustbin for my unwanted emotion by attributing it to you in my mind.' To the extent that the feeling is not dissipated merely by thought, they may need to do or say something that makes you actually feel it. Rat needed to be reassured by Suzy's reaction, her embarrassed, discomfited expression, to be able to avoid his fear of exposure. Had she not reacted at all he might have needed to expand on his comment until she was as visibly humiliated and vulnerable as he felt inside.

The whole operation was probably unconscious. Rat probably had no idea at all that this was what he was doing and thought he was simply making a bit of a joke, finding a jolly way to say hello after all these years. Whilst all of us project from time to time, psychopaths do it more often and are more likely to be compelled to commit the emotional rape of forcing their unwanted emotions into others, rather than keeping their feelings to themselves.

One of the key signs that you have been in the company of some-one with this habit is the unaccountable discomfort or dissatisfaction or depression they leave you with afterwards. You have been the dustbin for their emotional rubbish. Frequently, they are wrestling with a feeling of powerlessness. On the wall of Rat's office was a headline cut from a news-paper that seemed to back up his need for power that was fuelled by his insecurities. It read: 'BIG RAT IS BACK IN CONTROL'.

Bill found working with Rat a nightmare. Nothing he said could be trusted. Bill had to learn to make the assumption that anything Rat said to him was untrue unless proved otherwise. Rat constantly plotted with their colleagues and his lies about this made it hard to know what was going on. Bizarrely, he insisted on sitting in on phone calls that Bill made, clev-erly contriving the imposition in ways that were hard to challenge. Yet he was constantly going behind Bill's back himself. If challenged about his Machiavellian antics, Rat would lie but it was almost impossible to prove his duplicity. On one occasion, Bill happened to overhear Rat talking with a colleague, clearly hatching a plan to do a particular shoot in a way that Bill did not want. Bill triumphantly exposed them, yet when he took the matter to the boss, the boss upheld Rat's account and told Bill to calm down, supported by the colleague, whom Rat had managed to turn against Bill.

Rat's serious incompetence was glossed over: he failed, for example, to switch on a key bit of equipment, which lost them a day's footage. Sometimes his lies were to protect crude selfishness. Having eaten all the sandwiches one lunchtime when on location, he claimed there had been none. Five minutes later a colleague who had witnessed him eating them happened to ask if he had enjoyed the sandwiches. He replied 'delicious' without missing a beat, giving Bill a strange smile, as if defying him to say that he had just said there had been none. It was crazy-making.

The climax came when Bill was told that the advertisement he had come up with, executed and filmed was being given to Rat to edit. Rat had talked the boss into being given the opportunity to work on it, and the boss was determined to let the 'creative, young, exciting' Rat have a go. Incredibly, when he made a mess of it, it did not matter. Whilst Bill was finally given control back and allowed to complete the work, he emerged from the project portrayed as having been the weak link, and what credit there was, was given to Rat.

However, five years later, Rat's antisocial behaviour has caught up with him. Soon after his work with Bill he moved from advertising to feature film production, but he found himself increasingly unable to get jobs. A shift into television briefly bailed him out but today he has been forced to give up filming of all kinds, and works as a wedding photographer. His reputation eventually brought him down, because he was not skilful enough at concealing his malevolence.

Whilst the media and advertising includes a great deal of people who are primarily psychotic, they can be found in all areas of work. And like Rat, a great many triadic people who are primarily psychopathic eventually find it hard to progress in their careers because their reputation starts to precede them. Most become more or less unconstructive and malicious burdens on society. But there is a small and fascinating minority who manage to make a virtue of their characters and become hugely successful, for example, in the world of business. A key study* showed that senior American executives are four times more likely than the general population (4 per cent versus 1 per cent) to be subclinical psychopaths. These have been frequently portrayed in films and books, like the character Gordon Gekko in Oliver Stone's film *Wall Street*.

An element of implacable ruthlessness and heartlessness can help in reaching the top, especially in the economies of the English-speaking world, and in the emerging economies, like China, India and Russia. This most often comes into the public eye when they cross the line into criminality. It is far easier to actually swindle shareholders or investors if you feel no sympathy for them. This was true of some of the key players in the Enron and WorldCom scandals, who ended up in jail, or the corrupt figures who are periodically executed in China and India for their crimes, some of whom have been very publicly unconcerned about bankrupting relatives and friends whilst avoiding the same fate themselves.

But the key to being a successful psychopath is concealment about their personae and past deceits. The British newspaper and publishing magnate Robert Maxwell's fiscal juggling act was a perfect analogy for the way the psychopathic mind operates, even if his fraudulent behaviour did eventually sink him. None of the institutions that lent him money knew about the others. So long as he could keep them in the dark about his other creditors, he kept his head above water. Likewise he kept his different selves in separate mental compartments. David Astor, another newspaper proprietor of that time, a man of impeccable morality, once told me the story of a surprise visit he received from Maxwell in the early 1970s, illustrating this.

Astor hardly knew him but was aware of his reputation. It is a matter of public record that Maxwell was a narcissistic bully. His tyranny towards his sons, who worked for him, was little different to that meted out to his employees. One day, Astor was sitting in his office when he received a call from Maxwell, saying that he was sitting outside in his car and asking if he could come and visit him immediately about a matter of great importance. Astor ushered him in and Maxwell immediately embarked on an account of how he was failing in many different aspects of his life, including his marriage and his business, although this was many years before his eventual downfall. He became increasingly emotional, eventually bursting into tears. Astor was completely mystified as to why he had been chosen as the recipient for this state of vulnerable despair and eventually, Maxwell departed, Astor never hearing from him again. Maxwell probably operated through a menagerie of sub-personalities, of which this vulnerable person was but one, albeit rarely revealed to others.

Many years later, Maxwell was found dead having fallen off his yacht in the sea. It remains unclear whether he jumped, was pushed or had an accident, but a few days later it emerged that he had been siphoning off money from his company's pension fund to keep debtors at bay. Faced with the certainty of exposure, what eventually sank Maxwell was probably not a fear of humiliation but of madness. For those living multiple lives the worst nightmare is all the different personae being brought together in the same room, usually a court or a psychiatrist's surgery. A terrifying incoherence and sense of falling apart beckon. Just as the Boston Strangler (played in the film by Tony Curtis) went mad when the psychiatrists presented him with indisputable evidence of the murderous sides of his personality, so might Maxwell have done if he had stayed to face the music.

The violently criminal variety of psychopath is well documented in films and crime fiction. I once spent three months in a prison observing such a person, a psychopath called Al, for a TV documentary. This was someone who had groomed and raped his daughters and committed many other grievous crimes. He told me that from as young as he could remember other people seemed like 'Cardboard cut-outs. I remember thinking "How do I know people are real?" I'd get up during the night and go into my parents' bedroom to look at them. I would twist my sister's arm and she would say "you're hurting me" but I never really thought she meant it'. He told me he never believed that his parents were really his and that he trusted no one: 'I used to ask my mum [the same] questions just to see if she'd say the same as last time.'

I showed a video recording of Al to a television colleague whom I knew only slightly. His response so horrified me that I wrote it down afterwards. He asked me, 'As a psychologist would you say those sorts of childhood experiences mean he's different from most people in some way?' He continued, 'Surely all children think like that about their parents? I certainly was never sure if mine were real – or that other people were.' As we shall see in Chapter 6, the production staff of the television industry has more than its fair share of triadic people, including those who are primarily psychopathic.

Sure enough, when I got to know him better, this television producer turned out to be every bit as psychopathic as Al. Although I have since discovered that most of the people who have worked with him know he is like this, he continues to shuffle the pack with sufficient skill that, so far, he manages to stay ahead of the game in his career.

Whether successful or not, these people leave us feeling ripped off emotionally and they steal our ideas, money and anything that we value (especially the last, for they value nothing; their envy and destructiveness towards what we cherish know no bounds). A chief executive at a bank can inflict widespread damage; the risk-taking part of his personality means that he puts the savings and pensions of the people who bank with him on the line, whilst his incapacity for empathy means that he doesn't care when his schemes fall through.

Difficult as it is to deal with them, it may be some consolation that these people are deeply dissatisfied. They live in permanent fear of being exposed as the fakes they are convinced they are. Their inner lives are so barren that most of the time they feel desperate for any kind of human contact. Sadly, if they seek professional help, they soon realise that nothing and no one can assist them. There are no drugs that can enable them to feel for others. If psychotherapy is to work, the patient must be capable of forming emotional ties with the therapist, something they cannot do.

An interesting example of a conventionally successful triadic psychopath is Jan, a highly respected academic who is also a serial killer of the careers of the patrons who have helped her on her way, and those of her rivals. Although excellent at passing exams, she has little capacity for original thought. She has a great talent for acquiring, and taking credit for, others' ideas.

As soon as it was expedient, she dumped the two men who mothered her through her doctorate, and subsequently conspired to create false allegations of academic corruption by one of them who had shown her nothing but kindness. She accused her next employer of malpractice as well but only after she had moved to a powerful position in a research institute (whose director now rues the day he ever met her). She has never shown true remorse for her disloyalties, although she sometimes feigns it.

Today she is near the top of her field yet very few of her present colleagues know anything about these and her many other malicious transactions because, unlike Rat, she has a remarkable capacity for covering her traces. They would find it hard to believe such stories about her because, brilliantly, her persona is the quintessence of authenticity. It seems unlikely that she will ever be exposed.

On first meeting Jan, you could scarcely imagine a more unassuming, retiring presence. She is short of stature, modest in demeanour. Her clothing is functional and asexual. She speaks quietly, seems shy. There were no signs at all that she was a predatory subclinical psychopath when Gerald was first introduced to her.

Both were originally students of animal behaviour (known as ethology). A colleague put them in touch because they shared an interest in the harm done to animals by hunting. Jan had been employed as a research assistant following her doctorate, although at the time of their meeting, she was at home full-time caring for her second child, a newborn daughter. Gerald had trained as a vet and was eagerly seeking funding for a study to test the long-term effects of the stress on foxes and deer of being pursued by hounds and hunters. He had set up a charity to carry out this research, although as yet, it had no money. But having had a privileged upbringing, he had many contacts and believed he would be able to attract enough to support the work.

Over a couple of years they worked on a proposal for a major study. Gerald favoured a large-scale survey following several hundred foxes and deer over five years. Jan gave him good reason to suppose she agreed with this plan, although in retrospect he was able to recall odd comments she had made that subtly distanced herself from its details. He had many original ideas about what to study and how to do it, which he set out in a scientific monograph. This was sent to Gabriel, a leading authority in the field, who offered a favourable evaluation. Gerald and Gabriel met up and discussed the study. Jan was eager to meet Gabriel too, so Gerald sent him examples of her scientific work and arranged for them to meet.

Following that meeting, Gerald was puzzled to receive a letter from Gabriel stating that he did not believe he had either the scientific or administrative skills to conduct the study. Instead, he advocated something more along the lines, it later emerged, that Jan was suggesting, a much smaller-scale study. This was the first of many instances in which Jan was to use Gerald to advance herself. She had very deliberately poisoned Gabriel against Gerald. Alas, Gerald was not just innocent, he was naive. Although he was upset that Gabriel no longer seemed to support him, he was incapable of imagining that Jan could have behaved in this way.

At the next meeting of the trustees of the charity he had set up, he was astonished when Jan demanded that he present a copy of the letter from Gabriel to the assembled company. At that point it was obvious that she had schemed to have it written so that she would be able to use it to influence the trustees, who had control over the project. When Gerald expressed concern, she subtly deflected him, maintaining that they were still of the same mind and claiming she had had no influence on Gabriel's letter. Gerald naively bought this story.

He used his contacts to obtain funding for a pilot study by Jan at a top university. At this stage in their relationship, he was still blind to the real-ity of her self-advancement. She was not happy in her marriage and before taking up her new post, she sought to bind him closer to her. One night, when he was drunk, she seduced him. Still he was unable to see how manipulative she was. He later learnt that she was often unfaithful to her husband, when it suited her career.

Over the next few years, Gerald became very busy in activist interven-tions against hunting and had less time to spare for research. However, he continued to feel passionately that the research project he had in mind should be done and was led to believe Jan would conduct it, assisted by him but headed by her. To this end, he introduced her to a very wealthy man who was interested in these matters. This man was an aristocrat and when he described the benefactor to Jan, who affected a fashionable polit-ical rectitude in her values, she sneered at him, making jokes about what a pointless, privileged person he was. For once, Gerald showed some astute-ness, albeit on her behalf. He warned Jan that she would need to stop thinking like that and prepare herself for what would be the most impor-tant meeting of her life. A dramatic shift occurred in her attitude.

At the meeting she was charm itself, the benefactor was easily bowled over and developed an infatuation for her. A large sum of money was obtained to fund a study but, to Gerald's horror, the study was much less ambitious than the decisive one he had in mind. It was a study that suited Jan's ambitions, one that would advance her career and use up much less of her time. But it had none of the ground-breaking features he had hoped for, and was largely a repeat of similar work already done.

None of the work that Jan did was original, it was always targeted to the academic establishment in her field, enabling her to then obtain research grants for still more studies. Most of her concern for animal welfare was feigned.

Meanwhile, Gerald had finally got around to submitting the doctorate in order to have academic credibility. He consulted Jan as to whom to approach to be an independent assessor of the work. She recommended someone who she well knew would oppose its arguments. Sure enough, the doctorate was turned down.

Finally the scales fell from Gerald's eyes. It simply had not dawned on him that Jan would do something as harmful to him as to suggest an assessor who would reject his work. His mind did not work like that, so he had been unable to imagine a supposed friend and colleague behaving in such a way. Reluctantly, he acknowledged to himself that this was the kind of person she was. He realised now that Jan had betrayed every single patron she had had. Her doctoral supervisor had been appalled when she took the first grant she had obtained through Gerald to another university. She also plotted with enemies of three other patrons to expose them as fraudulent, successfully so, in two cases. She seemed to have no guilt about this, despite the great help these people had provided to her. There was something pathological about her destructiveness towards them, the opposite of gratitude.

By now, Jan had left her husband and married another researcher. Together they advanced, eventually obtaining professorships at a department in a university. Meanwhile, despite secretly despising the wealthy benefactor who continued to provide large sums of money, they had both become firm family friends. Also naive like Gerald, the benefactor and his wife perceived Jan as an authentic, decent person with no self-interest. With ease she outwitted their advisers and was able to spend the money as she pleased, becoming affluent as well as powerful, buying a large and expensive home.

From time to time, Jan still made overtures to Gerald. At one point, she suggested they jointly author a scientific paper, although it was simply a rewritten version of something by him that he had shown her. When he replied that he did not have time to do this, she went ahead and published it alone, under her name. Finally, Gerald was able to see Jan for what she was, someone with no moral centre. He also realised the lengths to which she was willing to go in order to further her interests. On one occasion there was a meeting between him, Jan and her second husband. Jan shed tears, making her husband defensive of her and implying that it was Gerald who was the devious one.

Many years later, Jan contacted Gerald, who had long since ceased to have dealings with her. She appeared at his home and declared that she wished to apologise for having misled him. Now much more worldly wise, he did not accept her apologies. Again, she shed tears and this only served to harden his heart: it emerged that she had only come to visit him in the hope that he could help her obtain yet another favour.

Interestingly, he came to the conclusion that on the two occasions she wept, there was an element of genuine distress. This was not the upset of true remorse, however. In both cases, in part, the tears served a pragmatic purpose, and were attempts to obtain something from him. However, based on his earlier knowledge of her, he came to the conclusion that this was a desperately unhappy person. The tears were of regret at being what she was: someone incapable of authentic dealings with anyone.

In terms of triadic traits, Jan was strongly psychopathic, actually stealing some of the money she was given to do research with, but able to get away with it. She was also a superb Machiavel, her game-playing invisible to almost everyone. Her narcissism was exceptionally buried. Unlike most narcissists, she had none of their usual tendency to want to be the centre of attention and to show off. At public events, for example, if she did make a comment on a scientific paper that had been presented by a colleague, she would do it in a way that aimed to hole the work below the water-line. That this was secretly a narcissistic desire to prove her superiority was wholly concealed by the low-key, modest and seemingly objective manner of speech and presentation. It was dressed up as a sturdy concern with the truth and as an honest attempt to engage with a scientific peer. Nonetheless, in a very rare instance of honesty, she revealed to Gerard late one night that, deep down, she felt wholly superior to everyone.

Jan is a lethal variant of the triadic psychopath. It takes exceptional perception to spot them and if you do so, the only solution is to keep well away. It takes years to truly know their psychopathy since they are so good at covering their tracks. If you know a high achiever with this modest, unassuming and unthreatening presence, what you see may indeed be what you get. But it's worth pondering how they got there. Their story will be that it's purely on merit and that may be true. But if there is more to their story than that, watch out. Do not share your ideas with them. Keep a close eye out for defamatory misinformation being spread by them to your peers and superiors. Jan is atypical of psychopaths, both in her success and skill in concealment of the tendency. But be warned, they are the most dangerous of predators in the office jungle.

Gerald was exceptionally naive but even astute people find it very hard to conceive of the malice and coldness of triadic psychopaths. If you are normally astute, it is vital that you allow the possibility of these things if you are to protect yourself. You must be alert to this as possibly existing in the most unlikely people.

The malice of triadic psychopaths is beyond most people's comprehension and therefore, very hard to factor into your dealings with them. It is especially triggered if you cherish something. I had a particularly strik-ing experience of this many years ago. I happened to be at a party where I met an actor who has since become world famous. At that time he was unknown and seemed engaging enough. We had a lively discussion about whether actors are people who lack identity and self-esteem, and use the performance of fictional roles in theatrical or cinematic productions to confer identity and make themselves feel loved. At the end of the evening he gave me a lift home. I had been asked by our host to bring my collection of Greatest Hits audiotapes to the party and, on getting out of the actor's car, forgot to take them with me.

Fortunately, we had exchanged phone numbers but however many messages I left, he never replied. We had friends in common, so I con-tacted them and asked them to raise the matter of my beloved tapes with him. After some weeks, eventually, one of them let me know that the actor was too 'embarrassed' to return them. This placed me in a bizarre position. Should I report the theft to the police? Should I go round to his flat and demand them back? In the end, I gave up, realising that there was nothing I could do. He had simply stolen something I had cherished.

Years later, after this man had become a Hollywood star, a mutual acquaintance told me that the actor was known to be a triadic man of great cruelty. He had held on to the tapes because he knew it would upset me.

If you have been forced into close professional proximity with a triadic psychopath, it should be clear by now that you can expect a lot of trouble. There is painfully little you can do to protect yourself.

The most important step is to identify that the person is as you suspect. With someone like Rat, that is relatively easy. Thankfully, plenty of them are all too obvious. One interviewee described an extraordinarily vicious executive he had to deal with whose psychopathy was manifest from the start. They met just after the executive had got back from a foreign trip. He had had to come back a day early because it was his forty-third wedding anniversary. The interviewee congratulated him and received the chilling reply, 'Thank you. As my father would have said, "Forty-three years of undetected crime."'

Once your astuteness radar has picked up that you are in the presence of someone cruel and cold, the next step is to do your best to put as much organisational space as possible between you and them. Of course, that is often not possible. In which case, as described, you must be self-conscious in taking care to identify their ploys as they happen:

⟩ When they project their own unhappiness on to you, using you as a dustbin, try to see it happening and in your mind, pass it back to them. If you are feeling humiliated or brutalised, that is how they are feeling. Whilst still in their presence, it may be strategically wise to pretend to look as if they have succeeded, and to allow your face to display being wounded, but as soon as they are gone, picture them as a dustbin and imagine yourself wrapping their unhappy emotion up in a tissue and dumping it back in their bin.

⟩ Learn to assume that everything they are telling you is a lie, until evidence to the contrary emerges. This *Alice in Wonderland* way of thinking is hard to develop, but it helps a great deal in understanding what is going on, even though it makes you feel as if you are going crazy.

⟩ Be at pains to establish what this person is saying about you to colleagues. Without becoming paranoid, you need to assume that they will be telling the most astonishing untruths about you. Having identified them, there is at least a chance that you will be able to clear your name.

In reading this account of the triadic psychopath you may already have noticed how much they overlap with the Machiavel. Nonetheless, there are some very important differences, insofar as the psychopathy of the

Psychopaths

Machiavel is relatively weak. Whereas there is disturbingly little you can do to protect yourself from psychopaths, if Machiavels cannot be beaten at their own game, you can at least get your head around the idea that they are game players.

Chapter 3

Machiavels

The classic Machiavel* has some or all of the following traits:

> ⟩ Resistant to social influences
> ⟩ Hides personal convictions well
> ⟩ Readily changes positions in arguments
> ⟩ Highly convincing when telling the truth
> ⟩ Resistant to confessing mistakes or lies
> ⟩ Suspicious of others' motives
> ⟩ Does not assume reciprocity in relationships – expects nothing back from you, does not return favours
> ⟩ Withholds judgement of others' likely motives
> ⟩ Able to change strategy depending on the situation
> ⟩ Exploitative, but not viciously so
> ⟩ Exploits more if others can't retaliate
> ⟩ Not susceptible to appeals for compliance, cooperation or attitude change
> ⟩ Never obviously manipulative
> ⟩ Prefers fluid environments
> ⟩ Preferred by peers as leader
> ⟩ Preferred by peers as work partner

Compared with Machiavels, those who score low on the Machiavel test, people who I call non-Machiavels, are like this:

> ⟩ Vulnerable to others' opinions
> ⟩ Wears convictions on sleeve
> ⟩ Clings to convictions
> ⟩ Confesses fairly readily
> ⟩ Less convincing when telling truth
> ⟩ Accepts others' motives at face value
> ⟩ Makes gross assumptions about what others are thinking
> ⟩ Assumes reciprocity
> ⟩ Believes others 'ought' to act in certain ways
> ⟩ Becomes locked into a single course of action
> ⟩ Tells it like it is
> ⟩ Sensitive to others' emotions
> ⟩ May appear unreasonable in negotiations
> ⟩ Reluctant to exploit
> ⟩ Reacts in socially desirable, sometimes people-pleasing, ways
> ⟩ Seeks stable environments

Not all Machiavels are triadic. Some are characterised as 'benign', because they ultimately use their game-playing skills for the benefit and others and the greater good. Some great leaders, like Nelson Mandela or Mahatma Gandhi, fit this profile. But when the Machiavel is triadic, their manipulations are predatory and wholly self-serving. That means that when you identify a Machiavellian colleague, you should not assume they are triadic but if you decide that they are, you need to take steps to protect yourself.

A measure of Machiavellianism is vital for self-defence and self-advancement, unless you really do not care about your career or are masochistic. The items on the list of traits of non-Machiavels, described above, which need to be changed if you have them are:

Vulnerability to others' opinions: you need to develop your own ideas, not just float along swayed by the last person you talked to.

Wearing convictions on your sleeve: doing so makes you vulnerable to unscrupulous colleagues.

Clinging to convictions: convictions are fine, but if you do not conceal them and appear to show flexibility where it is needed, you run the risk of being outmanoeuvred.

Confessing fairly readily: believing that honesty is always a good thing ignores the fact that others may be lying and that you end up being a mug who is easily exploited. Some white lying in all relationships is essential.

Being less convincing when telling the truth: oddly, if you are so earnest and honest, some people will assume it is a strategy and disbelieve you – you are too good to be true.

Accepting others' motives at face value: the word for this is naivety. Whilst innocence has it merits, in that you are playful and optimistic, naivety is simply failing to grasp what is going on around you, which is childish rather than the child-like virtue of innocence.

Making gross assumptions about what others are thinking: paranoia and wild attributions of motive are common among non-Machiavels because they are so unsure about what others are up to.

Assuming reciprocity: the best is not always for the best in the best of all possible worlds. Deal with the imperfect world you are in and be astute when doing favours. Triadic colleagues will not return them.

Believing others ought to act in certain ways: whilst it is fine to have your own moral code, expecting everyone else to live up to it is childish and egotistical. Never mind 'ought', you have to live in the real world of what actually happens.

Becoming locked into a single course of action: feeling at sea, the non-Machiavel withdraws into inflexible positions on points of principle. This may lead to some winning of battles but nearly always ends with a lost war. Prone to a faith in rationality, you risk excessive idealism about what can be achieved by being right.

May appear unreasonable in negotiations: outwitted by more astute and flexible colleagues, the non-Machiavel can become emotional, which is only an effective bargaining tool when done strategically, rather than driven by genuine beliefs.

Seeking stable environments: alas, this is increasingly rare in a shifting and unstable global economy. You must not expect the modern work environment to provide you with security, unless you live in northern mainland Western Europe. If you are an emotionally insecure person, alas, it may be best for you to get therapeutic help. In many countries today, you will be cut very little slack by employers or the job market.

Having said all this, even if you are moderately Machiavellian and astute, you will have difficulty outwitting triadic Machiavels who are skilled.

Terry is a textbook example of the triadic kind. From a poor background, he has built up a property empire worth half a billion pounds. He was described to me by someone who knows him well as, 'One of the five cleverest people on this planet, intuitively right on money, people, investments: he's really fucking sharp.'

Terry has reached a point where he does not often need to be

Machiavellian when dealing with his employees. He does not have to manipulate them, he just gives instructions. Being shrewd, he has a cadre of devoted employees who make his empire run smoothly. When making deals, he passes much of the work to investment bankers who do the politicking and negotiating of the details for him. However, if necessary, he can be charming or tough. His persona has a rich palette of colours.

At a lunch, Terry was introduced for the first time to George, a major business figure. George is still haunted by the spectre of a business decision he took some years ago, when he chose to buy Shelf Life, a seemingly very promising company which lost him a lot of money. Despite this, he remains a powerful and wealthy figure in the British establishment.

Long before the waiter had brought them the menus, almost immediately after shaking hands, Terry launched into a premeditated speech. 'I've looked at lots of deals around the world and you need to understand one thing about Shelf Life: if you had not done that deal you would be the subject of business school courses across the world, because turning down that opportunity would have shown a unique genius, no one else would have done it. I know your instinct was not to do the deal but you were way ahead of your time. Your advisers fucked it up for you, they should have looked more carefully at the books. You owe yourself no guilt or pain. It would have been a one in a million to see what was going to happen. Don't worry, there will be others that work.' No one had ever said that to George, the Shelf Life fiasco is the thing he cares about most. Does he now like Terry and do highly valuable business with him? Of course he does. Whatever Terry says now is very clever and insightful to George's mind, and has been achieved by that single initial speech.

As well as being socially astute regarding what will matter to others, Terry has a remarkable talent for cutting to the heart of the matter. He also has a willingness to do favours for colleagues. An associate wanted to buy somewhere to live in central London and Terry offered to look at it for him, going there in person. Afterwards he sent a succinct note explaining why it was overpriced and unsuitable. However, this is not altruistic or reciprocal in its motivations. Ultimately, Terry helps others to make himself feel powerful.

For Terry is triadic. He has been willing to deal deadly blows to his brother, whom he loathes. For example, he once set a private detective on his brother to obtain evidence he was having an affair, which was then passed to the wife. He treats women like cattle. He's unmarried and lives a restless, empty life, obsessed with increasing his personal wealth, with no real boundaries between his home life and career. Impatient and fidgety in person, his psychopathic component is most in evidence in his dealings with rivals, to whom he shows no mercy and some sadism. His narcissism shows in his desire only to be associated with the super-rich, of whom he secretly regards himself the emperor. Doing the odd favour is part of the way that he convinces himself of this superiority.

All Machiavels are chess players, regarding others merely as pieces to be moved around the board. However, the triadic variety often do not plot where they want to get to, so much as try to understand who they do not like. They then work out where the landmines are that will eliminate their enemies. They spend their time pondering how to manipulate X to fall out with Y in the eyes of Z. This may be less to promote themselves than to feel powerful. Ordinary Machiavels do these things for rational ends, triadic ones often do it because they are compulsive game players.

They find out things and use them to help other people blow themselves up. They might befriend an enemy and when trusted, give advice or encourage actions that lead to their enemy's failure. At its most devious, this might include encouraging a relationship with an unreliable girlfriend or mistress, or recommending a business plan that will fail. Often they do it just because they can.

Of course, a significant number of Machiavels are not very skilled at it. If so, they are easily spotted. This is the sort of person who is usually also obviously grandiose in their narcissism. The easiest way to spot that they are Machiavels is in their reasoning regarding the motives of others. Their vanity prevents them keeping quiet when you ask 'Why do you think X did this or that?' In offering convoluted and frequently fantastical accounts of what is going on, they reveal their Machiavellian mind-set. They will project on to the person a complicated set of motives and manoeuvres that tell you more about them than the person they are describing.

Highly skilled triadic Machiavels are few and far between. At least if you come up against one, you will find they are less motivated by malice than the psychopathic variety. The best hope is to keep off their radar and give them no reason to bother with you. If you do become a pawn in one of their games, you might be able to see how their mind is working. Once you realise that a lot of what they are doing is pointless game playing, it starts to make a kind of sense, unlike psychopaths, where it's much harder to comprehend the level of their malice and sadism and of the extent of their routine deceits. This brings us to the easiest to spot of triadic colleagues: the narcissists.

Chapter 4

Narcissists

Narcissism is an inflated self-estimation, imagining yourself to be cleverer or more attractive or powerful and compelling than is truly the case.
Whilst often charming extroverts, such people are uncomfortable with
warmth, intimacy and commitment in relationships. They go to great
lengths to boost their value in the eyes of others by 'me, me, me' attention-
seeking, taking credit where it's not due, courting high-status trophy
partners and friends, and chasing public acclamation.

Just as Machiavellianism has increased in the last twenty-five years,
so has narcissism. American psychologist Jean Twenge* identified eighty-
five studies of undergraduates that had used the same questionnaire for
measuring narcissism between 1979 and 2007. There was a significant
trend over that period for higher scores on the test.

Twenge found a 30 per cent increase in narcissism. In 1979, 15 per cent
of students had very high levels of narcissism; in 2006 that had increased
to 24 per cent. Twenge reports that the average contemporary American
undergraduate got the same score as the average person in the entertain-
ment industry – her sample included movie stars, famous pop musicians
and reality TV show winners: people don't come much more narcissistic
than that*. Interestingly, Twenge also showed that the rise in narcissism
was much greater in women than men. In 1979, men had been considerably more likely to be narcissists but by 2006 women had almost caught up.

But is narcissism all bad?

Arguable plusses* are that narcissists tend to report high self-esteem, happiness and life-satisfaction. They tend to be rated by others as likeable on first impression, and are good at performing in social situations. They are more likely to be accepted when applying as contestants in reality TV shows. They tend to win in brief competitive tasks and will put themselves forward as leaders (though they do not tend to make good ones in the longer term).

However, the news for narcissists is more bad than good. They are prone to sexual promiscuity, risky behaviour (condoms are for lesser beings) and compulsions (booze, shopping, gambling). The costs of their impulsivity and short-termism are often borne by others, as well as themselves, so that they are unreliable romantic partners, aggressive, prone to commit assaults and to perpetrating white-collar crime. Despite performing well in large groups of people, they are antisocial and selfish.

Above all, they have very distorted perceptions of their own abilities and deceive themselves and others about their emotional state. This is probably why they score highly on self-esteem, happiness and life satisfaction. They exaggerate how wonderful they feel.

In most cases, their exhibitionist tendencies make them all too obvious. Usually they are much easier to spot than the psychopathic and Machiavellian triadics. However, the cunning ones quickly learn that putting others down by building themselves up makes them unpopular. Their Machiavellian side curbs the tendency and they learn to conceal it. The necessity for this partly depends on the kind of organisation, profession and nation they work in. Public sector workers have to douse down the flames of their self-love if they are to progress, whereas in some financial services or marketing roles, narcissism can be a positive advantage.

National differences are the most profound*. In Scandinavia and most of the Far East, being perceived as modest is essential. Narcissists working in those countries have to be very careful to conceal their exaggerated self-love, like the psychopathic academic Jan who we met earlier.

*

Richard is the quintessential narcissistic triadic example. His long-suffering friend Simon, a school teacher, tape-recorded a meeting in a pub with him for me, so I could get the flavour of the self-absorption.

Richard is a senior figure in a large marketing corporation and is at his most relaxed in Simon's company.

Their exchange starts as follows:

Richard: How are you?

Simon: Not bad. I've been pretty tired from working too hard but I can't complain.

Richard: God, tired! I've been working nonstop for the last eight days. I've got four different projects all nearing completion and it's pathetic, I cannot find a single manager who really knows what they're doing. I have to go in and revise the plans completely from beginning to end. It's a nightmare.

For the next forty minutes, Richard itemises to the smallest detail the inadequacies of all the people who work for him. When Simon tries to change the subject, Richard ruthlessly cuts straight back to his problems.

Richard: So I told him I would not allow the plan to go to the client until he had made that change, but of course he paid no attention.

Simon: So anyway, what else has been going on? How's your sister, wasn't she trying to write a—

Richard: But that's really not acceptable, is it? I told him to redo it in the right way and he just paid no attention at all.

Simon: Sounds very tricky. I was having a few problems myself with a pupil who wouldn't do his homework—

Richard: And if they won't do what I say then I just don't know

> what to do. It makes me realise I really need to do more
> of the actual writing of the pitches myself but they don't
> like it …

Intermixed with the theme of his indispensability to the minutiae of the innumerable projects that he oversees, is the subject of how successful and wonderful he is. He tells tales of how much his bosses value his work and of how vital they say he is to the success of their organisation. He cuts between these subjects and the question of how to advance his position within the company, occasionally asking Simon's advice, but only for brief periods and paying little attention to it.

After about an hour Richard finally appears to be taking an interest in Simon's work but it quickly emerges that this is because he is thinking of pitching for a government contract connected with education. As it happens, Simon has sophisticated views on this subject. Richard listens carefully. This is virtually the only occasion during their meeting when his emotional transmission system is set to Receive, as opposed to Transmit mode. He files away the details and, it subsequently turned out, was secretly making plans to sabotage a project Simon had in mind, relating to his own. He feels no guilt in planning a manoeuvre that would be damaging to his friend; if anything, he takes some satisfaction at the thought that it will clip his wings lest he get too big for his boots. He is secretly envious of Simon for having a career that is satisfying and a home life that is relatively fulfilling.

Indeed, after this brief interim, Richard changes the subject to his love life. He is gay, and since his boyfriend had abandoned him for a woman several years ago he has been obsessed with attempting to seduce one of his employees. Unfortunately, the man who he has his eye on is not gay but he believes he may be, 'really'. He talks almost uninterruptedly for an hour about the various ups and downs of his attempts to misuse his professional power over his intended partner to get him into bed.

Narcissists

At closing time Richard has made only the most cursory of references to Simon's life. For almost the whole evening, the subject has been him. All attempts to go elsewhere, even the most strident and assertive that Simon can muster, have proven fruitless. Nor is Richard's tendency to talk only about himself limited to this kind of occasion, it is his normal mode. In social situations where there are several others present he is every bit as uncomfortable with topics of conversation that are unrelated to him or which provide him with no opportunity to stress the importance and success of his career. On many social occasions, Simon has witnessed him alienate groups of people by his insistence that he be the centre of attention.

On his way home, Simon feels both drained and hyped up. It has been sporadically exciting to be in Richard's company yet he feels unrewarded and slightly depressed. He has been a dustbin for Richard's emotional rubbish.

For narcissists to be successful, the Machiavellian component of the triadic traits is vital. Without that, they simply come across as Toad of Toad Hall, a grandiose fantasist. For them to take the practical political steps to convert their ambitions into reality, they need cunning. Unless deeply concealed, as it was in Jan, the psychopathic academic, their self-aggrandising tendency is all too plain to see. Bosses and peers alike will feel put down by their sense of superiority, preventing promotion. But they will also be that person, of whom we all know one, who lives in a la-la land of their own wonderfulness, so brilliantly evoked by P.G. Wodehouse's character Ukridge, a con artist with ludicrous pretensions.

Compared to the psychopaths and Machiavels, it is easier to manage a narcissistic triadic colleague. Apart from the fact that they are much more visible and therefore identifiable, they respond very well to flattery and other ingratiatory tactics, ones that most of us are capable of executing more or less well. For instance, Faisal is a very sharp Arab businessman but he has what would commonly be described as 'a big ego' linked to a great deal of insecurity. Faisal owed a lot of money to Charles, one of his suppliers, a shrewd but not triadic Machiavel. The problem was that the money could not be paid without the signature of Faisal's tricksy, triadic Machiavellian company chairman. There had been a long delay in getting this signature and Charles realised that this had reached the point where Faisal had lost face. This was partly a cultural issue, but it was mainly that Faisal was someone who hated to feel that there was anyone more important in the whole wide world than him.

As Charles put it, 'Faisal started avoiding me. He felt like he's got no dick because the chairman wouldn't sign off my payment. What should be happening is him writing to me saying "Great job, here's some money and a bonus." Yet he is not responding to my emails.' Astutely realising that narcissism was the cause of the fiscal roadblock, Charles also saw how it could be used to his advantage. He wrote to Faisal saying what an amazing project it had been, how the chairman and board were happy with him, how much he loved working with him and how much he had learnt from him. Near the end he added, 'Oh, and by the way, who should I deal with on the four outstanding points, just point me in the right direction, you owe me this, and this discretionary bonus, and for this vision work, which totals half a million.' The reply came straight back: 'Hey Charles, I am so happy we are where we are. Thanks for all the help you provided. Without it I would not have been able to do this. Charles: can you send me a separate bill for payment with each of the individual items? I will make sure the Office of Finance pays you. Warm regards, Faisal.'

Charles's email gave Faisal credit for everything that was Charles's, and that solved the problem. As Charles put it, 'He had had his dick chopped off and I needed to give him his dick back. Because he has absolutely no insight at all, if I tell him he had all the thoughts I had, he will feel good, powerful and not notice he has conflated himself with me. He'd lost confidence in himself on the issue of my payment, I was reminding him that he is a hero in everyone's eyes, no embarrassment there. I could have written saying "Listen, dog breath, I have sent you eight emails saying you owe me all this money. Why the fuck don't you sort it out?" It would have been ugly and unpleasant and he would have just retreated further. The Arab and Asian worlds are all about preventing the loss of face. He moved it away from the chairman to the Office of Finance, which he controls. He felt empowered to say "fuck the chairman" because I made him feel good about it. He fixed it. You have to make people like that feel good, making them feel bad doesn't work.'

When it comes to dealing with narcissists, Charles advocates reminding yourself of the American television series 24. It constantly wrestles with the tension between using violence and torture to get information, as opposed to using the information you receive from relationships. But, as Charles points out, 'The head of Israeli intelligence says that torture doesn't work because the suspect will tell you anything to make the pain stop. The most assassination-prone nation on the planet doesn't use torture! Instead, they build relationships, get their prisoners to cry about their kids. It's the same with narcissists. It's "What does this person care about, what is their identity, how can I make them feel good and become aligned with doing what I want them to do?" Power and influence are "the ability to achieve a premeditated aim without violence". The real geniuses don't use coercion.'

Charles believes that this way of approaching narcissists always works and that it can sometimes be applied to triadic psychopaths and Machiavels as well, if you can plug into their narcissistic component.

Chapter 5

Impostors

A final fundamental issue that needs to be kept in mind in dealing with triadic colleagues of all kinds is that they are very liable to feel like impostors*. Feeling imposturous is a common problem for people of all kinds, not just the triadic. It is particularly common among unselfconfident women. But among the triadic it is a strange and interesting feature that has important implications.

There is a spectrum of imposture in all human psychology. At one extreme is authenticity, in which a person's sense of who they are has the quiddity – the solidity – of a stone. At the opposite extreme are people who feel they are only pretending to be themselves, constantly at risk of being caught out, who feel imposturous.

Imposture surrounds us, in all sections of society: at parties, in pubs, at a desk near you in the office; people put on funny voices and other pretences that are the normal currency of play. But the full-blown impostor is a different animal. There are two kinds. 'Psychopathic' impostors are often con artists, people who assume the name and identity of another person in order to further their own interests. What sets the impostor apart from the ordinary con artist is that the 'true' (psychopathic) impostor never fears exposure when he is a swindler and feels like a fraud when he does honest work.

Jan Ludvik Hoch was born the son of an itinerant labourer in Czechoslovakia in 1923. He could not speak English when he arrived in Britain, aged fifteen, but in a remarkably short time he had become the pin-stripe-suited owner of a country mansion, often speaking with a British upper-class accent. Although by the time of his death he had earned the mistrust of much of the British establishment, there were still plenty of respectable institutions sticking up for him, unaware that he had been swindling hundreds of millions of pounds.

What marks Robert Maxwell (born Jan Ludvik Hoch) out from a straightforward case of an antisocial criminal is the fact that he reinvented himself. It is possible that he felt least authentic when transacting deals entailing no fraudulence, yet had a heightened sense of reality where gross deception was involved.

There is more of this going on than you might think. When a woman I was chatting up at a party in 1988 asked what I did, I proudly told her that I interviewed celebrities for a particular television programme. With great glee, she said, 'I happen to know that is not true. I met the man who really does those interviews only last week.'

Because my face was never shown on these programmes, she only had the interviewer's voice to go on. The man who had passed himself off as me had one sufficiently like mine for her to have been taken in. Whilst it might just have been a one-off case of a man using a lie to get a woman into bed, I have since learnt that this is his *modus operandi* and that in all aspects of his life he feels a fraud unless he is lying.

The other main kind of impostor also experiences themselves as an actor playing a part, their true social roles as father, mother or employee are treated 'as if' they are real, rather than being truly believed in. This is known as the 'as if' personality type. They differ from the psychopathic kind because they lack the cold, ruthless and antisocial tendencies.

Tony Blackburn, the British radio presenter, told me when I interviewed him in the 1980s that 'I only feel myself when I am pretending to be Tony Blackburn the disc jockey; I live for the daily two hours of broadcasting, you can forget the rest. I wish my whole life could be a live radio show'. Many other entertainers have said similar things, like the comic Frank Skinner.

This may seem very odd. But Oscar Wilde pointed out how self-expression is often achieved through concealment behind a facade: 'Man is least himself when he talks in his own person. Give him a mask and he will tell you the truth.' Stephen Fry, the British comedian and actor, regards Wilde as his hero and, indeed, described to me in detail how imposturous he feels. He told me in the same interview series in which I spoke with Tony Blackburn that his greatest fear is, 'Being found out – most men live in fear of a nameless "being found out".' In this, Fry is wrong. It is only the imposturous who dread it.

Instead of stealing or inventing a name as the psychopathic do, the 'as ifs' impersonate the style and colour of admired groups and individuals. They are Walter Mitty role players who can flit between identities without the slightest feeling of self-contradiction.

Both kinds of impostor share five characteristics.

Lacking identity, **the impostor is a composite of the feelings, ideas, expressions and mannerisms of others**. He is often a brilliant mimic, capturing accents and gestures to perfection, sometimes passing them off as his own. He skilfully adapts them to his immediate social surroundings, a magpie for clever-sounding ideas and turns of phrase whose form conceals their lack of substantial content.

To mask his fraudulence, **there is a dilettantism about him, an artificiality, which may base itself on a common cultural type** such as 'sporty', 'ex-army', 'camp' (even if he is heterosexual) or perhaps a Bertie Wooster-ish upper-class gaiety. As further camouflage he employs esoterica, using obscure words and speaking of little-known matters, like the habits of the Inuit in building their igloos or the rarity of certain kinds of cutlery. He is the first to pick up the latest trendy word of whose meaning no one is yet quite sure and that people are too embarrassed to show themselves up by querying. He also has smatterings of technical jargon, which he uses sparingly to imply insider skills or expertise in relatively arcane professional disciplines (post-modern literary theory or something really outré, which no one will know anything about, like anime trivia or 'cyberspace technology').

Thirdly **he can display astonishing verbal facility**: a fluency and range that bowls you over. It may be replete with exquisite puns and flowing metaphors, similes and analogies, or with witty aphorisms and paradoxes; or it may just be perfect for the specific situation you are in, dripping with innuendo and hidden promise. 'Language is reality,' he may opine.

Occasionally the fluency deteriorates under pressure, say, if he accidentally picks the wrong person to blind with jargon (like an actual cyberspace technologist). He may collapse into glib, disjointed and confused speech, a bizarre mix of non-sequiturs and gibberish reminiscent of schizophrenese – the way schizophrenics talk.

Fourthly, **he can be beautifully attuned, telepathically so, to what you are thinking** almost before you have thought it, likewise with your feelings, both profound and superficial. Yet for most of the time, he is frustratingly unaware of your emotional needs and obtuse in the extreme.

Finally, **he has a heightened sense of reality when pretending**, and feels detached, lacklustre and bored when he is not. He may feel that his real (as defined externally) roles – successful writer, merchant banker, husband – are fraudulent and they conceal or deny his true gifts.

Impostors with all five of these traits are at the imposturous end of a spectrum.

Next along come people who feel fraudulent even though they are not at all. Usually successful and often happy, they are guilty about their success and happiness or fearful of others' envy of it. This is especially common in women. Unconsciously it is safer to experience their real success or happiness as not real to avoid punishment or attacks.

Then come artists. Whether performing or using pen, brush, clay, film or other media, they must enter imaginary identities and make them real. The resultant truth is an artifice that their audience can enjoy.

Normal people cheat, lie and fictionalise but only insofar as is required to grow the carapaces of tact, discretion and self-preservation necessary for survival in adult reality, T.S. Eliot's 'face to meet the faces that you meet'. Where normal people fundamentally differ from the more imposturous is that they are much more the same person from situation to situation.

The final group, at the opposite end of the spectrum from the impostors, are the compulsive truth-tellers, incapable of deceit – these are often the non-Machiavels described in Chapter 3. Through a peculiar mixture of morality, desire to please, desire to feel superior and desire to inflict injury, they 'cannot tell a lie'.

Curiously enough, imposture is a close relative of emotional health*. Pretence is vital for much of the play we do. To be healthy, all of us must adopt personae and facades to some degree. Begin to notice it, and you soon become engrossed. As Helene Deutsch, a key researcher of the phenomenon, put it, 'Ever since I became interested in the Impostor he pursues me everywhere. I find him among my friends and acquaintances, as well as in myself.' This is not to say that all of us are impostors, only that it is a subtle distinction between the vivacity and creativity of the emotionally healthy, and the appearance thereof in the impostor.

Nearly all triadic people suffer from Impostor Syndrome to some degree. The psychopathic variety has already been described. The Machiavels and narcissists tend to be the 'as if' kind. Knowing this helps you when faced with a triadic person in your working life.

Once you realise they are triadic, look more closely at how they conduct themselves. In most cases you will quickly see how contrived much of their persona is. But most helpful of all, however much they may outwit and abuse you, there is always this reassurance: when they go to bed at night, they feel terrified of exposure.

Chapter 6

Toxic Professions and Organisations

Over the last thirty years* psychopathy, narcissism and Machiavellianism have increased in America. What is true of that nation tends to become true of other English-speaking ones, and subsequently, spreads wider. Whilst I believe there are considerable variations in the amount of triadic behaviour in different professions, and between organisations within them, my suspicion is that triadic functioning* is increasingly widespread in all workplaces in the English-speaking world and beyond. That changes our world of work.

Only a tiny minority of people are able to earn their living working alone and largely unaffected by relationships with professional colleagues. For most of most days a writer like me can largely ignore office politics, although even then it does sporadically arise in dealings with publishers or literary agents. However, before I became a writer, I had a number of other careers. I worked as a research fellow and organisational consultant in a university, as a clinical psychologist in a mental hospital, as a television producer and as a journalist. These careers have brought me into contact with a wide variety of other professions. For example, there was a period when I used to interview FTSE 100 chief executives for the financial section of a Sunday newspaper. My television career gave me first-hand knowledge of diverse occupations, from prison wardens and inmates to all manner of artists to politicians. In what follows, I shall do my best to provide a brief guide to the triadic toxicity of different categories of profession, based on what evidence there is, my experiences and the people I have interviewed for this book.

I shall start with the world of television, especially documentary making. This is by far the most triadic that I have personally encountered.

Television production

Sarah was the researcher on a television series called A *Poke With Pat*, made for a major British broadcaster in the early 2000s. She believes its story is broadly illustrative of the psychology and office politics of the business. With the exception of her, all the main players in the series were triadic, as was the culture in which they worked.

Pat was a famous TV presenter and she seemed perfect as the hub for an educational series about sex for young people. Her fame would make it easy to persuade other celebrities to contribute their thoughts on the subject. She was known for her sauciness, constantly appearing scantily clad in the tabloids with her equally famous husband. That she was ambitious, perfidious and shallow did not alarm the programme's commissioners, as she would simply be the presenter. Ordinary young people would also be interviewed and experts would provide authoritative comment. The programme was to be made by Egotista, a small independent company with no track record in this field but very well connected to the broadcasters.

The driving force for the series turned out to be Terry, aged thirty-four, originally a trained counsellor, who had made his way into television and had the dual roles of assistant producer and series consultant. Terry had the theory that, despite decades of sexual liberation, even now in the 2000s, people of all ages, including the young, still needlessly repressed their sexual desire. He hoped the series would help young people to feel more relaxed and enjoy their sexuality. However, in Sarah's view, and like all the other production staff, Terry was dysfunctional in his own sex life. A single man, if anyone was repressed it was him. He had no girlfriend and never seemed to have any sexual encounters.

His boss, the producer, was Anton. A gay man in his forties, he had very little experience of television production, having acquired his post through a nepotistic appointment by his close friend, the boss of the production company. Since the series was limited to heterosexual sex, Sarah was a bit nervous that Anton might be uncomfortable with that or insufficiently knowledgeable. Early on in the production, she was not reassured by his view that sex is best when done alone, masturbating, and that he regarded Terry's theories as pure nonsense. This did not augur well, in terms of potential conflicts between them.

Anton's previous career was shrouded in mystery. From a poor home in Northern Ireland, he had been clever enough to obtain a place at Cambridge University. Apart from this, all that he revealed was that he had had periods working in the Foreign Office and as a correspondent for Reuters, the international press agency, in various countries around the world. In fact, Sarah subsequently discovered, he was a member of MI6, the foreign arm of the British Intelligence Service.

The other key figure in this ill-fated enterprise was Bob, the director, who was in his mid-forties. He had worked extensively with Pat before and worshipped her. He drank heavily, was foul-mouthed and dressed like a student in jeans, trainers, T-shirts; Sarah maintains that many male middle-aged television personnel dress like this and that it is a sign of their emotional immaturity. His favourite way of introducing himself to a new acquaintance was to say, 'Hi – and I don't mean drugs!' Before Egotista were handed the contract, Sarah went with Bob to meet another possible company. Both of the producers were female and he proceeded to tell a series of lewd and sexist jokes (some of which, admittedly, says Sarah, were very funny). He was successful in his object of scaring them off the project.

Sarah's initial impressions of Pat were unfavourable. The first time she was introduced to Terry, she sat on his lap, rendering him speechless for the only time Sarah can remember. When she did the same on meeting Anton, it was less disarming, since he was gay. She was clearly a very insecure person, indeed, she was quite open about that, and used her faux-kittenish persona and exhibitionism to try to win men round.

In the month before filming began, tensions soon emerged between Anton and Terry. Much to Sarah's surprise, Anton disappeared on holiday for two weeks of that period, and Terry produced a detailed script for the series, incorporating his strongly educational agenda, largely based on Freudian ideas of repression. At a meeting with the commissioner, Terry revealed an astonishing lack of office political astuteness by announcing that he felt it would be best if Anton move aside to the role of executive producer and let him be the producer. Although Sarah felt this was not completely outlandish, in that Terry had done all the work and actually had more production experience than Anton, it was a disastrously inappropriate way in which to effect a coup. He was lucky not to be fired on the spot and Anton certainly never forgave him.

The first day of filming was with Tim, a lithe, handsome twenty-year-old lead singer in a band that was topping the charts. Pat was all over him but Sarah assumed this was merely her usual lap-hopping. It soon became apparent that she was head over heels in lust and they began an affair. This astonished Sarah, since there was hardly anyone in the country who had not read newspaper interviews in which Pat extolled the godlike qualities of her husband and the rock-solid stability of their marriage. It turned out this was pure fiction and in fact she was highly promiscuous. Awash with sex hormones, her already limited interviewing skills were severely diminished.

Strangely, since the start of the project, she had affected to be shy and squeamish talking about sex. She claimed to hate saying the word 'masturbate', for example. Terry proceeded to write out detailed questions for every interviewee, nervous that his serious educational objectives would get lost. Alas, it was not only Pat who put them at risk.

Once the filming got underway, Sarah noticed that Bob, the director, seemed to have a very weak bladder. Hardly an hour passed without him making a visit to the toilet. She mentioned this to one of the camera assistants who laughed at her naivety. The reason for the frequent trips to the loo was not incontinence but his cocaine habit. His drug use helped to explain to Sarah his wild fluctuations in mood. However, he was not so drugged that he was incapable of office political skulduggery. On many occasions, Sarah overheard him and Anton scheming to undermine Terry's earnest objectives.

A key tactic was to do their best to unsettle the numerous experts that Terry had lined up for interviews. On one occasion, they insisted on taking a psychoanalyst whom they knew had a fear of heights on to a precarious roof, high above London. On another, Bob barracked the expert so much that he became inarticulate. Anton also did his bit. A comedian whom Terry had signed up to tell a series of educational jokes was all set to be filmed when Anton told him that he would be paid only half what had been agreed. A rancorous dispute ensued, after which the comedian was so put out that he performed inadequately.

Anton proved to be a slippery customer in every way. Nothing that was agreed with him could be relied upon but in addition, he had no compunction in sleeping with as many as possible of the gay male teenagers that he came into contact with in connection with the series. Worst of all, he kept disappearing, mysteriously, for days at a time. Whether this had anything to do with his former role as an intelligence officer, Sarah never discovered. But when questioned about his lack of availability, he claimed, somewhat implausibly, that his telephone landline was not working, nor his mobile phone, nor his emails.

The climax of the *Poke With Pat* filming period was an interview with a sex therapist who actually slept with her patients as the main clinical intervention. She had been extremely reluctant to take part, persuaded only by Terry's all too evident earnestness. During the interview, she described the case of a middle-aged male patient who had never had a sexual relationship with a woman for fear of making her pregnant. Using Terry's questions, Pat teased from the therapist her account of how she prepared him to have sex with her. As the narrative proceeded to the point where he had become erect, had penetrated the therapist and was approaching orgasm, Pat got the giggles. Worse still was Anton's reaction. Just before the report of the orgasm, he started to cough. He did his best to hold back the cough, disgusted by this story (as he later confided to Sarah, he found the idea of women's genitals repulsive). His face became purple as he tried to suppress the cough and he proceeded to ruin the soundtrack by letting out a loud rasping sound just as the therapist reached the climax of her story.

A shy and retiring woman, not only was the therapist upset by Pat's giggles and Anton's coughing, she was extremely distressed when Bob insisted on cornering her after the interview in a nearby room and locking them in. He proceeded to question her in minute, lascivious detail about whether she obtained sexual pleasure from her therapeutic work. It was all Terry could do to persuade her not to make a complaint to the broadcasting authorities.

With all the material now filmed, Terry was given the job of doing the first edit, to cut it down to manageable slabs for each programme. He worked day and night, Anton disappearing for lengthy periods. However, on announcing the completion of this work, Terry was amazed to be told that he would not be needed in the editing room any longer. A few weeks later he was allowed to see the finished product. To his horror, all the experts had been cut out of the film and the vast majority of the material consisted of mildly suggestive anecdotes from the famous interviewees. There was no discernible educational purpose to the programmes and they seemed to lack any thread. This was also the view of the commissioners, who were appalled at the lack of substance when they were finally allowed to see the material. Eventually, after much toing and froing, the series was transmitted only once, in the middle of the night, on one of the broadcasters' least-watched satellite channels.

Sarah believes the *Poke With Pat* saga illustrates several points about the British factual television industry. She often found that the production staff employed to work on programmes suffered from the very problems they were documenting. On one about wife beating, she was horrified to learn that the executive producer had beaten his first wife. The exec believed himself cured of this abusiveness, having bought the sociological theory that it was something he had done purely because he had absorbed sexist values from his society, seeing women as chattels. But this theory was contradicted because it became apparent from the interviews with wife beaters that every single one had been severely maltreated as children, in most cases badly beaten by their mothers or witnessing abusive behaviour by their fathers against their mothers. This evidence suggested a reason for the abuse that the exec was not willing to accept. To make matters worse, his (much younger) second wife was a researcher on the programme. She and her husband went to great lengths to try and prove that the interviewees were lying about their childhoods and trying to shift the blame on to their parents. History does not relate whether that had been so in his case but he continues to be a highly sadistic executive in his treatment of employees.

Sarah acknowledges that the production team of *A Poke With Pat* were startlingly maladjusted as individuals, but she maintains that there are many TV production staff like this, the more successful they are, the more so. She has worked with no fewer than four producers who have received the highest accolade in their profession, the BAFTA. In each case, she has noticed an extreme level of ruthlessness and cunning. Their willingness to manipulate the lives of their subjects knows no bounds and explains the exceptional programmes they make. If it suits the plotline they have in the back of their minds, they will think nothing of encouraging a dissatisfied spouse to divorce, or an employer to sack an employee. Equally, if the story needs a delinquent, aggressive child to become law-abiding and sociable, they are clever enough to manipulate both parents and children to get that result.

They are also wizards in the edit suite, knowing how to tell a story. So prone are they to lying or fictions that they often conceive of their own lives as mere stories, as told to themselves or others, according to Sarah. They are always aware of what they are going to do with footage when filming it. If they need to slant events differently from what really happened, they are consummately skilled at doing so in the edit suite. This is no different from the way they edit their accounts of their own lives.

In every case, they have unstable marriages, some of which have ended as a result of their repeated infidelities. Having got to know all of them well, Sarah says they are desperately unhappy people whose only solace is their work. They find it extremely hard to live first-hand, real lives, they exist through the contributors to the programmes, obsessively pursuing the most intimate details of their existence and documenting them. They form very intense relationships with them – interestingly, hardly ever sexual, because that would spoil the film – but encouraging dependence at a deep level. As soon as the filming is over, their interest evaporates, although they are highly skilled at pretending still to care.

Sarah is at pains to stress that not everyone working in factual television is as triadic as this, but that most seem to lack identity and to be fluid, imposturous kinds of people. Highly Machiavellian, they are usually fast-changing chameleons.

I cannot vouch for the modern era, but, based on my time working, off and on, in TV production between 1982 and 2006, I would have to agree with her. I worked for all the major broadcasters and many independent producers during that time, first as a researcher and then as a producer, finally as a presenter. Quite a few of the people I worked with were intelligent, ambitious and had hankerings either to be artists or scientists but instead, found themselves lured into television. Most seemed attracted by the status and glitz, a few longed to be famous. Often they had little real life beyond their work. In the edit suite, they frequently sneered or joked at the ordinary people who they filmed, yet whom they depended on for the programme. They lived a second-hand existence through these people's real lives. They were like flies crawling up a window pane, desperate to escape from their dissociated, isolated lives, looking out on the world beyond, longing to be part of it but unable to tolerate the sustained dependence or intimacy that that would have demanded.

It seemed to me there was a chicken and egg element to the psychology of how the business could accumulate so many such people. The editorial component of television production (as opposed to the technical work, like that of the camera operators and editors) is a profession for which there is no real training. It is iconically emblematic of a modern service industry, largely dependent on skill in manipulating other people. It relies on sophisticated equipment that enables the producers to create remarkable effects. They have no idea how the machines work, but it gives them an almost magical feeling of power when the fruits of their work are broadcast to millions. It also makes them feel cleverer than they really are. Much of the impact of television derives from the equipment, not its operators. Almost anyone with an average intelligence can make a mediocre programme, with minimal training, although making a good one is much harder and extremely rare. As a channel controller once told me, he relied on a handful of people to come up with programmes that would make his tenure in charge memorably distinct from his predecessors. Most programmes were mediocre, he declared, and a fair few were actually bad.

Crucially, because there are no other criteria, you obtain your first job through contacts and your personality, pure and simple. If you can persuade a TV employer to take you on, you are on the first rung, as a runner, and after that, it's all about networking. Given that the industry is packed with people with triadic psychology, they favour others like themselves. Non-Machiavels or non-chameleons stand little chance in such an environment, or else, must have some invaluable specialist skill. They will never rise to positions of power. At every level, triadic people thrive. Even more than usually, the industry works through patronage and networks.

Another key factor about the industry is the ease with which skilled Machiavels can get credit where it is not due, and offload blame for their mistakes on to others. There is minimal evidence, no paper trail, to indicate who has contributed what.

Commissioners frequently have great difficulty in identifying why a project worked or failed, who was responsible. Everyone blames everyone else, or takes credit.

To the best of my knowledge, there is no hard scientific evidence regarding the psychology of TV production staff, so everything I am describing here is ultimately anecdotal. However, I did have one experience that provides support for the account I have given.

In the 1990s I was invited to address senior BBC management and key independent producers on the subject of taste and morals. I decided to use this as an opportunity to do an informal test of how aware these people were of their triadic tendencies. To this end, I made some fairly preposterous suggestions, beginning as follows:

'It's not surprising that TV producers find it hard to judge matters of taste and decency when you grasp just how profound a divide there is between them as a group and the general public. I am talking about the **kind** of people that work in TV, the sort of personality who's drawn to the profession.

'In the late 1970s, Richard Hoggart, the distinguished historian of broadcasting, teamed up with Professor Sir Michael Rutter, from the Institute of Psychiatry, to compare the values and morals of 200 randomly selected BBC and ITV producers – 100 of each – with 200 state secondary school teachers and 200 manual labourers in the building trade.'

I went on to present a series of spurious and more-or-less implausible findings of the differences between the groups. For example, 85 per cent of producers felt that sexual infidelity was wholly acceptable so long as it was successfully concealed from the partner, whereas only 42 per cent of teachers and 28 per cent of labourers took that view. Given these beliefs, the producers were three times more likely to have been unfaithful to a partner, and to be separated or divorced, compared with the other groups.

Based on such findings, I pretended that the researchers hypothesised that the producers had a deficit in their ethical development to the point of lacking any consistent moral sense. So the researchers supposedly mounted a further study.

'All three groups were observed in their workplaces for one week. A staggering 28 per cent of the producers qualified as having a full-blown psychopathic personality disorder, whilst a further 34 per cent were found to have psychopathic tendencies. By contrast, the teachers and labourers scored around the national average of 1 per cent.

'In seeking to explain the findings, Hoggart and Rutter posited that the nature of TV work and its surrounding structures and cultures encouraged psychopathy. They also discovered that more than average numbers of psychopathic people, *per se*, are attracted to the TV profession.

'When they explored the producers' backgrounds, they found them much more likely to have had broken or disturbing childhood homes, and to have been especially likely to have been the object of severe neglect or isolation, classic precursors of psychopathy. So, whilst TV culture and structures might cause normal people to develop psychopathic tendencies, the profession is also attracting more than its fair share of disturbed people, many of whom may already have been psychopathic before they enlisted.

'If these studies are correct, it means that nearly two-thirds of the people I am now looking at are technically as psychopathic as Fred West or Dennis Nilsen, and this must inevitably affect your judgements about taste and decency.

'Being a psychopath doesn't make you a killer or a madman. Lacking any sense of morality, of obligation and commitment to others, you see life and love as a game, and people as dispensable pawns, so relationships offer little fulfilment. This leaves you feeling empty and trapped in a desperate search for meaning, and filled with envy towards more fulfilled, mentally healthy people, like your viewers. To put it bluntly, no wonder that you as a group have difficulty in judging what the general population would regard as being in good taste.

'Doubtless many of you will feel the findings of these studies don't apply to you. Perhaps you are not particularly surprised to learn that your profession is filled with such people. Such reactions would, of course, be exactly what the research would predict: psychopaths are conspicuous for their lack of insight.

'Whilst that sinks in, let me ask you a question: how are you feeling right now? Assuming that you have not guessed that the studies I have been describing are in fact a total fiction – sadly, Hoggart and Rutter have never investigated the psychology of TV producers – I imagine some of you, at least, are feeling a little how the typical viewer feels just before reaching for the phone or pen after they have been insulted or outraged by one of your programmes.'

Ironically, this last sentence turned out to be wrong. There were two main reactions.

The first was that many of the listeners did not register what I said in the last paragraph and therefore imagined that the fictional study I had described was a real one. All these people told me how right I was, and that they believed the industry was crawling with psychopaths. In doing so, of course, the interlocutors did not include themselves, although in many cases I knew – because I had worked with them – that the person telling me this was indeed triadic.

The other fascinating thing was that, of those who had grasped that the study was a fiction, they were at pains to suggest that if it had been done for real, these would have been the findings. Not one person objected to my statement that two-thirds of those present were either psychopathic or had those tendencies.

Whilst by no means scientific evidence, I do think it is reasonable to infer that this suggests, at the very least, a great many senior television personnel at that time believed that psychopathy was rife in their industry.

Television production is jam-packed with untalented people who have managed to associate themselves with successful programmes and disassociate from failures. It is just one of a range of burgeoning professions where there are no objective metrics for evaluation of performance. These professions and professionals both reflect and reinforce the wider growth of triadic tendencies.

Broadly speaking, the more that there is a measurable output to the work for which someone is paid, the less opportunity there is for triadic functioning to prosper. It also helps if there is no ambiguity regarding authorship of specific pieces of work. An engineer who has been assigned the task of mending a piece of software, designing a transistor or supervising the building of a factory by a certain date, either does or does not do that work. Within manufacturing industries, therefore, at the lower levels, triadic tendencies cannot conceal levels of competence and if noticed by colleagues, may lead to unpopularity. As you move further up the food chain within these organisations, office political skills become increasingly important. Triadic people who manage to conceal their less savoury aspects will still be able to thrive.

Nonetheless, I suspect that the more measurable the output, the more that expertise and hard work are rewarded. A sign that this might be true emerged from a survey I did* of leading British CEOs in 1992. First-class degrees were commoner among CEOs in specialised manufacturing industries, ones like pharmaceuticals and engineering. This suggested that measured technical skill – merit – did count where the industrial sector demanded advanced knowledge and skill in a scientific discipline.

An interesting distinction exists between the psychology of entrepreneurs and people who spend their entire career in corporations. Studies show that successful entrepreneurs frequently have minimal educational qualifications and are much more likely to start off in relatively low-income homes. Whether ultimately successful or not, anyone who runs a small business is forced to prioritise survival far more than in most corporations. For entrepreneurs to succeed, some measure of triadic tendencies is probably vital.

Within the media, there are interesting variations in the extent of triadic tendencies. For example, journalists are very different animals from TV producers. Even those working on tabloid newspapers have a camaraderie that is lacking in television. Of course, there are the same patterns of patronage and of intricate politicking: the more senior the role, the more central that becomes. But unlike in television, accountability for output is usually clear-cut. Either you do consistently write good articles or you do not, because your name is on the by-line. If it's badly written or poorly researched, you are clearly to blame.

Generally, journalism is a less itinerant profession than television. Particularly today, television personnel tend to be on short contracts relating to specific projects and they are constantly hopping between employers. Journalists tend to work for several years for one paper, sometimes for decades, without necessarily reaching senior positions. An interesting difference in cultures shows up in the traditions relating to someone leaving a newspaper. Whereas, at most, a TV production team might meet up for a drink or a meal at the end of a project, when a journalist moves on there is a leaving event to mark the occasion. A member of staff will make a more-or-less humorous speech about the departing journalist, to which the leaver will (more-or-less humorously) respond. Colleagues are ultimately comrades. The leaver is presented with a mock front page from the newspaper written especially for them, humorously and subtly memorialising their time there. Whether it feels like a funeral or a wedding, the ritual gives off a broader message of 'Whatever our differences may have been, we are all in this together.'

Journalists also tend not to take themselves as seriously as TV producers. This might partly have to do with the 'here today, gone tomorrow' nature of newspapers. Whereas TV productions take months and sometimes years to create, journalism is on a much faster turnover. For the most part, journalists are acutely aware that today's news is tomorrow's fish and chip paper.

How workers in media professions regard their motivation is key. Journalists generally enjoy the buzz of daily stories and the pleasure of finding the right words for expressing them. In other media, commerce is king. There is no confusion about the commercial object of advertising (with its many sub-disciplines), marketing, sales, commercial artists and designers, and public relations. The more senior the managerial position, the more triadic the person is likely to be.

The arts are also affected by commercial motivation, prompting more or less triadic functioning. Publishers, literary agents and writers vary as to how much they prioritise profit, and are concomitantly triadic. Filmmakers also vary according to that principle, though no one is likely to play an important part in the production of a feature film who is completely lacking in triadic skills. Numerous books (and several films) have chronicled the elaborate shenanigans and ruthlessness of life in Hollywood. In the music industry, performers may vary in the degree to which their desire is artistic or financial, but very few record company executives really regard the music as anything more than 'product'. I recall the chief executive of a record company once telling me that he was selling 'the soundtrack to your life'. I did not have the impression that he saw himself as primarily motivated by the desire to make me happy. The world of modern art is the same, with some very commercially minded artists alongside ones who make art for art's sake, but nearly all the gallery owners (and agents for artists) are concerned with earning money. In short, triadic traits flourish the more that money is the motivating force.

The professions

Running alongside manufacturing, retail and service industries are a set of support professions, like law, accountancy, management consultancy and security companies. The more global and the more prestigious the company, the more triadic its employees. Having said that, in some branches of some professions, like the law or actuaries, it is true that levels of proficiency and of hard work are more important than office political skill, and that triadic tendencies do not advance a person's career. A revealing example of someone who works in one of these is Natasha, aged thirty-two, a senior associate in Span, an elite global commercial law firm based in New York.

Natasha achieved top grades at school, graduated from an Ivy League university, and was a star pupil at a leading law school, which gained her entry to Span immediately afterwards. At entry level, the majority of the employees were women with very similar CVs. Natasha's initial period at the firm was frantic, like a two-year job interview. Every one was acutely aware of the competition: for every one that would be offered a staff contract as an associate at the end of the two-year probationary period, there were two who would be 'let go'.

Like nearly all leading companies in the professions, Span was pyramid-shaped: the vast majority of the employees making up the wide base, on relatively low pay working very long hours; a tiny number at the top – the partners – earning spectacular multiples more. On joining this system, the premise is that if you work hard and display talent, you will beat your competitors and in due course, take your place among the elite of the elite, the partners. The actual odds of this happening at the outset are around ten to one. As we shall see, they are considerably worse than that for women, although they do not realise that when they begin.

The 'winner takes all' remuneration model drives the probationers, alongside the fact that they are a carefully selected group of hyper-competitive young people used to doing all they can to be first, all having had that experience during their education and training, and prone to assuming they will be one of the special, chosen ones, even among such hot competition. Natasha did indeed manage to be one of the winners as a probationer. Through a mixture of extreme conscientiousness, effective networking and luck, she gained a high appraisal mark. However, things did not proceed so smoothly in the succeeding years, once taken on as an associate. Interestingly, in some respects, the reason was because the specialism she chose was a true meritocracy and she simply was not good enough in all the ways needed to become a partner.

In the first instance, to be in line for the crucial promotion to partnership, it was essential to work extremely long hours. As she moved through her twenties into her early thirties, she was not prepared to stay late every evening and often at weekends. On top of that, it was vital to take on yet more work than that allocated by your boss. To have a chance of becoming a partner, you needed to write articles and give lectures to client groups. This raised your profile within your department, making you more noticeable to senior figures, whose attention it was hard to attract. Effectively the lectures are a form of marketing, a way of keeping the organisation's profile high. When an email goes round asking if someone will do one, there is usually a race to get the job among the most ambitious associates. They volunteer for everything beyond the call of duty, willing to travel anywhere that their boss suggests, including secondments to distant places which play havoc with a normal person's social life.

It is not all a matter of hard work. In a law firm as elite as this, all the associates are assiduous and among the brightest young lawyers in the world. However, a few have truly outstanding technical legal brains and breadth of knowledge. These nearly always seem to become partners. In many cases, they are conspicuous for their lack of ability as team players, often being humourless and charmless. Their social skills with clients can be almost non-existent: they are quite incapable of selling either themselves or the firm. Socially, many of them resemble people with Asperger's syndrome, seeming largely unaware of either the thoughts or feelings of others when in their presence. Yet by dint of their astonishing capacity to analyse case law and their encyclopaedic knowledge, they get to the top. This was a very rare example among the professions I encountered in which ability combined with conscientiousness – true merit – was rewarded more than office political skill.

A few fall by the wayside through misfortune. Natasha knew one woman in this über-lawyer class who simply had the bad luck never to be noticed by the partners. Lacking any office political skills, she was a gem that needed to be discovered and the extremely negligent, dog-eat-dog system failed to spot her sparkle.

It is a big motivational problem in the firm (and in that profession generally) that, within a year or two of becoming an associate, it becomes apparent that the great majority of people will never become a partner. A logjam builds up of discontented associates and the firm is constantly looking for a reason to cull them, because there are too many at that level. An associate lives in constant fear of being dropped as there is nowhere to go. A move to another similar firm will not improve their chances because other firms are in the same position as Span: looking to fire associates, not hire. Effectively, despite having been among the most gifted and hard-working lawyers of their generation, these go-getters feel as if they are on the rubbish tip, with no chance of getting the pot of gold – a partnership – that incentivised them as a callow and often slightly arrogant probationer.

Advancement did depend on attracting the attention of the partners, the more senior the better. In Natasha's department this was hard because there were only two social events a year, the Christmas party and the summer barbecue. Beyond that, there was virtually no socialising outside of the office and virtually none there. During the working day, everyone was working in isolation and your only contact was with your PA and your boss, either a senior associate or a partner. At best, you might get two minutes of a partner's time if you had a query that was essential to raise with them. The social interactions by which office politics could be exercised, whether face to face or electronic, were so minimal it came down to the number of hours you were able to clock up on the firm's behalf (all logged scrupulously, since this is how legal firms calculate bills for clients), the quantity of articles and lectures you gave, and the excellence of your actual legal work.

Other departments offered more opportunities for politics. The transaction department, for instance, often worked in small teams for two-month periods, drawing up contracts for the merger or acquisition of companies. The teams worked closely together late into the evening, and at the end of the project, the partner would take them out for a drink or a meal. There was nothing like that in Natasha's department.

However, even in these departments opportunities for self-advancement through politics were limited. As in so many global corporations providing legal or other similar services (accountancy, consultancy) to industry or commerce, it was an impersonal culture. Natasha learnt to trust almost no one. Within the organisation she became true friends with a couple of other women but, apart from that, she was acutely aware that almost anything she said and did could come back to bite her. Nearly all her relationships with peers were coldly professional, with her bosses knowing a minimal amount about her life history or current circumstances beyond the work.

There was one junior partner with whom Natasha felt she had a reasonably amicable relationship. As a junior associate, she found herself faced with a particularly knotty legal issue that she knew he could explain in no time. She popped into his office, as she occasionally did at the end of the day, and asked his advice. He gave it in a few minutes and it seemed as if he was quite happy to have done so. Yet when her appraisal came through at the year's end she was startled to learn that her score had been marked down for failing to do her own research. It turned out the partners had been looking for reasons to not give her a high score because they already had too many in that category and her 'friend' had piped up with the story of her advice-seeking. She learnt to be completely self-sufficient, if possible, and never depended on anyone else for help in doing her job. She realised that you can never show any signs of vulnerability or that you are anything less than 100 per cent devoted to the firm.

Purely for the sake of appearances, the firm makes a pretence of being concerned about the welfare of its employees. Every so often the employees are asked to fill out computer questionnaires on issues like their work–life balance, job-satisfaction and career prospects. The results are analysed (for a huge fee) by an organisational psychology corporation whose computers crunch the numbers and supply statistics, which are then completely ignored. Natasha's department had the lowest satisfaction ratings of any of the firm's departments, globally, but off the record, its managing partner was overheard commenting that he could not care less. The reality is that as an associate, you must subordinate your life to the firm, even after you have realised that you have no chance of becoming a partner. To do the work and to cope with the atavistic culture, you have to become emotionally detached.

Natasha was constantly suppressing her emotional reactions to situations, it was heavy-duty emotional labour. A partner would shout at her because he was stressed and in a normal social situation, she says, she would have 'told him to fuck off'. Instead she had to seem impermeable. She was regularly asked if she would do jobs at the end of the day and the partner would affect regret that this meant she was missing a theatre or ballet event, hardly bothering to conceal that he really could not care less. Even more extreme, when she booked holidays, more than once she had to bite her lip in accepting that she had to cancel it abruptly. In one case, it was a long-awaited trip to Rome, where she had been on honeymoon. Instead, she was forced to spend the week preparing an everyday brief for a partner that could easily have been done by one of her peers. She had to appear professional at all times. She was suppressing her reactions to these personal disappointments, never ever complaining, feigning total commitment.

Natasha is sufficiently resilient to cope with this but it is so common for her peers to break down that there is a well-established system for dealing with burnout. One of her peers found herself at the company's doctor, reporting that she could not sleep, could not concentrate and was having bouts of dizziness. She was immediately signed off work, given antidepressants and sent for a course of cognitive behaviour therapy. Although the human resources staff affected sympathy, the whole response was designed to get the faulty robot reprogrammed as quickly as possible and back at its workstation.

What is striking about Natasha's firm is that, although triadic traits cannot help much through the office political skills that Machiavellianism can confer, psychopathy could be most helpful in surviving and ultimately flourishing. A lack of empathy for others would mean your work would be unaffected by the distress of other employees and you could treat them as impersonal instruments for achieving goals. Being cold and ruthless would enable an exclusive focus on work, and you'd be less likely to miss intimate relationships. Whilst narcissism would have to be buried deep, this is a system in which those triadic people in whom psychopathy is uppermost will find it easier to reach the top. As Natasha pointed out, the exceptional lawyers also often had elements of Asperger's syndrome, which overlaps in some respects with psychopathy: lack of awareness of the emotions of others.

An additional triadic component of the firm, and of nearly all top global corporate professions, is the systemic bias against women who become mothers. That strongly favours the triadic tendency not to place a high value on the emotional component of relationships and life beyond work. Of course, parenthood is something valued by many men, as well as women. But for obvious biological reasons, it is more feasible for men to ignore their emotional and intimate lives until their mid-thirties or later than it is for women. It is no accident that at Span the great majority of partners are male. The most recent appointment was one and so is the one most likely to be next. Both of them, as Natasha put it, 'have no life whatsoever'. When it comes to the articles, lectures and secondments, men are far more likely to volunteer. Whilst it is true that when women first become associates, usually at around the age of twenty-five, they may be as eager as men for about a year, in the vast majority of cases, this peters out as they find their love-lives and friendships are wrecked by the long hours. Within two to three years of becoming an associate, nearly all the women realise they are never going to be partners because they are not willing to sacrifice their selves and their personal lives to that extent. There were just as many outstanding women as men at Span but a significant proportion of them could not progress for that reason.

Natasha found it fascinating that, having realised this, the women still continue to compete. They vie to obtain a high mark in appraisals, even though they realise that the partners are looking for excuses to mark them down in order to save money. Whereas in their educational and training careers they had been at or near the top, they were now in a system where all of them were extremely capable but only a very few could rise. It was also a system that demanded more from them than most were willing to provide, precluding them from consistently being the very best, which they were used to. As Natasha summarised it, 'We all live with repeated disappointment because we can only sometimes be assessed as superior. A lot of this is the constant desire of women to be acknowledged. It is my opinion that women love to be told they are doing a good job, more than men. Praise is so rare in the firm, we long for those scarce compliments. Even so, the prospects are so poor you wonder why women push so hard. I can't understand why we care about our appraisal grade when all it could mean is maybe a three grand bonus.'

As it happens, a plausible explanation for this does exist. In an account of 'burnout' in cases of young (twenty-nine- to thirty-eight-year-old) female corporate lawyers, the New York psychoanalyst Brenda Berger* demonstrates the way firms exploit emotional insecurities. She prefaced her account with a quote about large law firms from the novelist Scott Turow: 'The only sure ingredients of growth are new clients, bigger bills and – especially – more people at the bottom, each a little profit centre, toiling into the wee hours and earning more for the partnership than they take home.'

Berger presents the case of Meg, in her twenties, who was working sixty hours a week and at the end of her brutal day, would 'zone out' in front of the television. Despite having had less savage alternatives, she had chosen her top firm because she felt more 'at home' with it. She came from a family in which her mother was a fragile, self-centred woman whose love Meg could only attract by acting in accord with her perfectionist demands, ones based on living out her own ambitions through Meg. Her father was no better, taking any signs of independence as a personal affront. Berger describes how Meg had developed a masochistic need to repeat this scenario in her work life: 'Her firm's stance – "I will pay you a hundred grand a year if you don't tell me you feel strained, exhausted, bored, powerless and lonely" – is remarkably consistent with the messages she felt she received from her parents'. In her appearance and conduct of her life, Meg was utterly chaotic, all domestic work having been taken care of by her mother until well into her twenties. Indeed, other than when executing her tasks at the firm, she was helpless, angry and incapable of thinking for herself. Similar patterns were found in Berger's other cases and in summarising her conclusions, she points out that the pathological need to please and to join cruel working environments is viciously exploited by such corporations. When I put this to Natasha she said it rang many bells regarding her female peers.

This account of life in a top legal firm could be replicated by countless examples from the other top firms in the professions. Whilst they vary in the degree to which political skill can be used, all have strongly triadic psychopath-favouring structures. The demands for total commitment to the firm and the gruelling hours discriminate against people who want to have a social life and for whom parenthood is also important. The march of the triadic into these professions is global and has accelerated* during the last thirty years.

The public sector

Careers in the public sector have always entailed some office politics, but this has become increasingly important in the English-speaking world, with the attempts to improve efficiency through targets. This applies as much to the emergency services (police, fire, ambulance), the civil service and local council provisions, as to health and education. In Britain, during the period after 1999, the New Labour government began to greatly increase public spending, especially on education and health. The targets were intended to increase efficiency. But measurement of performance ran the risk of becoming an empty ritual. The vastly increased need for documentation of performance could lead to a 'tick box', 'going through the motions', 'watch your back' mentality, with large doses of cynicism from all concerned, except from some politicians and senior civil servants.

Alongside this, there was an increasing tendency to outsource functions to private companies, such as cleaning and catering, to save money. But this created long chains of responsibility, so that it was hard to exercise authority or to establish who to call to account. A school headteacher who was dissatisfied with the upkeep of their school or with its cleaning, could no longer simply sack or otherwise discipline the relevant person. A revolving door of private service companies would have to be contacted, ones selected by someone at the town council and managed by the companies. Because the outsourced sections of the system were profit-driven, the workers had no commitment to the institutions, nor did their bosses.

These changes, along with several similar ones, meant that being cunning became more and more important for those employed in the public sector at all levels, the higher the level, the more office political. There was tremendous potential for toxic triadic individuals to exploit the new arrangements to their personal advantage or out of sheer malice. If they become powerful, they create toxic organisations and if very powerful, can even toxify large chunks of their professions or parts of the country where they hold sway. Non-Machiavels and non-chameleons are at great risk of being relegated or ejected, by such systems.

For example, Tom was that rare thing, a male primary school teacher. What originally attracted him to the school was that its head was a warm person and the approach was child-centred, meaning that there was a big emphasis on finding ways to make the subjects appealing to children.

However, the head was ousted and in his place came triadic Sheila. As with so many Machiavels, initial impressions of her were favourable, in fact, Tom really liked her. As a non-Machiavel and non-chameleon, he was undoubtedly naive. Sheila seemed to agree with him about basic educational philosophy but he was not the only member of staff to be lulled into a false sense of security.

It did not take long for them to realise all was not as it seemed. Initially, there was a 'consultative' period, seemingly inclusive, with lots of questionnaires for the staff about which age groups they most liked teaching, their favourite subjects and so on. Half-jokingly, Tom said he would resign if he was asked to teach Year Fives. That was soon put to the test. He was moved from his preferred age group of the Year Twos to Year Fives. What was more, nearly all the other teachers were similarly allocated years and subjects they disfavoured. It was almost as if she was trying to get rid of them.

Within a week came another major shock: Sheila went to the county education inspectorate and placed the school on 'amber alert', meaning it was on the brink of being deemed failing. This was based on inadequate record keeping, never the previous head's priority. The county school improvement team were invited in to help. Sheila's rationale was that the involvement of the inspectorate would ultimately result in better funding and support for tidying up the record-keeping systems. It sounded plausible – who could not be in favour of raising standards – but it slowly emerged that Sheila had other goals.

The initial inspection occurred without prior warning. Sheila had reassured the staff that they would not be observed in the classroom but this was not the case. With Tom the observation was cursory, perhaps five minutes sitting in on one of his classes. The consequent report included accounts of events that the inspector had not witnessed and was based on prior reports from the scanty records. Since it was the same for the other staff, there was uproar. Sheila was impressively articulate in reassuring them; she could talk her way out of anything. She was also forceful and assertive, so no one was willing to stand up to her, except Tom.

Gradually he began to understand her strategy. She was intending to show that the school was failing and then present herself as having turned it around. She was very ambitious, one of those heads hoping ultimately for high honours. The trouble was that she could neither lead nor teach. She spent most of her time in her office on her laptop. She was obsessed with time keeping, although poor at it herself, rarely on time for meetings and her staff meetings invariably overrunning. She did virtually no teaching herself, despite a staff shortage. Prohibiting the use of worksheets for lessons, she used them herself on her rare ventures into the classroom. It was clear she had no talent for the work, boring the children stiff with her dull and rigid use of the syllabus sheets. Their nickname for her was Borling, which rhymed with her surname, Dorling. Oddly, when they were ill-behaved and sent to her for disciplining, she never imposed penalties and the children became increasingly out of control. Tom started to realise that was exactly what she intended. She needed the school to be seen to be failing before she could emerge as its saviour.

Much to her annoyance, when the scheduled OFSTED inspection occurred they were initially rated Good. It subsequently emerged that her strong relationship with the inspectorate enabled her to get them to reclassify this down to Satisfactory. That provided her with justification for calling in the inspection team again. Following their subsequent visit, she told the staff that they could relax, that they would no longer be endlessly having to provide the documentation of performance that she had introduced. But by now none of the staff believed anything she said and sure enough, a few weeks later, she was calling in the inspectors again. From then on, recalled Tom, 'None of the teachers could even fart without being assessed.' Every twenty minutes of every class segment had to be planned, put on a sheet and emailed to Sheila in advance. Tom found himself working evenings and weekends to keep up with the paperwork, a relentless grind of lesson plans, worksheets and assessments of children's performance.

The hardest evidence Tom obtained of Sheila's strategy emerged when he handed in his class's results. She responded that it was too much improvement, too fast. Pressed to explain why this was undesirable, she was frank: it would reduce the likelihood of the school having an emergency status. She lowered the marks, so much so that it presented some of the children as having lower standards than the previous year.

A cunning way to decrease the school's standing was to reduce the pupil's SAT scores. This was done by simply not warning the teachers that the tests were coming until two weeks beforehand. Unsurprisingly, the results were poor. When a further inspection occurred, it was all too clear what was happening. In league with the inspectors, Sheila's newly appointed and favoured teacher, Stella, gained an Outstanding, as did another recent addition to the staff. The other teachers were rated in direct proportion to how much resistance they offered to Sheila. Tom was horrified to receive a Satisfactory, having always been rated Good or Outstanding in his career until Sheila's arrival.

Morale at the school was hitting rock bottom. One of the staff was so depressed that she not only had to be given sick leave, she was admitted for inpatient psychiatric care, on suicide watch. Tom decided the time had come to call in the union. Never the best of politicians, he made a series of big mistakes, not the least of which being to underestimate the extent to which Sheila had established excellent relations with the education authority. Through them she got wind of his objections and was easily able to overcome them.

Today, only two of the original seven teachers who were at the school when Sheila arrived are still there. Tom has changed profession and, sure enough, having been praised as the resuscitator of a dead school, Sheila has moved on to greater things.

The moral of this story is twofold. On the one hand, it illustrates how much triadic individuals have prospered* as a result of changes in the organisation of public services. Thirty years ago, the likes of Sheila might have found it harder to work the system. On the other hand, it also shows how vitally important it is for us all to develop better office political skills if we are to survive. Tom was grievously lacking in this department. Had he been better, he would have been more able to resist Sheila, failing that, at the least, he could have been defter in escaping from the school to a better one.

This story is not exceptional. Public services have always entailed a measure of politics, but the new targets and other measures provide a playground for the triadic. Whether it be social workers watching their backs, doctors worrying about budgets or highly paid chief executives of local government areas, the triadic are liable to thrive.

The bigger picture: triadic nations

Triadic behaviour flourishes where ruthless, devious selfishness is advantageous and where an individual is very concerned to gain power, resources or status. It might be supposed that these conditions exist everywhere, at all times, but that is not the case. Societies vary considerably in how much they encourage or demand that people improve their lot relative to others. They also vary in their tolerance of the triadic, or specific traits thereof, as a tactic. However, it is true that in almost every nation, the ruling elite is more triadic than the rest of their population.

In general, the least triadic are the Northern European nations, especially Scandinavia. English-speaking nations, particularly America and Britain, have become much more triadic in the last thirty years* and the traits have spread widely through those populations. For urban dwellers in emerging nations, whether trying to achieve upward mobility or just trying to survive, Machiavellianism is taken for granted and a measure of psychopathy unsurprising – these are tough environments. However, since narcissism is strongly disapproved of in Asian countries, it must be highly concealed in that part of the world. Rural populations everywhere are less triadic but especially so in the developing world.

There are two key factors that determine how triadic a nation is*. The first is the extent to which it is collectivist. Collectivism demands a high degree of dependence on others, of give and take, reciprocity. You must be dutiful to parents, both as a child and having grown up. Cooperation and contribution to community are highly valued. You are loyal to your in-group and are careful to avoid shaming your family or work unit by behaviour which is disapproved. Conscience is regulated more by shame than guilt. Standing out from the crowd is disapproved, if you do well you give credit to the group. Boastfulness is abhorred. Examples of collectivist nations include Japan, Sweden and Nigeria.

By contrast, individualist nations require you to place the self apart from the group. Through education and subsequent career, you establish a unique identity, supposedly distinguishing yourself from your family and breaking free from assumptions made about someone of your gender and social class. Individualism takes different forms. The American variety emphasises 'bigging yourself up' to the point of arrogant boasting.

Danish and New Zealand varieties also strongly foster uniqueness but not at the expense of others. Collectivism does not necessarily preclude this kind of individualism: they co-exist in those nations. A high measure of consideration for others is demanded, including commitment to the family, yet at the same time, there is strong support for thinking independently and remaining true to what you believe even if it contradicts conventional wisdom.

In nations like this (which are a small minority) – ones that are both collectivist and individualist – triadic people will have to conceal these traits and since this is hard, fewer will thrive. In nations that are collectivist and do not tolerate any kind of individualism, like many Asian ones, they will discourage any overt narcissism. For triadic people to prosper in those settings, their Machiavellianism and psychopathy will need to be presented as for the good of the group, not the individual. Displaying these traits in Denmark will rapidly lead to rejection, whereas they may be applauded in China or Korea, so long as they are correctly represented as for the group. Cunning leaders who show ruthlessness in helping a factory to survive against competition or in gaining foreign sales of a product will be seen as acting for the collective, even if they are really self-interested.

The form of political economy* is the other major determinant of how triadic a nation is. Ones that permit insecure employment conditions, have privatised public utilities, health and education, and favour short-term share price as the means for measuring business success, are what I call 'Selfish Capitalist' (Thatcherism or Reaganomics in popular terms, also known as free market, neoliberal economics). They have large numbers of people working on low incomes and huge differentials between the average pay of a worker, and that of a senior manager. In many respects, when it comes to their tax systems, these systems rob the poor and average to give to the rich, often permitting corporations and individuals to avoid tax through offshore havens. Considerable inequality develops. They tend to smash collectivist components in the society and to create an 'every man for himself' ethos, presented as opportunity, freedom and permitting economic aspiration. America is the most extreme illustration of this with a wide variety of nations adopting some elements. For example, Sweden has high taxes for the wealthy but it has also privatised many of its public services.

Selfish Capitalism strongly supports and indeed nurtures triadic traits. Americans are the most narcissistic people on earth*. They have high rates* of psychopathy and Machiavellianism. What is more, through their universities and business schools*, they have strongly influenced the ruling elites in the developing world. Many of the leaders there have had American education and impose Selfish Capitalist political economics on their populations. However, the spread of triadic psychology into the general populace is limited by the collectivism of developing nations. For the vast majority of Africans, for example, selfish ruthlessness is a less successful coping strategy than altruism and communality. When the food or water or money runs out, if an African has behaved cooperatively and supportively to their family and community, that will save them. If the person has a reputation for self-seeking ruthlessness, they will find themselves on their own. With that reputation there is little hope for survival without turning to crime. Hence, although leaders in most developing nations have had triadic traits encouraged by the American example, it remains an ineffective strategy for most of their citizens or employees.

None of the mainland European nations are fully Selfish Capitalist and they present an alternative, what I call Unselfish Capitalism*. This offers state support for health and education and stronger employment security. Whilst there are a wide variety of ways in which this is implemented, it works against triadic traits becoming widespread among the populations, even if the ruling elites possess them. In northern Europe, triadic behaviour must be concealed. In some parts of southern Europe, where there is widespread corruption and a long tradition of ignoring national laws, conspicuously triadic behaviour among leaders is more tolerated, even if the general population are not like that because of the longstanding collectivism still found there. I suspect that Silvio Berlusconi, the former Italian prime minister, may be an example of someone who does little to conceal his triadic tendencies. Some Spanish and French politicians and business figures are also blatantly triadic. Yet collectivism continues to act as an antidote to this becoming a widespread trait in businesses and public services, as well as in personal lives. Southern Europeans still place a high value on family life and cultural pleasures, like food and opera, and on keeping their weekends free from work and shopping.

So, what are the implications of this trend? Clearly, we live in an increasingly triadic world. Some nations are less so than others and the same is true of professions. If you live in a relatively non-triadic society, or work in a profession or organisation that is similarly free of triadic psychology, you are fortunate. You will still need office political skills but they will be less important. But if you are surrounded by triadic systems in a triadic society, office politics become imperative. They are the only way in which you will be able to protect yourself from massive stress. Without them, you will not be able to carve out a meaningful, satisfying way of pursuing a worthwhile career.

Part Two

Improve your Office Political Skills

Introduction

If only it were possible to provide a sure-fire list of wizard wheezes by which you could magic yourself around the office, casting spells left, right and centre, enabling you to manipulate anyone and everyone into doing as you please. Alas, it is an illusion that office politics can be achieved by learning clever tricks, just as there are no failsafe devious ploys for sexual seduction or 'right' methods for getting babies to fall asleep. The manipulation of others is not the behavioural equivalent of a card trick, it's much more complex than that.

Scientific studies have not identified one single* political tactic that can be relied upon to work in all situations. Whether it be ingratiation, chameleonism, sabotage or anything else, whilst there is evidence that they can work, it all depends. It depends not just on which method you use, but when, with whom, using what words or method of communication. Get any of those wrong, and the method may not work or, worse, backfire. Political skill is crucial*, not specific manipulative tactics, nor your mental ability or your personality: a high IQ does not predict who will be good at politics, nor does the kind of person you are.

For example, you might assume that to be a good car salesman you should be outgoing, or at the very least, pretend to be. One study measured the personalities of car salesmen* and their levels of political skill. Only the skilled were aided by an extrovert (outgoing, friendly) personality; on its own, extroversion did not increase car sales and sometimes it backfired. Who wants a chummy, gushing car salesman that does not adapt the spiel to your particular case? Indiscriminate joviality can actually decrease sales. The same principle applies in all services. We may prefer low-key, sympathetic funeral parlour personnel or upbeat nurses, but only if they adjust themselves to our set of circumstances.

The technical term for tactics is Impression Management: ways to create, protect and alter your image. There are at least thirty-four Impression Management strategies*. Any of them might be useful sometimes but none will always be applicable in all circumstances.

Tactics are classified as hard or soft. Soft ones entail using personal persuasion methods, like ingratiation, whereas hard tactics rely on more dominant behaviour or positional power, like the intimidation of a subordinate by a manager. Studies suggest that soft tactics are more likely to bring about a desired result than hard ones. Two soft tactics* used in combination are generally more effective than one. But even these very broad statements have to be qualified. For example, much depends on the culture of the company you work for, or the country you work in. On the whole, people in America who act tough* (hard tactics) and are often disliked by colleagues actually rise higher than likeable folk who use soft methods. The opposite is true in Denmark and Japan.

Tactics also vary in their efficacy* depending on what outcome they are seeking to influence. For example, ingratiation is more likely to work on subordinates than on bosses, because bosses often see you coming if you suck up to them, whereas subordinates are not expecting it. Except that … if you are soft all the time and constantly ingratiating with subordinates, there is a danger that they see you as a soft touch and take advantage, in the same way that over-indulged children will become ill-behaved.

In meetings with your supervisor regarding your annual pay package, if you use self-promotion*, 'bigging yourself up', it is more likely to succeed than when being interviewed for a job: you are liable to come across as an arrogant prat if you are boastful in an interview, whereas your supervisor will expect you to be telling a success story when discussing pay. Except that … what if your boss is a vain narcissist who must constantly have his ego massaged? Ingratiation is far more likely to work with such a person, including pretending that your achievements were only possible because of the wonderfulness of your grandiose boss.

It's not what you do, it might be said, it's the manner in which it's done, likewise the timing and the choices of target and location. Neither talent nor personality in themselves are good predictors of who will succeed. In every study*, office political skill trumps tactics, ability and personality. Just as you may always have suspected, that's why some very stupid, lazy or pathological people rise to the top. They know the way, time and place to make their pitch: that's what gets results.

How, then, are you to work out which tactics to employ? They are essential, but how do you decide which to use, on which targets, at what point in time? Self-help business books have a tendency to isolate behavioural techniques that will do the trick, will Win Friends And Influence People. This is snake-oil salesmanship. There is no best way. First, you have to become more self- and other-aware: astute. Then you need to work out what kind of actor you will be best as, and when to act. Only then does the question 'Which tactics should I use?' arise.

Since the most difficult skill is effective implementation of tactics that is where we shall begin: being able to act.

Chapter 7

The Importance of Acting

For many of us, the nearest we get to being aware that we are deliberately acting is when we mask a hangover on a Monday morning and put on a cheery face for the boss. At work, most of us tend not to put enough thought into how to use acting to get our way, yet even at low levels in organisations, it can be important. If you want to work a particular shift, the more that you can generally get your boss to like you and the more persuasively you perform when making your request, the greater your likelihood of success. It's important to admit to yourself that deliberate falsehood is required for this – acting – and not to feel guilty or self-conscious about it.

To succeed in office politics you have got to be able to act*. Oddly enough, the more you can acknowledge that you do it, and the more conscious you can become about when and how you perform, the more authentic you can be. Only if you know you have switched it on, can you also switch it off.

Ideally, acting is something that you do to achieve specific goals. Indeed, for most of the time during working hours, most of us are not acting. When you are, you may still 'be yourself', using a persona you have self-consciously adopted in order to express something that you truly want. Simulated emotion or views do not necessarily mean you are betraying who you really are, they may be the only way of achieving what you ultimately intend.

There are whole professions, or sectors within professions, that are heavily dependent on acting skills, obvious examples being salesmanship and the media. The higher up the system, the more important acting becomes. To ascend to management or all the way to the top, you need to be as conscious as possible of what persona you are assuming in various contexts, and of the personae being used by your peers.

What you are looking for is a career in which you are as comfortable as possible with the script, and the role and lines assigned by it. But even where the fit between the real you and your job is as good as imaginable, there will still be a need for you to be alert and quick on your feet, every day, in working out who you need to be in order to get your way.

The very best political actors are rarely admirable people or good models for average workers. Some are ruthless predators, others are fragile types who act because they lack much sense of who they are beyond their facade. But there is much for the more normal person to learn from these people.

Charlie was once an Oscar-winning office political thespian. He has much to teach us about how to improve our acting performance at work; however, few of us would be wise to emulate him completely.

I shall use his story as the only one in this chapter but I would not want the reader to gain the impression that the rest of the book is going to be largely concerned with such unusual stories, or with banking. In fact, there are virtually no other stories from financial services. The vast majority of characters you will meet in later chapters are much more ordinary than Charlie, with his somewhat privileged background and exceptional acting skills. It would not be possible for most of us to behave like him, nor desirable, he is an exceptional case. Nonetheless, from this extreme we can still learn a good deal about how to improve our political skills.

The interview
When Charlie arrived to be interviewed for his job in the trading department of a leading New York financial institution based near Wall Street,

let's call it Heiger, he had only had a week to prepare. They were looking for a bright young thing who could make investments in a new financial instrument which was being traded, known as a PTSD. The problem was that Charlie had never even heard of it.

He rootled around on the Internet and asked a couple of people who did at least know what a PTSD was. He would not be able to demonstrate any track record using the instrument but, despite being only twenty-six, he was an old hand at dealing with interviews and a dab one, at that. All he needed, he believed, was to know more than the person he was speaking to and he was sure PTSDs would be Greek to the interviewers. They would just want to feel that in employing him, they would be at the cutting edge of financial innovation.

His strategy was to present himself as much nerdier than he really was, much more technical and statistical in his use of language, speaking in deliberately convoluted sentences. They would want to hear certain words like 'correlation' and 'integrated trading', and would expect complicated ideas. That is what he gave them and by the time he had finished he was positive they were thinking 'that is exactly the person needed for this role'. It was a version of who he really was and set the template for who he became at the firm. He maintains that you can get almost any job if you work out who they want you to be and become that person.

The scientific evidence for what tactics work in interviews* is very inconclusive. It's hard to generalise when the issues are so different from job to job and company to company, and given how much depends on the fit between the personalities of interviewer(s) and interviewee. Whilst on the whole, as you might expect, the studies show* that being agreeable and outgoing help, there is just so much more to it than that. Ingratiation can work, but only if you are subtle about it. The interviewer must not feel you are sucking up them. It has to be done cleverly. Likewise, chameleonism may work with some interviewers. For instance, narcissists will tend to feel warmly towards people who mirror them. If you spot a narcissistic interviewer, you can try using their buzzwords back to them and adopting their mannerisms when directing answers to them personally, like their minimalist or extravagant body language. But it is so complex. In doing that, you would need to be careful not to alienate the other interviewers, assuming there is a panel of them. In that situation, different personal strategies are likely to be needed for different interviewers in order to make each one feel you have connected with him or her, individually.

Overall, Charlie has got a point. If you carefully work out who the interviewers want you to be and can convince them that you will be the person best able to perform the tasks (whatever the truth), you are most likely to be chosen, so long as you act that role effectively. The more you are able to use your networking skills to have advance warning of what they are looking for and the more you can deliver it, the better your chances.

I was once on a panel interviewing candidates for the job of running an influential organisation. We eventually appointed a woman whose curriculum vitae seemed to tick all the boxes. During the interview, I asked her some specific questions relating to an area I cared about and she appeared to be singing from the same hymn sheet as me. Alas, she was lying, and in fact was bitterly opposed to almost everything I felt was important. But it took me several years to grasp this and she was such a good actor that the other interviewers were similarly duped. She went on to waste quite a few millions of pounds on pointless projects, simply feathering her own nest and employing like-minded chums. It was a good (if painful to me) illustration of how right Charlie is: presentation and fitting the interviewers' preconceptions gets you the job.

Establishing your role in the company drama

Who Charlie really is: a tall, personable, patrician-looking, scholarly and rather emotionally sensitive twenty-six-year-old American from a privileged background (a top-drawer private school, followed by Yale University, although, as we shall see, he actually comes from quite a modest background, despite having been to these establishments). Whilst he is capable of abstruse mathematical calculations, that is only a small part of his abilities. Nevertheless, from day one at Heiger, he played out a role, just like an actor on a stage. An important component of his success was his understanding of the scriptwriters' – his colleagues' – reading of his persona's motivations.

This was a company that had bought the support of elected politicians from across the globe. Numerous ex-prime ministers and presidents, or their relatives, were on the payroll, giving the company all manner of more-or-less unethical advantages over rivals. It had gone to tremendous lengths to establish itself with the corporate brand of being greedier and dirtier than anyone else.

At the outset, Charlie believed it was vital to show he was like that himself and to reflect the emphasis on branding at the corporate level by pointedly establishing a personal brand. He had to decide which category of person he wanted to appear as, what kind of commodity. Then he had to make people think about him in that way, controlling how they pigeonholed him in the organisation. It helped that from the outset he knew he was being brought in as a star trader who had made money (or was perceived as having done so) for his previous company. He used people's perception of his brilliance (whatever the reality) to reflect badly on others; this was how everyone in the organisation got ahead. He was constantly seeking to reinforce positive opinions about himself whilst undermining the people around him.

Charlie felt that, at an emotional level, beyond the practical functions that had to be fulfilled, bosses tend to have a dream of who they want their staff to be, a sort of fantasy team with different personae filling different roles. It was just a matter of identifying which one you were supposed to impersonate and then performing it. His boss, Jerry, cast him

as the intoxicating wizard who understood the intricacies of the mysteri-
ous PTSD market. As a top trader he needed to be someone 'ballsy' who
would rub people up the wrong way (which wasn't remotely Charlie's natural tendency).

He is careful to stress that acting a role to this extent will not work for
most people. At Heiger, he was having to dissemble almost all the time
and does not recommend this unless you are a very good actor. There was
another man at the company who had also sold himself as being a bit of a
whizz kid in a particular area, but it very quickly became clear that he was
not because he did not conceal his ignorance cleverly enough. The story
very quickly went round that he had lied about his CV, although he had
not, because everyone had been fooled and was looking for an explanation that blamed him, not their credulity. So taking on a role beyond your
expertise can backfire if you lack the skills to control colleagues' perceptions of you.

As with all actors, costume mattered. Charlie paid close attention to
his wardrobe and styling, as well as self-presentation (posture, gesture,
facial expression) when speaking or being observed. He had been brought
in to work alongside a much less glamorous, tubby man, somebody who
wore commonplace suits from a chain store, a person of slovenly appearance. Technically, and in his level of commitment, this man was much
better than Charlie in every way, a perceptive guy who could look inside
a market to what lay beneath the surface. Yet the boss contrasted this rival
with Charlie as inferior, and consistently undermined him. Within a short
time Charlie was promoted over him, even though his rival was better at
the job.

Charlie believes that something as simple as wearing Brooks Brothers
ties and expensive suits was important. Class can be valued in American
financial companies because there is still a sense that this is where they
came from, their preppy origins (a preppy is the stylistic American equivalent of the British upper-class Sloane Ranger). Apparently, that is why so

many brainless duffers are to be found on the boards of so many investment banks and brokerages. The right suit can confer a sense of class – in both senses of the word – and of being in touch with the foundations of the industry.

Realising that a component of his boss Jerry's fantasy about him was of blue-blooded, Ivy League, 'old money', Charlie played to that. Never mind that there was nothing especially posh about his ancestry (in fact, his parents were first-generation professionals, a doctor and nurse, and had never been wealthy). If the boss had been looking for something rougher, Charlie believes he could have supplied it. Having been involved with many theatrical performances at school and university, here was another part to be played.

Of course, enacting poshness was a delicate balance, double-edged, for as Jerry was himself from a working-class background, he admired and resented these features. It had to be done subtly, with care. Charlie dropped occasional references to a *Great Gatsby* or *Brideshead Revisited* lifestyle when younger, to decadent weekends at grand and historic houses. This let Jerry enjoy some voyeurism, but Charlie also was careful to appear a bit embarrassed about it too, affecting a shyness and reticence in the telling. He needed also to reassure Jerry that underneath his preppy exterior he was a commercial animal, just like him. The worry was that he could slip into seeming a fey amateur, a hedonist, not really committed to making money, not mercantile, not hungry enough. If you were too much someone who did not care about money, you might not make any.

Charlie was also very aware that his boss was not the only person in his audience. In communicating with other colleagues, he made it clear that his family no longer had riches but implied it once did. He intimated he was someone who was trying to restore the family fortune, its capital base. He did this in such a way that it was never spelt out, always inferred by the audience, so that they could knowingly say to themselves and each other 'that's what drives him'. He believes you need to give your colleagues a fairly obvious psychological motivation for your ambitions, one that they think they have worked out for themselves. It's very like being a spy in which you cultivate a plausible cover story, based as much as possible on the truth. It's all about slight shadings of the truth. Added up, they amount to an enormous lie, but no individual distortion is too large to stand out. It could seem playful and fun, in that we'd all like to be a spook for a day. However, there can be dark consequences of doing this for longer than that, as Charlie was to discover.

It's worth noting how sophisticated Charlie was. Firstly, he had the astuteness to sense his boss Jerry's desire for him to occupy a certain role, that of a star with posh origins. Then, playing out this role, Charlie was also perceptive in realising that it could backfire if he was not careful. Both his boss and his colleagues might resent and envy him. Turning this part of his character's narrative into a plausible explanation for his ambition was a shrewd use of it.

It is helpful for all of us to think through how we come across to our colleagues and how they might analyse our motivations. Depending on the kind of organisation you are in, you can work with the reality of who and what you are, and adapt for the workplace. If you're a social worker, for instance, it is likely that a desire to help others will be valued by your colleagues but perhaps they will need a bit more than that if they also can see that you want to be the area director. An obvious scenario might be to mention how your own difficult childhood has affected you, making you someone who feels the need to shine because you felt neglected, perhaps. But leave it to your colleagues to join up the dots, for that was another crafty element in Charlie's approach: enabling others to reach the conclusions he wanted them to.

Whatever your line of business, being self-conscious of how your boss sees you in relation to your rivals in their fantasy team is worth thinking about. Charlie is probably right that many bosses do have some kind of template of this kind in the back of their mind, even if it's not conscious. All of us have internal worlds based on our childhood experiences: the tyrannical father, the much-loved sibling, the unfairly advantaged older sibling and so on. If you look closely at how your boss relates to different employees, you may be able to work out what they are projecting on to you and you, in turn, on to them. On the surface it might seem that the boss is just reacting to how annoying or charming, how incompetent or capable, the employees are. But if you look deeper and draw a psychic map of the different psychological and social roles you all play for the boss, you might be surprised what opens up for you.

The actor takes the stage

One way for Charlie to play upon his star image was by taking people subtly beyond where they were comfortable and familiar, using technobabble to get them to cede authority to him. When he first arrived at the firm, he set up a series of deliberately bewildering PowerPoint presentations about what PTSDs are. He encouraged everyone who might matter in the progression of his career to attend, knowing that they would probably want to understand a new financial instrument and to be seen to be showing an interest in such matters. They had to endure three hour-long presentations which he knew would confuse them but which no one would dare challenge, to avoid seeming stupid or out of touch. That would build up his mystique and create a world in which he was master. It would wrap him in an aura.

Indeed, his audience did pretend to understand what he was saying, even though some of it was close to gibberish. He took great care in preparing the language he used in these talks. There were phrases and terms that the audience would be sure to have heard, but most of which would be only partly understood. Charlie acknowledged to the audience that he quite appreciated these words were somewhat arcane and to 'help' he explained them using other jargon that was even more abstruse, yet still terms that would be common enough that no one would dare simply ask what they meant. With great care, he deliberately ensured the audience were always just at the edge of their knowledge.

The presentations worked a treat. Not only did they result in instantly sealing his reputation as a whizz, they created for him a unique niche, a domain in which nobody ever dared to challenge him because they were convinced he could crush them with his superior expertise. Since there was hardly anyone else in the financial world at that time who knew anything about PTSDs, it was extremely unlikely that his colleagues would run into professionals from other firms who might blow his cover.

The other critical early step Charlie took after arriving at Heiger was to embark on a nineteen-day round-the-world trip where he visited a different country every day. That was thought 'really cool and interesting' by his colleagues, almost legendary in terms of the sheer amount of work, distance travelled and evidence of commitment to the Heiger cause. That the trip itself was a total failure in terms of drumming up PTSD business went unnoticed. From then on, Charlie had an image of 'businessman meets James Bond adventurer'.

An interesting feature of Charlie's success at Heiger is the extent to which he was freed to be an actor by not being truly committed to his profession in any deep sense. For example, he was immune to titles. Although he was made head of various departments, none of this interested him at all, whereas many others would put elevation of title ahead of increased financial reward. At one point, Charlie was passed over for a particular title and it was seen as very strange that he did not care. So strange, in fact, that in order to maintain his facade of an ambitious star, he had to pretend that he was pretending not to care. He went into Jerry's office and almost feigned tears for not having got it.

Charlie believes that the fact that he didn't really care about any of it, even the money, was a vital reason why he did well. There were so many people who felt deeply about their position and what they were doing, and had a lot of fear. Charlie felt it was all ridiculous. He did not understand the markets, and nor, he believes, did anyone else. He did not know what he was doing but, unlike others, he knew that he did not know. So it was all politics for him, the acting out of a role.

There is no doubt that it is beneficial for everyone to arrive at a new job with as much as possible of a plan for making a specific impact. In some cases, it might be hard to gain much foreknowledge of what the situation is and what will work, in which case, it may be necessary to wait a week before devising the plan. It also depends on what kind of person you are. A shy one who finds acting hard would obviously be very unwise to try Charlie's kind of strategy. If eager to develop acting skills, there is nothing to stop you imagining a specific exchange you are intending to have with a colleague and acting it out in front of the mirror, observing your body language and speech. You could even consider joining an amateur theatrical group and get some experience of actual acting. If you feel you have a real problem in this area and are very serious about it, you might want to visit a transactional analyst for a few sessions. They can be brilliant at helping you to understand the different parts of yourself and acting them out. Beyond that, you could consider a brief (sixteen-session at most) period of cognitive analytic therapy, focusing on the childhood origins of your shyness and lack of acting ability, with a view to changing. I realise the therapy options take time and money, and that most of us really do not have the spare capacity. Of course, if you are quite happy with how you are, there is no problem. But it will limit what you can achieve if you have minimal acting capacity. Why not try a bit of extempore messing about with your best friend or partner? It could be amusing!

For those of you who feel more confident, the important thing would be to take care to read your company and your position in it, and then to find a plan that will work for you, and for the persona you are assuming. This is not to suggest that full-scale adoption of Charlie's approach is desirable. What you can learn from him is that it is feasible to look at your work environment and, through acting, become much more proactive in managing it to your advantage than you realised was possible or even necessary. Part of this may entail some deliberate use of obfuscation in the creation of fiefdoms. If you can gain a reputation as a specialist it always helps to keep both bosses and colleagues from interfering, allowing you greater autonomy.

The unimportance of professional competence in gaining rewards and recognition

Charlie characterised Jerry, his boss, as 'pretty B-Minus, intellectually', yet, nonetheless, in some respects 'a very, very good operator'. In conventional terms, Jerry had done badly at school, getting poor results. On intelligence tests he would have scored low on many of the areas tested. He had minimal knowledge of the wider world, like international or national politics, let alone books, art or high culture. He was barely even conversant with popular culture (incredibly, on one occasion he looked askance when a colleague mentioned that he had enjoyed *Sex and the City* the previous evening; he truly had not heard of this television series and supposed the speaker was talking about actual erotic activities). Like almost everyone at Heiger, he was a philistine. Charlie never heard him express an interesting, imaginative idea about anything substantial, even in the areas of finance about which he was knowledgeable. He was also ignorant of other people, their thoughts and feelings, having no interest in them.

But he was talented in sensing the financial market trends that people were getting excited about very early on and investing accordingly. Being a neophiliac (lover of novelty), he was one of the first to latch on to PTSDs, saying 'this is the future' and bringing in Charlie to deal them. As it happened, it rapidly became clear that PTSDs were just another scam, a dodgy financial instrument that, within a year of Charlie's arrival at the firm, was swept away by the economic tsunami of 2008. As a result of that there was a return to basics in a desperate attempt just to retain money, but Jerry hung on to the fiction that PTSDs were the next big thing for a considerable time after it was obvious that they were toast.

Jerry's greatest skill was in devising narratives regarding trends within the business, which he would then market to people both within and outside Heiger. Of Polish descent, he played to that shrewd, tough, canny Polack stereotype when interacting with others. He had risen on the flood tide of soaring stock prices in the first half of the noughties. Actually, his was a very ordinary business but he dressed it up as something interesting and sexy. He was a fantasist who worked at making the fantasies correspond to some reality, a compelling salesman and self-publicist, good at creating stories and getting other people to buy into them, and had attracted a lot of capital into Heiger. So he was an extremely capable salesman in one specific domain.

When it came to people and office politics he was nowhere near as perceptive as he believed. He liked to think he had a good nose for what others were thinking, but the swiftness with which he was taken down, the collapse of his reputation within the firm, suggests otherwise. At Charlie's very first company conference call, there were about one hundred key employees listening in from around the world. The clues to Jerry's eventual demise were already present. One of the top bosses said Jerry's department 'doesn't seem to be winning the plaudits it used to'. He was very publicly shaming him, the first of a series of hints and slights, such as not being invited to certain dinners. Jerry lacked the human skills to fight back from that position.

Towards the end of Charlie's time there, one of the CEOs unilaterally brought in a rival from the UK to run both the UK and US parts of the business, without telling his other CEOs. Jerry was effectively finished. He stayed on for six months with nothing at all to do. No one in the section had any real jobs any more, everything was put on hold. Jerry was playing computer poker alone in his office, getting in at ten o'clock and leaving at three. He had failed to read the political runes. His sacking was nothing to do with his effectiveness or otherwise in managing his department, or indeed, its profitability.

Jerry never had an inkling of what Charlie really felt about him, but then Charlie was pretty good at concealing it: he really did know how to seem the part he was playing. But as Charlie says today, 'One of the things I have had to learn since giving up that career is how not to act. In the rest of your life, and as a way of existing for years on end, it isn't helpful, to say the least, quite apart from what it does to your human spirit.' Whilst at Heiger, he maintains that it was absolutely essential, far more important than actual skill in the tasks of the job. Beyond a certain level in the company, without personae you hit a ceiling. It was very difficult for people to stay alive, career-wise. Once you rose beyond the dealing coalface, it was about your abilities as a political animal because you were no longer specifically accountable for making money. You managed the money-makers and could always find a scapegoat if things went badly: 'This guy messed up so I am going to chuck him out.' Anyone who did not act could not get beyond a certain point in the firm. There were plenty of people in the lower reaches who were 'straight up', what you see is what you get, but they got passed over for promotion.

Partly this had to do with the particular field they were in. In other areas of finance Charlie has friends who are relatively genuine, but he thinks there are very few who have no artifice. Even the genuine ones are brilliant game players. One of his mates doesn't seem to tell any lies, but Charlie knows he does, it's just that his friend is so good it's seamless. Indeed, for much of the time most of us are oblivious of the fact that we are politicking, doing it automatically. Being more honest with yourself about that, more self-aware, is something we all need to work at.

A startling example of the unimportance of actual skill in Charlie's organisation – that is, the job of investing borrowed capital so that it increases in value – and the importance of politicking, occurred about six months after Charlie went to Heiger. Jerry, at that point still very much the golden boy in his own bosses' eyes, carried out a putsch on a rival in the Frankfurt office. Just as dictators have to be very wary about leaving their countries for foreign diplomatic meetings lest rivals carry out coups, so too with senior financiers and holidays. On the day the rival went off on two weeks' leave over Christmas, Jerry put a proposal to the top brass to merge their departments. When the rival returned, he was already ousted. As a result, Charlie was promoted and had a team of people working in Frankfurt reporting to him. Not only did these traders know much more about the work than him, they were all much older. Yet in his boss's fantasy, they were idiots who did not really understand what was going on. His whizz kid was the one really in the know so it made sense that they were reporting to Charlie.

Then along came the credit crunch. Real performance became even less important. Nobody did well. There was not a single person within the organisation who was in a good place; it was just relative extents of horrific performance. Insofar as it had ever been possible, now you could no longer differentiate people by the value of their portfolios, or their skill in playing the market. It became about how you presented the story of your mess and how you made the mess of those around you seem worse than your own. Because the work that Charlie did was so complicated it was very easy for him to say 'Well, it's fine, it will all get better because …' and then come out with some guff about Gaussian curves that nobody understood. The people who were doing uncomplicated stuff were the ones who got really hammered.

However, whilst you needed to act to rise up the system, in the longer term, Charlie believes that ultimately the players were most vulnerable. Those people who stayed on and were wrapped into the new business after the credit crunch, the people who survived, were often the ones who were not at the forefront of the politicking. The tubby, slovenly dressed one is still there, chugging along. Some of the people like him had always claimed they were playing the long game. By keeping their heads under the radar they would have job security, even if they did not get the huge bonuses. They presented themselves as plodders, and bosses like to have some such people in their fantasy teams. There is a much faster turnover of the stars at the top than the plodders at the bottom. The plodders pose no threat and in reality, you do need people who will get work done, rather than devote most of their energies to politicking. There is more money to be saved by sacking expensive senior figures.

Most of us were brought up to believe that if you work hard and are talented, this will be directly reflected in your pay and level of promotion. Once we get into the workplace, it rapidly becomes obvious that matters are not so simple. You start to notice some very untalented people are in positions senior to you. You feel deep resentment if peers get promoted who have contributed far less than you. What is more, it is soon apparent that the system by which employees are recruited is often deeply flawed, or at any rate, that there is a large discrepancy between the claims made for that system's capacity to predict who will be effective and what actually happens. Although corporations spend billions every year assessing the capabilities of new and existing employees, it is a fact that, overall, neither tests of ability nor tests of personality* are good predictors of who will succeed. Office political nous is. But perhaps that is caused by intelligence? Not so. Contrary to what you might expect*, when the relationship has been tested, no link has been found between intelligence or 'general mental ability' and office political skill. You might imagine that skill reflects cleverness as conventionally measured. You would be wrong. The truth is that office political skills are far more important than being good at IQ tests.

There are some professions that are striking exceptions, but they prove the rule. In professional sports, for example, like golf, tennis, baseball and soccer, there are objective metrics of performance, and whether they are attained is very much a matter of public record. You either do or you do not win Wimbledon, or score goals if you are a striker. But the vast majority of people in the developed world do not work in such fields. Rather, they are employed in largely unmeasurable service industries. The theory goes that those who do well in the objective exams administered at school and university will subsequently also do best in the workplace, and it is true that there is a correlation between level of education and income*. However, a great deal of this reflects family background* and the contacts, social networks and cultural membership that is conferred by social class and expressed through educational establishments. Going to a top private school buys you an old-school tie, a place in a top university and, subsequently, an expensive business school, and all of these things plug you into a powerful network. What is more, once established within these elites around the developed world, talent and hard work alone do not ensure success. The level of achievement in most fields reflects the kind of processes identified by Charlie: acting and cunning in dealing with peers and bosses.

Recently I was contacted by a man who worked in human resources at a major British corporation. Whether based on fact, I cannot say, but broadly speaking, his observations are supported by a good deal of evidence. He wrote:

You might be amused by a few gleanings from my forty years of personnel work at Corpitum. Our assessment techniques are wholly ineffectual.

a) 'IQ' tests of fast-track graduates at recruitment, end of selection, end of training and end of first year in post do not predict success. The test design (arithmetic, geometric sequences, word definitions, logic tests, etc.) and the kind of test is totally immaterial.

b) 'Personality' tests of entrant scientific specialists have the predictive value of tea leaves. The 'presented personality' in one study of staff changed as each individual met a different interviewer for fifteen minutes. Plasticity seems a weak word for this kind of slick social response. Chameleonism busts face-to-face assessments of personality.

c) Follow-up of expensive specialists' performance measures (engineers, IT experts, section heads, etc.) do not work. The probable hard fact seems to be that your careful 'measurements' will be of the wrong things at inappropriate times in the self-development sequence.

I am only surprised to see 'IQ' still talked about. I could never make it mean anything. The ancient statistical tests are of course fraudulent. As for interviews and personality tests, the whole idea of getting an individual to declare the unknown sources of their life motivation is daft beyond the reach of words.

This man was deeply sceptical of the value of the tests he had been trained to use. The truth is that they only endure because there seems to be no alternative and they are self-perpetuating. There is a huge industry of people within and outside corporations and government departments who depend on such tests for their livelihood. There is a curious reluctance on the part of organisations to notice that these human resource and consultancy emperors are scantily clad. Scientifically speaking, the predictive power of these tests* is minimal and in many cases, non-existent. Office political skills, not predictably measurable abilities in the execution of tasks for which employees are paid, are what determine success in the great majority of professions in the developed world.

Playing the assessment game

Although titular positions were important to the employees at Heiger, earning a lot of money was the ultimate marker of status and the main reason most people worked there. Core salary was often a relatively small part of the total earnings. The overall amount of money was decided every Christmas when the bonuses were agreed, following a period of assessment in the preceding months. Whilst the basic Heiger salaries were enormous by the standards of an average public sector employee, let alone someone working at a checkout in a supermarket, the critical issue was the size of the annual bonus.

These were decided in a tournament system, judged by the boss. The section within which you worked would have a limited pot of money. From an individual competitor's standpoint, the key was to persuade the boss that you deserved more of it than your rivals. The more you got, the less they were given, and your standing in the tournament could be measured this way. The more money you got, the more prestige you had.

Very few employees had a job with a specific amount of profit or loss attached to it. For most, there was no objective metric by which their contribution could be measured. These were the support staff, people like analysts, accountants and secretaries. As they were not frontline combat soldiers, it was much harder for them to claim a particular number of 'kills', so how much they received was even more a matter of self-presentation and of their relationship with bosses.

With the traders, like Charlie, there was still a good deal of basis for argument about how much they deserved. In theory it was possible to put a figure on the amount of specific profit their annual trading had resulted in. But it was always possible to blame other individuals or market conditions for trades that had gone wrong and to take more credit than was your due for successes. In theory, it was a case of how much you had made and what percentage you should be given. But in practice, this was always remarkably unclear, even in the good years, and in the bad ones, more so. Then it was about how much you had lost and how much you had managed to minimise the damage, protecting money that hypothetically might otherwise have been lost.

If deemed a failure, a 'derisory' bonus gesture would be made, perhaps 30,000 to 60,000 dollars (more than the national average wage, yet regarded as negligible in this opulent world), though actual figures were never revealed by peers when talking with each other. If someone was given no bonus it was a way of saying 'you're fired'. In the end, the degree to which you were admired or liked by the boss was the principal basis on which your slice of the cake was decided.

Charlie recalled a particular individual whom Jerry did not like. He was a Harvard graduate, quiet, softly spoken and highly intelligent. He did not ingratiate, having neither the talent nor the inclination to suck up to the boss. He believed in calling a stick a stick. He was not rude or crass or prone to speaking out of turn. It was simply that he did not compliment Jerry, or do anything to make him feel good, like chameleonism or flattery. After each review Charlie could see this man's position get a little bit worse. Although he was contributing considerably to the overall pot, he would be fobbed off with a meaningless promotion or new title, and slowly edged towards the least profitable areas of dealing. By contrast, Jerry thought Charlie loved him, that they were the greatest of mates. For example, they always went out to lunch on Fridays, with Charlie taking great care to make him feel there was a personal bond between them. He was careful to mirror his use of certain words and to parrot Jerry's prized ideas. However, Charlie did not play the game in every respect, and could ultimately have been penalised for failing to do so.

The annual review was done by the system known as 360-degree assessment. You had to write a report on everybody who reported to you, whilst they did one on you, and your bosses also reported. It was not name-specific, so you could not see who had reported what. You were marked on all sorts of things, from your performance to your character. It took Charlie about three weeks every year to do it, for twelve or so people. He felt it was gruesome and his policy was to write nice things about everyone because he could not see a reason to do otherwise. He would get some reports about himself that were horrific but that did not lead him to adopt the same strategy.

There would be a mixture of panic, fear and excitement as Christmas approached. Almost invariably, Jerry would begin the annual meeting with a phrase that made Charlie want to punch him: 'Don't poach a gamekeeper.' At first, Charlie just did not know what it meant, it sounded like drivel to him, and in fact, to this day he is not entirely sure what it means, presumably something to do with poachers having turned gamekeepers. Following on from that, Jerry would come out with torrents of sub-MBA management speak. He would say in a hushed, conspiratorial voice, 'I've always referred to you, Charlie, as a three-pronged threat. You're making money. You're raising money from investors. And you're manoeuvring politically within the firm. If you can do all those really well, you will make *billions*.'

Oddly enough, they never discussed specific trades he had made during the course of the year, the actual job for which he was employed by Heiger. Rather, there was a focus on how he could improve his conduct, a bit like a headmaster disciplining a naughty pupil. There would be critiques of his personal style, such as, 'During that conference call you weren't polite enough.' It was all about politics and presentation. The issue was his capacity to work within a modern 'ethical' office. There was also a certain amount of berating of Charlie for giving insufficient time and attention to his position in the wider international company. It was explained he would not be promoted to the upper echelons if he did not devote more energy to ingratiating himself to the top management.

During these annual assessments, it was as if Jerry felt that the person occupying the Charlie role in his fantasy team should have an annual ritual criticism, like the self-criticism sessions conducted in Maoist China. Throughout, Charlie would also get a sense of Jerry stacking his players against each other and always near the end he would throw in a really barbed question about somebody else, encouraging Charlie to be cruel towards his colleagues.

Although Charlie felt that the process was miserable, part of him did not care. The thing he hated most was that he had to appear to care. So Jerry would say 'What do you think to the fact that someone says you don't give enough time to reading credit reports?' and he would have to adopt a *mea culpa* persona, 'I know, I know, I just have so many things I have to do, I am going to start coming in earlier, leave later.'

Of course he would try and work out who had shafted him, and would have a good idea who it was, but the uncertainty was frustrating. One problem was that he was high profile in his trades and public persona, another was that his office was right at the front, so it would be obvious if he had his feet up on the desk. The commonest smear was that he was too interested in the showy trades and didn't do enough of the plod work. That knitted into Jerry's fantasy of Charlie as a star player, so an ineffective smear. But Charlie would have to pretend to be affected by it, even though the whole exercise was very ephemeral and soon passed. He would make a token gesture by coming in early for three weeks and very obviously be seen to be reading credit reports. Then he would just stop doing it and no one would notice.

Overall, Charlie's view of 360-degree assessment was that it was an outlet for a lot of unpleasantness, pure office politics. It was a way of encoding your ability to manipulate the system in a document that would be kept on file for five years. It was clearly something he was not that good at but he did not care. What kept him safe was his boss's star fantasy, which withstood any amount of evidence to the contrary.

This fantasy also meant he could hold the threat of leaving over Jerry. Every November he would make a point of going out to lunch a great deal with people from other companies because it would give the impression he was planning to jump ship. In fact, he would just be messing about, talking about sport or favourite films, but it was assumed he was being wined and dined by headhunting companies.

*

Charlie's degree of detachment from his profession is obviously not recommended. Ideally, you are engaged with your work, find it stimulating and challenging, and do not have to be an actor at all times. However, a measure of detachment, an overview of how your organisation or profession works, is desirable. Because Charlie was so detached, he could see through the system to an extent that enabled him to work it. He realised that in his company, when it came to the amount of money he would be paid, his actual performance was less important than his relationship with his boss. Whilst in most workplaces pay is more efficiently related to actual productivity than this, you can still learn a lot from Charlie. The vast majority of work today is in service industries and truly objective metrics of performance are hard to establish. As a result, whether or not done by 360-degree systems, to a large extent, assessment comes down to personal relationships and to perceptions. If you analyse your situation, you will almost certainly see that by far the most important consideration regarding both your pay and promotion is how your boss perceives you. Hopefully, that does reflect your actual contribution to some degree, but it also is usually heavily dependent on how you get on with that person. Through self-conscious adoption of personae, you can probably increase the degree to which the boss likes you personally, and that will feed into the decisions they take about you, relative to peers.

Apart from doing your job well, the main tactics by which you can improve relations with the boss are chameleonism and ingratiation (see Chapter 3). Chameleons (known technically as 'high self-monitors' because they pay close attention to what impression they are creating and what others want to hear) ask themselves 'Who does this person want me to be?' when they meet someone. They then do their best to find the buttons they can press that will make the other person feel they are like them and are, therefore, desirable. Interestingly, this is an important component of sexual desire, of attraction and seduction in sexual relationships. Couples often are attracted by similarity. The cliché that 'opposites attract' is generally incorrect.

Ingratiation entails making another person feel that they are admirable, important and attractive. This is mostly achieved through flattery. Through a variety of methods from the verbal to the behavioural, you 'big up' the person's attributes, suggesting how clever or sensible or shrewd or impressive they are. Blatant compliments do sometimes work, perhaps simply by saying, 'That was smart, the way you dealt with Joe Bloggs.' At other times it needs to be done much more subtly, for example, by making complimentary remarks to a third party who is likely to repeat them to the target individual.

By mirroring the right features of your boss and by flattery, you can increase how warmly they think of you. However, as already noted, you have to make sure the boss does not realise* this is what you are doing, so along with the specific imitations and compliments, you need to create a warm vibe, so that the person feels comfortable with you. The problem with all this is that it depends so much on what you are like, what the other person is like and the organisation you are in. A rich combination of tactics are required, and rarely will any single one be effective. The way in which you get your boss to like you is no different from how it works outside the office. It's all about saying the right thing at the right time, and succeeding in doing this over an extended period. That is why we have much to learn from Charlie's fundamental idea, that personae are crucial. Whereas with a lover or a friend, you are not mostly engaging in this level of manipulation, with a boss you need to be honest with yourself about what you are doing. To sustain it, it needs to be based as much as possible in what you really feel in your heart and what the boss is truly like. But given that you may not get along personally with a boss, a persona will be helpful in providing a way to keep yourself consistent and seemingly authentic.

As I shall describe below, there is persuasive evidence that tournament payment systems* are liable to increase the amount of office politicking among employees. From an organisational standpoint, this is highly inefficient. Time and energy that should be devoted to substantive tasks gets diverted into attempts to get a larger slice of the pot. What is more, as an employee, when it comes to pay and promotion, in many organisations, your gain is someone else's loss. Alas, unless you do not care about career progression, if you work in such an organisation it means you must learn how to engage in the sabotage of rivals and how to protect yourself from their machinations.

Getting down and dirty: sabotage and other tricks

Heiger worked by pitching its employees against each other. There were lots of competing teams essentially doing the same thing. It was divide and rule, a deliberately Darwinian survival-of-the-fittest approach. The team that won gained the most money and power. As we shall see, many studies show that this tournament system for employee motivation engenders sabotage. It can mean that more effort is being devoted to undermining competitors than to generating wealth for the company.

Since Charlie was cast as a star, he naturally became a target. His main internal competitor did his best to undermine him from day one. He spread damaging rumours and generally sought to harm Charlie's reputation. But he also took active steps to try and mislead Charlie into making mistakes. He made sure he was on conference calls when Charlie was discussing how much cash he had available to put into various positions. He would suggest bad strategies: 'Why don't you put less money there, put more into emerging markets?' hoping Charlie would be conned into taking bad dealing positions. Being older and more experienced, he would also adopt an avuncular, apparently cooperative stance: 'Listen, why don't you let me help you with some of these calls with clients? I know how their minds work.' By speaking like this in front of colleagues, his real intention was to make Charlie seem callow.

When the markets crashed in 2008, sabotage became much more important than doing your job. It was about finding people other than yourself to be thrown to the wolves. During this intensification of politics there was an inflation of public flattery and private backstabbing. A lot of the time it was strangely transparent, as if enemies wanted you to know that they were out to get you, even though outwardly they were seemingly supportive. You had people sucking up to you who you knew were stabbing you in the back.

There was one rival whom Charlie vividly evoked with the words, 'He had a voice like nails down a blackboard. He was prone to copious sweating, dripping with perspiration, a constant sheen on his upper lip.' During the crisis of 2008 he became almost unpleasantly friendly and kept suggesting they go out to lunch. Charlie had to do that once a week, knowing they loathed each other. Of course, the rival was hoping that Charlie would let slip something that he could use against him, and that Charlie might accidentally reveal how he was trying to sabotage him.

Charlie's main protective tactic was getting the little guys on his side, everyone who was involved in the minor decisions, which sometimes ended up being major. He particularly concentrated on the people whose job it was to measure risk, ostensibly fairly menial work. Yet on certain occasions their views could be critical. There were monthly risk committee conference calls during which the traders had to state their strategies. These were attended by the lowly risk assessors but also by the top brass. Charlie would put forward his proposal and his enemy would start spluttering and coughing, but the risk guys would say, 'Well, actually, we think Charlie is on the right path here, we support this.' He would take the risk dogsbodies out for a beer at the end of those days and they would talk about what a 'wanker' his enemy was. His enemy's approach was to give the risk dogsbodies a really hard ride, using shouts and commands that alienated them, making it easier for Charlie to get their vote over a few beers if his nasty voice was still ringing in their ears. In fact, Charlie did actually like them, enjoyed drinking with them, whereas he never liked the people at his own level.

As with everything else, though, his relationship with his boss was the key to sabotage. They always sat together on the numerous flights around

America, taking the first plane out, the last back. On the return trips, Jerry would like Charlie to sit next to him, to have a drink and talk things over. Jerry's secretary booked the seats in advance to ensure he could have his 'star' beside him.

Jerry would ask 'How do you think Colin's getting on?' (Colin being the ill-dressed portly rival) and Charlie would say, 'I think he's doing really well, I've been kinda surprised at how well.'

Jerry:	Why surprised?
Charlie:	Well, the way he presents himself.
Jerry:	Yeah, I know what you mean.

By saying 'surprised', Charlie could plant a seed of doubt. Getting Jerry to think that he had arrived at his own negative assessments of his rivals was crucial. Charlie would always appear to be speaking positively of his prey, yet in doing so, steer Jerry towards faults and limitations. Charlie would ask 'I was thinking about promotions. Are you going to promote Stewart?' (The sweaty rival who insisted on having weekly lunches) and Jerry would ponder 'Do you think I should?'

Charlie:	Well, he is awfully good at what he does.
Jerry:	I worry sometimes that he doesn't think outside the box enough.
Charlie:	You need that kind of guy, though.
Jerry:	Yeah, you need him at a certain level, not beyond it.

Thus did Charlie reinforce the idea that his rival was not a high-flyer.

One of Charlie's more unusual dirty tricks was to discuss office politics. There was an unwritten rule that you just did not refer to the fact that politicking went on. People would be terribly shocked if you said, 'Have you noticed that this or that is being done by so and so, that's a bit weird, isn't it?' Charlie made the breaking of this rule part of his persona when he wanted to unsettle people. It had to be done piquantly. So he might say 'Isn't it odd that Bill seems to be acting against the interests of the company?' to stoke up the paranoia of an enemy, like the sweaty man who insisted on having lunch with him. The man would be mystified as to why Charlie was acknowledging what was unspoken: that everyone put their own interests ahead of the company. He knew Charlie was manoeuvring against him. The paranoia could be used to deflect the man from realising what was being done to him. When made to feel out on a limb, the man sometimes made rash judgements or even became overtly aggressive when he needed to seem charming.

The persona Charlie presented to his bosses was not necessarily the same as the one he assumed with his peers or juniors. Temperamentally, he was not someone who was naturally comfortable in the role of a showy, belligerent wizard. Given the choice he would opt for a less prominent, less hyped-up part to play. Then, he also felt it was very obvious to some of his more able colleagues that he did not really know much about his business. So he had to act differently according to who was there. If his bosses were present, he would adopt a brisk and domineering stance as if in control: 'You report to me.' As soon as the bosses left, he would switch to, 'Right guys, I am not going to get in your way, tell me what you think you should be doing.' He would make it implicitly obvious that he was only putting on a show for the boss and so they gave good feedback to his boss on what a nice guy he was and supported his plans. Meanwhile, his seemingly dictatorial performances in front of Jerry left him thinking, 'Charlie's really got them under his thumb'. He led a double life.

There are some interesting studies* of the conditions under which sabotage is activated, and when different kinds are likely.

In one experiment*, students were formed into groups of eight and given a simple task: printing out a letter, putting it in an envelope and hand-addressing it from a list, taking about seventy-five seconds per letter. They were asked to continue doing this for thirty minutes.

After the production period, in one of the experimental conditions, an opportunity for sabotage of others was provided. The participants were asked to examine the output boxes of the other workers in their group, counting the number of envelopes completed and giving a score for each one's quality of production. Quality was assessed on one envelope chosen at random from each box (handwriting legibility, sealing and so on), on a scale from 0 to 10. An official letter-carrier from the US Postal Service was employed to provide independent evidence of the actual 'deliverability' and quality of all the completed envelopes. At the end of each session, the students filled out a short survey.

The groups of students participated in one of three conditions that differed with respect to the method of compensation and the opportunities for sabotage.

In the baseline piece rate condition, participants were paid $1 for each envelope produced, evaluated by the independent assessor.

The second tournament condition was identical to this, except that a bonus of $25 was paid to the person who managed to complete the most envelopes. The assessor judged who had done the most. Any changes in performance in this tournament were compared with the first, could be wholly attributed to the competitiveness created by the bonus.

In the third tournament with sabotage condition, workers were compensated based on the average score given by their peers in each group, as well as the assessor's appraisal, and a bonus was given to the winner. Here, your pay and chances of winning the tournament depended on your peers' assessment, as well as that of the assessor.

In this case, at its most brazen, saboteurs could simply undercount each other's output. From a strategic point of view, it should be obvious that each worker has the incentive to report zero units produced for each of the seven other competitors in their group. This is how one maximises the chance of winning. However, it was not expected that many people would risk such obvious acts of sabotage, since they would inevitably be detected.

To provide an environment more conducive to real-life office politics, the participants had been asked to hand-write the addresses on all of the envelopes so that there would be subjective differences in the assessed quality of the output, as well as the objective one of the crude number produced. This possibility of subjective peer assessment is at the very heart of office politics. Just as one has the incentive to undercount the output produced by one's competitors, one also has the incentive to underrate the quality of their output. Because quality (of handwriting) is so much more subjective than counted envelopes, saboteurs might feel more comfortable using it to lower the perceived productivity of their peers. Their sabotage would be less blatant and detectable.

The results did indeed provide strong evidence that sabotage is triggered by differing conditions. In the piece rate one, far from sabotaging, people actually made small gifts to each other. On average, they slightly overestimated the number of envelopes and the quality of production, compared to the independent assessor's scores: when nothing is at stake, there is no harm in being nice to peers.

The same is not true in the tournament condition with the $25 bonus for the winner. Here we find that people sabotage each other even though there is no material incentive to do so, since only the assessor's view matters. On average, competitors undercounted rivals by one envelope. This seemed to be a simple emotional response to competition for a bonus.

In the tournament with sabotage treatment, the peers gave each other even lower scores. Compared to the assessor's evaluation, peers credited each other with producing an average of about two envelopes less. Interestingly, the researchers estimated that sheer spite or other emotions account for 47 per cent of the overall sabotage that occurs in the tournament with sabotage condition. The remaining 53 per cent is likely to be strategy-driven, properly political. It would seem that much sabotage is malevolent or irrationally emotional, as well as a self-enhancing tactic.

It is one thing to miscount by one or two envelopes but in the tournament with sabotage there were twenty-two instances of the target's output being evaluated by peers as less than five units (where the average was around twenty being completed) and nine instances in which the peers reduced the target's output to zero. The researchers were amazed that people were willing to engage in such flagrant deceit that was very likely to be detected. That nearly half of it was motivated by malice was also shocking. Other, more subtle, forms of sabotage were available. It shows how crude many people are at office politics.

Another interesting finding was that the different conditions affected overall output. The workers were much less productive if the possibility of sabotage existed. It is true that, as others studies have found, adding the $25 bonus for the highest producer increases output. The number of envelopes increases by 1.125 on average when we move from piece rate to tournament. The difference may not seem large, but remember that participants only produced for thirty minutes. Over the course of an 8-hour day, the 8 workers would produce 144 more envelopes in the tournament.

However, what is most significant is that raw output actually falls in the tournament with sabotage compared to both the tournament and the piece rate conditions. It is bad enough that it engenders sabotage but to find that just the potential for it acts as a large disincentive to productive effort is striking. On average, workers produce 2.475 fewer envelopes when sabotage can alter the outcome. The tournament with sabotage condition also yields lower quality compared to the piece rate and the tournament.

Also interestingly, those students who were measured by questionnaire to expect co-workers to report their output correctly, sabotaged them less: If A expects B to report A's output correctly, then A will correctly report B's, and so on. This suggests that if there is an office culture in which trust is present, there will be less sabotage and politicking.

On a practical level, the obvious question is whether managers should foster competition among co-workers and whether they should set up promotion tournaments. One clear answer is that if office politics can have an effect on output, either directly or indirectly in terms of lost productivity due to political manoeuvring, then competition between workers should be avoided. Workers have good reason to be wary of 360-degree peer review. This study suggests that when there is any ambiguity in the performance of a competitor, workers are likely to engage in sabotage. Not only will time be spent on unproductive tasks, the atmosphere itself created by a tournament can be a disincentive to work hard.

It is far from clear whether one should use tournaments even when office politics can be kept to a minimum. If the bonus is substantial, it is not clear that the increased productivity provided by the competition outweighs the added costs of energy expended on sabotage. Recall that as soon as the bonus was added, in the tournament condition, workers started undercounting each other's output even though it could not affect the result, which was decided by the assessor alone.

Sabotage results from the fact that workers can choose between intensifying their productive effort or deteriorating their competitors' performance by destructive activities. Sabotage is pervasive whenever relative performance pay is encountered. It is easy to find examples from real life. In some American presidential election campaigns, so much effort is exerted to damage the opponent's reputation via negative campaigning that there is a failure to convey the positive merits of your own candidate.

Many leading American and British companies use tournaments to decide pay. In some cases the bottom 10 to 20 per cent of low performers identified by relative performance evaluation are advised to leave the company, a practice known as 'rank and yank'. Students of business suggest that cooperation* among employees is put at risk by such incentive schemes. The kinds of sabotage they foster include actively withholding valuable information, deliberately providing false information or even damaging tools, which are necessary for the work done by other employees. The gap between wages received by employees* with high- and low-performance ratings influences the amount of sabotage being exerted. One analysis reveals that the larger the spread* between winner prize and loser prize, the greater the sabotage. For instance, a study showed how the creation of the British football Premier League* resulted in a substantial increase in negative tactics devoted to sabotaging the performance of the opposition. The league was much more economically inequitable and tournament-driven than its predecessor.

The implication for employers is that smaller spreads in the gap between winner and loser – more equitable pay structures – will reduce sabotage and maximise effort. Charlie's experience strongly bears this out. Heiger created a system in which a great deal of energy went into sabotage rather than productive work. The implication for employees is that, if you are in an organisation which has large inequalities between the highest and lowest paid, and in which there is a tournament system of payment, if you want to get the best pay just doing a good job may not be enough. Sabotaging peers may become a significant part of the job itself, and you will be sensible to devote considerable energy to doing it effectively, as well as to defending against the destructive actions of peers towards you.

Networking

Charlie always did well with his bosses and when he met them, their bosses too. He knew how to talk a good game. However, there were some important respects in which he did not perform as required by Jerry or the system he was in. He understood very well what he was supposed to do. He just felt it was a performance too far.

The greatest deficit was in his behaviour at the three or four company weekend retreats held during the year. They were his idea of hell. He was supposed to be prominent in these situations. All the delegates put on their name badges and were expected to actively press the flesh, introducing themselves to senior figures, appearing friendly to peers, putting them-selves about with a wide smile on their face at all times. Charlie would retreat to his room and drink the minibar.

What he found so gruesome was the pretence during these weekends that you felt a personal interest in all these people. There was minimal dis-cussion of work. A prominent activity and topic of discussion was golf, a game Charlie abhorred. The retreats would be held all over the world and you were supposed to turn up a day early to play a round or two. His refusal to take up golf was mentioned a number of times by Jerry as a specific rea-son why he was not progressing, hierarchically, in terms of titles.

Charlie even went as far as to try to get out of going to some of the retreats. He would say 'Listen, I've got a young family', and because of the politically correct, lovey-dovey sheen behind which all the corporate killing occurred, they weren't allowed to say outright what they thought, which was 'sod that'. It was done by implication. When his daughter was four weeks old, he did not want to leave his wife for five days. Although lip service was paid to this uxoriousness, it was also made very clear that fail-ure to attend could end his career at the company.

The retreats were all about forming relationships across the firm on a national and international level. Jerry was appalled when one of the senior managers just below the CEO asked him who Charlie was. Charlie was told it was shocking that he had not made sure this man knew him. If Charlie was doing a good job of putting himself forward he should be pressing the flattering buttons of the key figures. For example, one of the most powerful had purchased a very rare picture by a famous Impressionist painter. If you were 'lucky' enough to get a few moments with this impe-rial presence, it was mandatory to ask what it had felt like at the moment when he knew his bid of tens of millions of dollars had won him the paint-ing. Never mind that the man must have been asked this specific question by dozens of junior employees, it seems he could not be asked it often enough.

Such stories of corporate and personal expenditure were rife and expressing enthusiasm for them was a way of showing you shared in the worship of the god Mammon, Heiger's driving force. Some of the most powerful company figures spent a total of 150 days a year airborne in their opulent private jets. Bosses boasted about the comforts of these planes, detailing the gizmos and exotic food cooked by the chefs on board. You were supposed to express jealousy of such perks. Since none of it mattered in the least to Charlie, he found it impossible to act the part of someone who cared. Whereas he could cope with impersonating a star, this was an impersonation too far.

Another weakness was his reluctance to shun unpopular peers. Once someone was a pariah, it was expedient to avoid them. There was a woman in the office who was undoubtedly bad at her job, as well as lacking political skill, but then many at Heiger were not very talented. She was being scapegoated for mistakes that had nothing to do with her. Charlie thought she was nice enough, so did not shun her when she was being edged out. If he happened to run into her in the kitchen he would talk to her, if he passed her office and she said 'Hi', he would say 'Hi' back. During her last couple of months at Heiger most of his colleagues would not speak to her, not one word. You were never thought of as a nice guy for not cold-shouldering her; politics trumped everything else. Jerry would comment on it, saying 'You're quite friendly with Suzy, aren't you?' Charlie would have to pretend he was shunning her like everyone else.

There was a queer fish Charlie knew who was very good at his job but didn't advance because he did not join in as part of the team. Someone at that lowly level could not afford to eschew staff jollies or trips to the pub. Charlie could get away with it because he was at a more elevated level, and could plead wife and kids. Whilst he did his calculated post-work pub visits with targeted groups like the risk assessors, he did not make a habit of it. People lower down could not do that. When Charlie had been starting out in the profession, he had gone to great lengths to seem like one of the lads and lasses.

*

Networking is, of course, a vital component of career progression. The evidence shows that high-flyers* tend to expend considerable energy making contact with people in other organisations who may eventually prove useful. They do their best to go to conferences and other events where they can socialise with them, like having drinks or meals. Studies show that high-flyers* tend to move between companies and between departments within companies much more than their less successful colleagues.

That Charlie did not engage in networking was one significant consequence of his lack of core commitment to a career in broking. He did not see himself as having a long-term future in it and was already stretched to the limit by his daily acting. He simply did not have the spare capacity for yet more performances.

As we shall see, the moral of Charlie's tale is that such an extreme level of subterfuge and inauthentic role-playing is not sustainable. For a more satisfying, enduring career, it is vital that there is a better fit between you and your work than was the case for Charlie.

Shafting enemies under cover of the politically correct corporate canopy

Heiger was extremely eager to present itself as a frontrunner in a new era of corporate responsibility in which everyone acted as responsible employees in a socially valuable, egalitarian, meritocratic company. If you transgressed any of the obvious no-nos, like sexism and racism, and were successfully convicted of these crimes, you became a Dead Employee Walking. There were stellar guys in the company who were had up for, in Charlie's view, very minor misdemeanours, like not promoting a woman although her gender had nothing to do with it, or making a derogatory remark about the performance of someone who happened to be a person of colour, and the off-the-cuff comment was unrelated to the person's ethnicity. These people were instantly marginalised. The company was very keen to plug itself as on the side of matey inclusiveness whereas in reality, it was a shark tank of corporate killers. It was imperative to be visibly and audibly politically correct, greatly complicating when you did what, to whom and how.

One example was a senior figure, a sex addict, despite being married with three children. He was widely known to visit prostitutes and lap-dancing clubs, as well as sleeping with the receptionist. It had got to the stage where it was common knowledge they were going to hotels at three in the afternoon and that, as a result, there would be nobody to greet visitors when they came in, a significant problem for a large company.

The first thing Charlie found weird was how long this was allowed to continue with the tacit agreement of the bosses. The second thing was that there was an internal rule that if a relationship occurred between colleagues and was regarded as a problem, the one with the lower salary would be fired, nearly always a female. This was not actually legally enforceable, but it was the custom. So it was that when their affair was finally brought into the open, she was fired and he was kept on for a few weeks and seemed to be operating just as normal. Suddenly, during a conference call with all the senior staff listening in, it was announced that he had cancer. He was temporarily allowed sick leave. Some of the secretaries in the office were crying; it was taken seriously. Charlie saw him a week later and he was absolutely fine. Eventually the cancer was reported to have been a false alarm and the executive continued in his post. The official line of equality of the sexes was simply ignored.

One of the most vicious examples of office sabotage that Charlie ever witnessed entailed use of the politically correct corporate code. There was a senior woman whom Charlie felt was a decent person but who had made a couple of enemies, including a savage head of a related department. They worked closely together but hated each other. This odious man had started lowly in the firm. He had a wife and young children and when he had suddenly made an extraordinary amount of money, he had simply dumped them. He was that kind of person.

He had been trying to undermine the female colleague for several years but because she was generally well thought of within the firm, people were getting fed up with his campaign against her. One day they had a very public row during a conference call. About twenty minutes later an email was sent from her email address. It was 'accidentally' forwarded to various people. The email expressed grossly racist comments about a person of colour working in her department.

The two rivals had worked together for a long time and years back, before they had become enemies, he had found out what her computer password was when she had asked him to check her emails when out of the office. After the acrimonious conference call she had gone to the toilet. He had logged on at her computer and sent the killer email. What was interesting was that it was very obvious that he had done it but, because it was clear that he had won that battle, nothing rebounded back on him. She was fired and he kept his job even though everyone knew what had happened. He just denied all knowledge and nothing could be proven. She had been prosecuted in the court of political rectitude and, although innocent, office politics convicted her.

Legislation to prevent sexism and racism in the workplace was, of course, never intended to be distorted in these ways. Yet it is exploited by office politicians, depending on the individual and the organisation. Wall Street firms and, indeed, those in the City of London, are notorious for their sexism. There have been many high-profile legal cases in which female employees have been given large settlements for unfair dismissal or for suffering grossly discriminatory abuse. Acutely aware of these payouts, financial services companies make great play of their codes of conduct and being seen to avoid discrimination, because the reality is much closer to what Charlie describes. This is by no means the only realm in which it happens. For example, it is a matter of public record that foul-mouthed obscenities were the norm among senior members of the British New Labour government, including frequent victimisation of individuals for their gender, as satirised in the comedy programme *The Thick of It*.

Equally, it is true that employees in many different organisations sometimes play the system by claiming victimisation where there has been none. For example, many women who become pregnant tell employers they intend to return to work after the birth, but only do so briefly after their babies are born, knowing that they are exploiting the legislation for financial advantage. If employers try to get rid of women who they suspect are going to play this game, they are sometimes heavily penalised. However, many women would understandably argue that the system in Britain gives them little alternative but to engage in this deceit. In mainland Europe, for example, this does not happen because there are much more supportive arrangements for mothers of small children.

We can learn from Charlie's account. There is no use burying your head in the sand regarding politically correct practices in organisations. It is much better to be astute as to what is going on and be sure not to be a victim of the system, whether a manager or an employee. That means becoming a better office politician.

The actor leaves the stage

In all, Charlie lasted seven years on Wall Street, three of them at Heiger. When Jerry's job was effectively ended and Charlie's death by inactivity began, Charlie believes he could easily have found another slot in the company, or else an equivalent one at another. But he was done acting, his life was becoming intolerable.

Whilst at Heiger, he would have a crisis a couple of times a year, spending a day in bed, crying, shuddering, a sort of breakdown. The necessity of living a lie, however consummately executed, had become such a big or part of who he was that it was no longer emotionally sustainable. Whilst he had managed to keep his home life separate from work, the strain of putting on a face to meet the faces that he met in his office was too much for him. The heart of the problem was that he did not have one single authentic relationship with anyone at Heiger.

There were no conversations he could have which were not political and manipulative, nobody he could have an unguarded chat with. His guard was up, constantly. It was a massive psychic drain, untenable in the long term, because there were no intimates. He was also standing up for things he did not believe in and behaving in ways that he felt were morally reprehensible. He justified it to himself by saying everyone else did it and that it was for the money, but neither of these was enough for him. It was a Jekyll and Hyde existence. He was this 'shape shifter', a monster during the week in Manhattan, not seeing his family, then there would be the weekends when he would be himself with friends and family at their countryside home.

Today, although he earns thirty times less than he did at Heiger, he feels much less stressed and far more fulfilled.

Heiger is a company in a professional sector where office politics are king. As a whole, people working in offices in which a lot of politicking goes on report lower job satisfaction and greater levels of stress. There is evidence that being a skilled politician greatly reduces the adverse impact of such environments. In a study of 105 managers*, the more that they felt they were being forced to base their decisions on office politics, the lower their job satisfaction if they were politically unskilled. Being skilled meant you reported higher satisfaction.

Another study was of two large samples* of shop assistants and customer service workers. If they felt there was little organisational support in doing their work (e.g., servicing of equipment, help if suffering domestic crises), political skill minimised the problems that created. They used the skills to reduce the stress created by lack of support and they were able to work more effectively.

In a sample of financial services workers* who had just suffered 25 per cent of their company workforce having been sacked, political skill was crucial for reducing stress. The study followed the employees over a one-year period. Those with political skills were less likely to find being highly accountable for performance in a precarious situation increased job stress. Overall, the skilled were rated to perform better partly because they felt less tense at work.

Perhaps the most sophisticated study in this field* was of nearly 200 workers at different levels of diverse occupations. It first of all measured the motivations of the workers, dividing them into two groups: those who were achievement orientated and those who were intrinsically motivated.

People who are very strongly focused on being achievers are driven by the wish for mastery, whether over physical objects, resources, human beings or ideas. They seek to gain it as rapidly and independently as possible. They overcome obstacles and attain a high standard. They rival and surpass others, increasing their self-regard by the successful exercise of talent. The fear of failure may vie with a wish for success in pushing them on. Given such ambition, they are more likely to employ political skills in order to succeed.

However, political skill may also be a response to a different kind of motivation, known as intrinsic. These people pursue work that is inherently rewarding because it serves to invigorate important emotional growth-fostering activities, such as seeking challenges, demonstrating competence and pursuing one's interests. It is true that this kind do need to look outwards for feedback on their competence, to feel relatedness and to confirm their sense of autonomy. Although the objective is to satisfy internal psychological needs, feedback from external sources is also necessary. This makes the intrinsically motivated more likely to develop political skills insofar as their self-created goals are judged by externally ordained criteria and authorities. On top of that, some of their goals may conflict with that of the organisation's and they will need politics to realise them. For instance, if there are a lot of lay-offs or frequent organisational restructuring, the intrinsic must be quick on their feet, using skills to prevent the disruption encroaching on their goals.

The study also measured the extent to which the workers were having to engage in 'emotional labour': having to suppress how they actually felt and instead, present a false face, as we saw in Charlie's case. For example, customer service representatives must display 'happy smiles' to customers who have just insulted them when they actually feel hurt and angry at the rudeness. Emotional labour results from the conflict between emotions we are forced to display and what we actually feel.

Those adept at office politics feel less emotional labour. Although they may have to simulate emotion, they will do so less because they are better at obtaining positions that have autonomy and access to resources. They are also more skilful at being able to distance themselves from necessary work personae and stay conscious of their true selves. They are more flexible and cope better with changing environments. A skilled customer service representative is less likely to be abused in the first place and if it does happen, can allow their persona to take the flak, feeling much less upset by the experience as a result.

The display of emotion itself may be a strategic ploy or a form of impression management. It is impossible to engage in any political action without expressing an appropriate emotion. For example, expressing ingratiation is incompatible with displays of anger. All politicking includes a level of 'appropriateness'. If the actor is skilled it enhances feelings of personal security and reduced internal turmoil and emotional labour. Job tension and anxiety diminish.

Sure enough, in the study of intrinsically or achievement motivated employees, the skilled suffered less emotional labour and performed more successfully.

Having a strong will to be political is not the same as skill, you need to be good at it and that means something less extreme than the continuous adoption of a false persona, the carapace behind which Charlie hid. Although a brilliant actor, you could say that in the end, Charlie's exceptional skill was not enough. He lacked intrinsic motivation. In the end, he was carrying such a heavy load of emotional labour, he could no longer sustain his role. He had to change career. A further body of evidence* suggests that people who are intrinsically motivated have better lives in every way. Not only are they more fulfilled by their work, they are less prone to mental illness. In moving from his achievement-orientated career at Heiger to a more intrinsically satisfying one, Charlie found a better way.

The object of this book is to help you to live a less emotionally laboured working life and often that means becoming more intrinsically motivated. But whatever your motivation, office political skills are the means for reducing grief at work and increased likelihood of achieving goals.

It boils down to this: you do need to learn how to act and how to simulate appropriate emotions; but you also need to find a career and a post within it where you can still be yourself to a sufficient degree. That way you avoid a crippling weight of emotional labour which, at worst, could leave you physically as well as emotionally dead. Indeed, as I shall explain in the concluding chapter, it can be a crucial building block in improving your emotional health.

Chapter 8

Astuteness

An eleven-year-old boy is part of a seven-a-side rugby team. The squad contains eleven players, of whom half are conspicuously better than the others. Despite this, the team manager by no means fields the seven best players every week.

A mother of one of the talented players is mystified. She cannot work out why the manager would not put forward the team most likely to win. Alas, she lacks the social and political astuteness to figure it out. Without this, she is completely powerless to do anything to change the situation, to engage in the politicking that might lead to the strongest team being fielded, or else, to move her son to a different club.

On a social level, she cannot 'read' the manager. Perhaps there is some malevolence in his actions, perhaps it's something to do with him wanting to feel he is in control? She has no instinct for what he is really like. Nor does she have political astuteness. She cannot work out what practical gains might be achieved by his decision. Is he doing it because he sees the team as a potential vehicle for boosting the confidence of relatively unskilled players, by making them feel good through selection? This is essentially a benign motive, even though their lack of ability is all too plain to them, as well as the spectators, so it does not seem very helpful? Perhaps it is because the unskilled players come from the same part of town as the manager, meaning he is doing it as a form of nepotism, to help the children of his friends?

Without astuteness we are lost in any situation but especially so at work. Your boss gives you a look. Your colleague does not copy you into a vital email, leaves you out of the loop. An article appears in the business section of a newspaper quoting one of your competitors' views of your company's quarterly results. What intentions lie behind these actions?

Astuteness provides the answer: being able to accurately perceive and then interpret the thoughts and feelings of others, and of yourself. Having read these correctly, you can make practical plans. Without being astute there can be no effective office politics or indeed, capacity to get your way in other domains of your life.

You need to be astute in three respects*:

1. **Reading others**: You have to be able to read the thoughts and emotions of the people around you on a second-by-second basis. Based on what you read, you make realistic guesses about their motives and future intentions, constantly updating these as you develop a picture of your colleagues' plans and their characters.
2. **Reading yourself**: you have to be good at monitoring the way others are making you feel, how you are responding to them and, most fundamentally, have as good an idea as possible of what your motives and goals are. In your career, the clearer you are about where you are trying to get to in the short and the long term, the easier it will be to work out how to get there. At the personal level, you need to work out what you enjoy, as well as what you are good and bad at. You also should know your idiosyncrasies, how and why you react to people and situations, for good and ill.
3. **Reading the organisation**: being able to see how the organisation really works is not just a matter of the chart mapping the structure and line management. You need to grasp who counts in relation to your specific role within your area, whom you need to impress in order for you to achieve promotion and better pay, and who your ri-

vals are. Beyond this, you develop an awareness of the potentiality of the wider organisation for you, including key individuals who need to be networked with (assuming you have greater ambitions), and beyond that, which other organisations in your field matter, from suppliers to competitors, with whom you need to develop links.

There are also important subtle other factors, the cultural flavours, like whether your company aspires to an easy-going or a highly conscientious style. Some organisations portray themselves as relaxed, friendly places, such as the dotcom technology companies with their ping-pong tables and relaxation rooms. At the opposite extreme are the commercial law firms or puritanical consultancy companies, where the vibe is all work and no play: no one cares whether Jack is a dull boy so long as he earns the money by doing the hours.

These official narratives must first of all be recognised, since they are often implicit, having to be inferred rather than something that is explained to you when you first arrive. But a further level of organisational astuteness is required. There is always some gap between the declared culture, whether fun or dour, and the reality of what actually goes on. Quite a few 'fun' cultures conceal shark-like workaholia, just as some ostensibly earnest, diligent cultures are more or less ignored in practice, with a surprising amount of slacking or hedonism. Sussing out these things and then working out how you want to fit into or deviate from them is vital to both the success and enjoyment of your job.

You can achieve astuteness by two psychological processes*, one automatic, the other deliberate.

From around the age of two onwards, most of us begin to intuit what is in the minds of others and also their likely intentions, based on their behaviour. As a toddler, you chuck the food on the floor and without having to give it any thought at all, you immediately grasp from your mother's reaction that she is going to place you on the naughty step. She does not need to say anything, past experience has taught you that when she looks or behaves the way she is right now, it's naughty step time. You know this automatically, without giving it any thought. In later life, in the office, you sometimes 'just know' that someone is lying to you, or that when your boss asks you to come and see her, something about the way she says it means promotion. These understandings seem to arrive out of thin air, they enter your mind without any deliberation.

The second kind of astuteness is conscious and reflective, a slower, more complicated process that requires attention, intention, awareness and effort. It starts around the age of four. Your father lets out cries of joy as his soccer team wins the match on TV and he says to you, 'As soon as you're old enough, son, I will take you to see them play.' Using your mind, you make a number of inferences from this statement and the jubilant emotions that preceded it. You clock that this team matters to him, that it pleases him if they win. You infer that, 'If I show an enthusiasm for this team, he will be nice to me. He will take me to a football match and I will have him all to myself.' Using words inside your head, you analyse his intentions and work out how to use them to your advantage. Thirty years later in the office, it is much the same when you remember to ask your boss if she enjoyed last night's visit to the cinema. You have twigged that this is one of her interests and deliberately use it as a way of cultivating her.

Whilst nearly everyone manages to develop both these kinds of astuteness to some degree, how good they are at them varies considerably. If you are skilled at the automatic kind, you will not necessarily be smart at the deliberate.

Some people 'get' what is going on without having to think about it, yet find it difficult to consciously work out a political situation when it can only be achieved through deliberation. Others are the opposite. They seem incredibly insensitive, downright 'thick', when someone tries to use implication to convey a message to them. Colleagues soon realise it is no use assuming they have understood almost anything that has not been spelt out. Yet this same person may be a wizard at analysing others' intentions and coming up with clever wheezes, so long as it is all based on forethought and planning and does not depend on reading the immediate words and actions of real people in the present.

At one extreme, severely autistic people have virtually no automatic astuteness whatever, because they do not realise that other people have minds at all, that they exist as people with thoughts and feelings like themselves. Experiments show that if you ask autistic people to work out what someone else is thinking or feeling based on first-hand experience, they cannot guess because they do not suppose the other person has any mental life. Just as I assume that the laptop on which I am writing these words has no consciousness of me, no thoughts or feelings, so with an autistic person in the company of another human. With training, they can be taught to use their conscious minds* to work out what may be going on if they learn to hypothesise that others have experience. In some cases, they can become highly sophisticated in their understanding of what might be going on. But their automatic astuteness is so poor that there are always going to be unfortunate gaps between theory and reality. As so vividly portrayed in the film *Rain Man* and the lead character in the television drama *The Bridge*, it can lead them to make embarrassing or insulting social mistakes.

At the opposite extreme, there are people who are very largely only able to be astute through the automatic mode. Some of these are extraordinarily intuitive, almost able to read others' minds. They can be a bewildering mixture of exceptional astuteness and a disastrous lack thereof. Colleagues may characterise such people as 'emotional'. Their febrile nature sometimes seems to lack a 'pause' button. Words come out of their mouths before the consequences of speaking them have been considered, the sort of person who is liable to be told they should 'think before you speak'. They may be largely incapable of advanced plotting of their careers or day-to-day office political moves.

About 40 per cent of people* are liable to find that their astuteness – whether automatic or deliberate – is impaired when emotions run high, especially if they feel threatened by isolation or rejection. Usually because of disturbing experiences in childhood of feeling unloved or maltreated, their emotional reactivity stops them being able to read what others are feeling and thinking, and deduce their intentions from that. They may respond with anger or paranoia or tears, and they are liable to start making wild and unsubstantiated assumptions about what is going on in others, usually based on what they feel or would like others to feel, rather than on external reality.

In a few cases of extreme insecurity, it triggers a false self* through which the person develops an office political virtual world in their mind. This can lead to a disastrous misalignment with reality, but in a few cases it fosters exceptional perceptiveness and astuteness. The real person is feeling terrified, but the false one is distanced from everyone and from this remote position, sees others as pawns on a chessboard. They can be consummate Machiavels, sometimes charismatic actors, hatching elaborate schemes. Whilst it may result in their peers seeing them as cold fish, unpleasant or self-obsessed, their detachment makes them more skilled at seeing where their interests lie and how to exploit others to further them. They may also be subclinical psychopaths, oblivious to the pain they are causing others and without this restraint, freer to do and say as they please.

Depending on our childhood histories*, we vary considerably in how astute we are in different contexts, automatically or deliberately. Very few people are astute in most situations in both ways. We might be brilliant at reading our spouse at home yet useless if it entails self-advancement at the office. At the simplest level, this is a matter of what we learnt from the model provided by our parents.

If you had a mother who schooled you to be cunning, the chances are you will be too. However, you may also have blocks. Your mum was devious in dealing with you, so perhaps when you encounter a woman boss who triggers memories of being messed about by your mum, suddenly your mind is paralysed. Because it is such a complicated mixture of childhood historical experiences, made more so by what happened at school and afterwards, each individual's personal history results in an uneven picture.

Just from reading the contents of this chapter so far, you should have already realised a few things about yourself. Perhaps you have recognised that you are better at one sort of astuteness than another, be it automatic or deliberate. Perhaps you have noticed that you are better at reading people than networking or self-awareness. Whatever your mix, the best way to improve astuteness skills is through examples, rather than specific training or theoretical ideas. In reading the stories that follow, you should be able to identify areas where you are stronger or weaker, and apply the lessons to yourself, a bit like learning from experience, which is by far the most effective way to acquire office political skill.

Jill is a well turned-out, confident thirty-three-year-old mother of two. If there are cat-like people and dog-like people, she is a dog person, running up to say hello and showing she is pleased to see you, wanting to be your friend in an uncomplicated fashion. I felt at ease in her company and her enthusiasm was infectious.

Rational and highly conscientious, she gained a doctorate in English literature at a young age before opting out of the workforce for six years to care for her two children. In her early thirties she decided to start earning money and went in search of a career beyond academia. She got a job at Faithful, an organisation that promotes understanding between religious faiths through public events like seminars and exhibitions. She plans and executes these with two colleagues, her supervisor, Jim, and with Geraldine, who has been at the organisation for a similar time to her.

Her relationship with Geraldine is an interesting illustration of the complexities of automatic astuteness. Geraldine is in her early twenties and, according to Jill, from the beginning 'deliberately or unwittingly' made her life difficult. Jill intuited from the start that Geraldine's reaction to her arrival was 'Uh-uh, I'm not going to let you come in here and be better than me.' Jill believes that Geraldine perceived her as a threatening rival who was seeking to displace her. However, this may be a good example of an automatic perception being incorrect. Jill's criticisms of Geraldine's subsequent behaviour during the year in which they worked together were of a lack of productivity, unstable irascibility and unprofessionalism. She provided few examples of actual rivalry.

Whilst preparing for a seminar, both women had the job of finding speakers to attend. Being so assiduous and competent, Jill came up with twice as many as Geraldine. At a meeting, Geraldine infuriated Jill by suggesting it had been easy for her because she merely had to call universities to book 'B-grade' academics. Jill thought, 'You bitch, you backstabbing bitch.'

Subsequently, Geraldine went on a week's holiday in Barbados. Jill picked up the slack, attempting the difficult task of booking a famous individual on Geraldine's behalf. For this she got no thanks and had to stick her heels in hard in order for the job to be passed back to Geraldine on her return.

There were occasional weeks when Geraldine worked conscientiously but most of the time she did not seem to have her heart in the job, resentful of the long hours they often worked. When she proceeded to have an affair with another employee, her output almost ceased completely for a few weeks. Attending a Faithful exhibition in a foreign country with her beau as well as the rest of the team, Geraldine sloped off with him leaving everyone else high and dry for prolonged periods.

What was more, Geraldine turned out to be prone to aggressive outbursts. On one occasion, she was speaking about something and Jill made a passing remark. This was an open discussion regarding what was the best subject for a talk, not a presentation by Geraldine, so interruptions were common and acceptable. Geraldine responded to Jill by slapping her hand down on her knee and shouting loudly, 'Don't interrupt me! I hate it when people interrupt me!'

Geraldine mocked Jill as being a 'teacher's pet' for working hard and doing her best to get along well with her bosses. She also sneered at Jill's diligence, implying that the organisation did not deserve such devotion. These criticisms and similar ones indicated disdain for Jill, not that she was competing with her. Overall, far from her initial intuition that Geraldine perceived Jill as a threatening rival, she turned out to be someone who was mostly uncommitted to the work and consequently, inefficient. She also appeared to be somewhat febrile and louche.

In terms of automatic astuteness, the interesting lesson may be that Jill's initial perceptions might have been more based on herself than Geraldine. It is important to be careful to check one's first impressions. Jill mentioned that when she initially arrived at the organisation, she had recently fallen out with her closest, dearest and oldest friend. This meant she would have been glad to have been on friendly terms with Geraldine. She also said that, when faced with rivals, her strategy is to cosy up to them, try to make friends. These factors may have meant Jill felt rebuffed when Geraldine did not reciprocate the overtures, but Jill did not seem aware of this.

In speaking with me, it was not that Jill simplistically and instantly assumed it was all Geraldine's fault. She spontaneously searched within herself to find reasons for the difficulties. Jill was conscious that Geraldine's abrasiveness could have been triggered by her. Coming from a large family with many sisters, Jill knew that she was prone to be forthcoming and even dominating in conversation, and she worried that Geraldine's rage at being interrupted might have been a reaction to her assertiveness. However, she did not seem to realise that her childhood might also explain her initial misperception that Geraldine saw her as a rival. This might be because she does not fully acknowledge rivalry with her successful sisters: as it turns out, it may have been Jill, not Geraldine, who felt in the presence of a rival.

A further clue that this might be the case was that Geraldine is very attractive and was educated at Cambridge University. Jill is also strikingly good-looking and did very well in her academic career too, although she did not go to Oxbridge. It is possible that on first meeting Geraldine, Jill was the one who felt rivalry, both in terms of looks and achievement.

So, it's important not to assume our automatic impressions are astute. We may have to dig deeper to work out whether they are, or whether, in fact, they tell us more about ourselves than the other person. Research shows that when we are asked to make judgements* about others after a brief initial meeting, all of us invariably bring some baggage from our childhood histories to bear. To take two crude examples, if you were bullied by parents or siblings, you may be prone to assume hostile intentions where there are none; conversely, if you felt unconditionally loved, you may be too trusting, slow to recognise real hostility.

If a group of strangers are put in a room together* and then asked what their impressions are of randomly selected others, they often have strong views. There is wide variation in how accurate these intuitions are. Those who are careful to stick to observable evidence, like the clothing and manners of the others, and who are wary of extrapolating too much from these signs, are the most accurate. Yet it is also true that we are constantly picking up unconscious signals from each other. If we are able to make these conscious, we accurately infer a great deal. It's a tricky old business and there are several tips that might help with sorting out the veracity of first impressions:

> In doing the interviews for this book, it was striking how professional peers competing for resources (money, status, promotion) tended to attract the most poisonous vitriol. Nearly everyone had a tale to tell of a 'bastard', 'shit', 'slimy creep', or some other pejorative term, who was a direct competitor. Whilst there were some

bosses and a few subordinates who also attracted attributions of madness or badness, rivals were much more common. This might suggest you should be especially cautious of gut feelings about a rival (sibling). Just as there is a big part of us that feels intensely protective of parents, eager to protect them from criticism, so we may be less eager to think ill of bosses.

⟩ If you have a very strong feeling about a new acquaintance, as Jill did, and if, on further deliberation, you feel very certain your perception is right, that tends to indicate two extreme possibilities. Either you are bringing past baggage to bear on your perception and something about this person has caused you to dump it on them, or, this person has triggered your unconscious radar, which has enabled you to intuit a remarkably insightful true understanding. The key thing is that where there is particular intensity of feeling, be careful to test out those theories, using the person's subsequent behaviour as evidence, keeping as open a mind as possible. Bear your automatic assumption in mind but, like a scientist, treat it as an hypothesis rather than a proven fact and seek further data to confirm or reject your supposition.

⟩ Develop a habit of noting your initial impressions of people and see if you can find any patterns. Perhaps you are excellent at astutely reading some kinds of people and prone to mistakes with others. In Jill's case, for example, she may have an abiding problem in reading attractive, academically successful women in her age group, prone to assuming they are rivals regardless of the evidence. There can be whole classes of people about whom we are clueless. Some men are hopeless at 'getting' women; other people's radars shut down when presented with an authority figure. The more you can establish the areas where you can trust your automatic judgements and the ones where you cannot, the sooner you can start to take remedial action. If you can identify a group who are a blank, you can start digging in your childhood to find out why. Write these categories down on a piece of paper: Gender, Peers, Bosses, Subordinates. Ask yourself which group is easiest for you to read and which is hardest.

⟩ The next time you go to a party, a simple and entertaining game is to identify a stranger who interests you. Ask yourself precisely what predictions your instinct tells you about the sort of person they are, as specifically as possible. Put aside whether you find them physically attractive, concentrating on whether you expect them to be ambitious in their career, loving parents, someone who can be trusted, that sort of thing. Then go over and talk with them, and compare what you assumed with what you have found out. If you get along well with them, you could even ask if your initial appraisal is right, in their opinion. Of course, you can take it further by asking their friends what they think of them. At the end (if you are still sober enough), or the next morning (if you have any memory of the game), you can explore the extent to which your initial instincts were right and what parts of them were imposed on the person by you, including baggage you may have brought from your past.

In our psychobabbling culture, it's all too easy for us to use clever theorising to justify our emotionally driven, unconscious drives. As the psychoanalyst Ronald Laing put it, 'We are the veils that veil us from ourselves', and that is especially true of the highly educated who can use fancy theorising to justify just about anything.

That does not mean we all need to undergo programmes of de-education or, for that matter, have therapy. The simplest and often most effective assistance comes from intimates whose judgement you can trust. If you have a friend or colleague who knows you and your history well, whilst they will always have axes they are grinding arising from your relationship with them (e.g., your spouse or siblings may find it especially hard to be objective), they can give you telling feedback if you hack through your feelings about a problem person at work. The loudest alarm bells should ring when you become shrill, emotional and overly insistent about that person. Who knows? You may be completely right in your intuition. But do not assume so, check it out with someone whose judgement you can trust.

Jill is someone who is better at deliberate astuteness than the automatic kind, at least with regard to rivals. When she has time to work out what is going on, not having to rely on the here and now, she is more accurate. She may also find men easier to read than women. Her astuteness about her organisation, its culture and her boss, seems to have been excellent, one proof of which being her rapid promotion. Her rise is not just down to office political skill. She is both a hard worker and an effective one, someone who actively enjoys rolling up her sleeves and getting stuck in. But it was also important that Jill astutely analysed the gaps between the official narrative presented by Faithful about itself and the reality, and was then able to work out how this might benefit her.

The official story was that Faithful was successful and vibrant in sparking public discussion and ideas. There was an intention to make it something like TED, the organisation that sponsors brief talks by new thinkers. The reality was that Faithful was startlingly unproductive and inefficient, considering its resources. It was really the plaything of its sole owner, Ahmed. He used the proceeds from his other businesses to fund it, along with a substantial inheritance from his entrepreneurial father.

A man with an MBA and a theology degree, Ahmed had a sincere interest in religious ideas, and in encouraging multi-faith cooperation. Jill felt that his intentions and ideas were good, and when she explained them to friends they would say 'wow', and seem jealous that she had such an interesting job. Except that the actual productivity was remarkably small, considering there were eight people working full-time in the organisation, with Ahmed also devoting considerable attention to it. In Jill's first year, they managed to organise only two events.

The first problem was obsessive micro-management. At the end of every single day, Jill was required to submit an Excel spreadsheet of how she had spent each hour. Keeping records of how long she had devoted to different activities was itself time-consuming and fruitless for all concerned. She also had to provide detailed briefing papers of the views of every potential contributor she spoke with on the phone. In developing ideas for events and debates, she was required to set out the ideas in excessively minute detail as proposals. That the vast majority of the proposals and a large proportion of the potential contributors were never used did not seem to concern Ahmed. What was more, he had a curious pattern of work.

He would only arrive at the office at midday and it would not be until the evening that the team would meet for their discussions. These could run on for hours, putting considerable strain on Jill's husband, who, fortunately, was able to care for the children because he had a flexible occupation. The discussions would ramble obsessively from one detail to another as Ahmed thrashed about, trying to decide what debates to have with which contributors. On one occasion, they spent two hours discussing which font should be used on a document that was being sent out. Jill realised that however successful a businessman Ahmed might be, in some respects he was 'incredibly stupid', even though that seemed hard to believe since he was the boss of several successful companies.

Because he was terminally indecisive, it was extremely rare that any conclusions were reached and once they were, they were liable to be reversed. On top of all that, despite his apparent desire to hear the opinions of his employees, in the end Ahmed largely ignored them. He liked to explain that nothing should be acted upon without working out all the implications, like playing chess. Before making a move, it was vital to try to foresee what consequences could follow from every move.

Astuteness

Ahmed believed he was running a super-efficient office, with delegation of tasks and efficient monitoring. The reality was that only his opinion mattered and he was a recidivist procrastinator who spawned organisational paralysis.

Jill realised all this after a few months. She also grasped that whatever the rhetoric, Faithful was really Ahmed's plaything, his bit on the side. She seems to have been able to read his psychology based on observing him over time, different from the automatic first impressions with which she evaluated Geraldine. Ahmed had a wife and family but seemed to have little desire to return to them in the evenings, perhaps preferring the feeling of significance and power gained in the office. He may have been an insecure man who actually was incapable of intimacy and just felt lonely, gaining some sense of companionship from the endless discussions with his young employees.

Her deliberated astuteness in reading Ahmed and the organisation enabled Jill to make the best of the bad job: astuteness is the foundation for effective political action. Like all the other employees, her salary was very low, which became a serious problem since her husband's income was unreliable. She had formed a good bond with Jim and received positive appraisals from him (in this micro-managed system, these were monthly, not annual). The role of Ahmed's executive assistant became available because the latest in a long line of predecessors could no longer put up with his tendency to let meetings overrun and his sporadic outbursts of cold abruptness. Because he was secretly loathed by most of his employees, there were no internal takers for the job. Knowing it would be a substantial pay rise, Jill agreed to do it when Ahmed sounded her out. She negotiated that three-quarters of her time would still be devoted to her previous duties, which were relatively interesting compared to being his assistant. She realised it would look good on her CV and that it would give her a useful insight into the other companies Ahmed ran. It would also make him dependent on her and she would become his gatekeeper, giving her some power. Since she was an excellent time-keeper, she would find it easy to organise him and had a thick enough skin not to be bothered by irascible outbursts if she interrupted an overrun meeting and told him, 'Your next meeting is already late. You need to go to it.'

Jill's astuteness was threefold: she worked out how the organisation really ran (Ahmed's inefficient toy); she correctly divined that, although Ahmed was undoubtedly a difficult person, he was not a bad or malicious one (not triadic), so she could tolerate close contact with him; and, she knew herself well enough to realise that she could cope with his difficultness and that her conscientious efficiency would be helpful to him (something he may have intuited, in asking her). It also meant she had triumphed over Geraldine, with whom she no longer had to share an office and was barely on speaking terms.

Because she had spent so many years after university caring for her children, Jill is effectively a beginner, in terms of office politics. Nonetheless, she has politesse. Perhaps she will evolve into someone as successful as Giuseppe, an Italian-born astuteness-machine. At fifty-one years old, he is a hardened corporate warrior.

His thirty years in the pharmacology industry have entailed several changes of company and continent. He has carved out a niche for himself, sourcing and buying chemicals and other commodities used to make drugs, heading in-house broking departments within drug companies. In doing so, he was alert from early on to the fact that his loyalties would be divided between his employers and the suppliers. His career antennae are constantly directed towards the wider industry, as well as to the particular organisation where he is employed at any one time.

Effectively Giuseppe is a go-between, a trader between his company and suppliers. On the one hand, he represents his company, spending much of the day deciding what prices to pay for quantities to be delivered by a certain date. Using his contacts, his team do the legwork of finding out what is available and then he takes the final decisions and conducts the negotiations with his equivalents in supplier companies all over the world. Ostensibly, his first loyalty is to his employer, to find the best price.

However, he regards the suppliers as more critical to his long-term career and in this sense, he looks upon them as his real 'franchise', the people who he is ultimately more concerned about pleasing. In making upward moves from corporation to corporation for ever more attractive remuneration packages, frequently relocating to distant lands (he has spent years in both India and China), he is acutely aware that the corporations ultimately buy his relationship with, and understanding of, the suppliers. That means it is extremely important for him to be well thought of by them. He is therefore constantly playing a double game.

He has to persuade his chief executive, with whom his role brings him into close contact, that he has obtained the best price. Yet he has also to convince the supplier that what is being paid is the most his company is willing to. Both must believe he is being truthful and yet, in order to curry favour with them, he sometimes must deliberately lie to both (although 'lie' is not the word he uses). He will tell his chief executive that the supplier will not budge on the price, and vice versa, although that may not be true, and he is careful to use words in such a way that they cannot be portrayed as deceit. He has to be able to stand by what he has said without hanging anyone out to dry, including himself. To misjudge whom he can trust would be, as he puts it, 'career limiting' (corporate life is full of these euphemisms; why he does not just say he would be sacked is itself interesting, as use of language is an important part of corporate office politics). Because his relationships with both parties have been built up over many years, he has become finely attuned to what he dare say, and to whom. Astuteness in these matters is essential. Whereas you can be trained as a chemical engineer (as he was), he doubts you can be taught automatically to read people, but he believes it can be learnt from experience, and especially the astuteness of the deliberate kind, in which he so excels.

His patron was Carlo, a chief executive who promoted him to his first head role. Through both automatic and deliberate readings of this man, Giuseppe made the crucial shift from a senior respected buyer to a boss. He describes Carlo as 'brilliant but mercurial'. Sometimes Carlo makes people feel very small in large groups, will pick on someone and tear strips off them. He easily loses patience, can be dismissive. He is a details guy, so when preparing material for him, everyone produces masses of information. Of course, it's never quite right so at the subsequent meeting, another layer of information is added, submerging everyone under a pile of paper.

Giuseppe spotted that his colleagues were managing Carlo reactively, none were being proactive. So he took great trouble to find out in advance what Carlo really cared about and then gave him just one sheet of paper, rather than the fifty with which faults would be found. The consequences were that Carlo felt his agenda was being addressed, that he did not get waylaid by spelling mistakes, and that it took half the time to get a decision. To top it all, Giuseppe says with a smile, 'No one got a bollocking.'

This is a prime example of how astuteness about another person enables someone to work out a practical strategy to achieve a goal. But Giuseppe's cunning in cultivating Carlo went far beyond that. He introduced him to the woman who eventually became his third (and, so far, final) wife, showing his ability to anticipate the sort of partner his boss would like, not an easy thing to predict at the best of times, as anyone who has tried to fix a friend up with a date will know. Most astute of all, Giuseppe worked out that there was one thing in the world that Carlo wanted more than anything and gave it to him.

In Italy there are certain operatic events to which only members of the aristocracy have access. Giuseppe is part of that elite, whereas Carlo is from a poor home in southern Italy. His dearest wish was to attend such an event, a sign that he had 'made it'. In organising this, Giuseppe won a special place in his boss's heart.

This proved crucial in his most important company transfer to date. For several years Giuseppe had had his eyes on a similar job in an even larger corporation, a direct competitor that Carlo loathed. A straight move would alienate Giuseppe's patron so he had to shift sideways first, to another company. Within a year of the shift, the job he really wanted came up. At the interview, his new potential boss asked, 'What would Carlo say about you if I phoned him now?' Giuseppe was able to reply 'He would say hire me' because he had already anticipated this by texting Carlo the day before the interview, asking if he would back him. Within ten minutes of doing so he heard back from Carlo that he had 'bigged me up' to the new boss.

By not alienating Carlo with a premature move to the new company, Giuseppe was in the clear. He argues that timing, when you play your cards, is important and admits that, 'I played a blinder, if I am honest.' But he goes on to stress that what was even more important than the timing was the prior bonds he had established with Carlo, achieved through match-making and opera tickets. These were the product of both automatic and deliberate astuteness.

If you are astute, like Giuseppe, you gradually build up a clutch of generalisations about offices that can prove helpful. Such assumptions must always be flexible: it is vital not to assume that just because people tend to behave in X or Y ways, in Z situations, they will always do so. But as long as you retain that caution, the patterns you believe you have identified are useful.

It is Giuseppe's conclusion that a great deal of what goes on in offices and business is deeply irrational. There may be a thin veneer of rationality to the decisions people make, but he argues that in evaluating the motives of others, and yourself, it's important to allow the possibility that someone's behaviour is downright dysfunctional. If you assume that they are acting in their best interests or for the good of the company, that can blind you to what he calls the 'fuck you factor', a left-field, completely illogical malevolence.

For one thing, he believes most people assume the worst about their colleagues, not the best. More often than not, he finds, they will assume you are trying to do them down or make them look foolish, rather than you have benign intentions or an open mind. This is emotion-driven, he maintains, and often leads to hostile actions towards you.

To a certain extent, Giuseppe believes there is a simple explanation for this pattern. Multinational corporations are insecure work environments. A large proportion of employees are either on the way in or on the way out. Whichever it is, that makes them anxious. When you first start, you are scared of making mistakes and made nervous by so much unfamiliarity, both by the new people you work with and differing organisational practices. Higher up the food chain, many are watching their backs, terrified that their inflated salary will mean they are a casualty in the next round of redundancies.

Giuseppe finds that corporate managers are very territorial. When someone new arrives they assume it's a threat. He once asked a relatively junior member of a different departmental team if they wanted to get involved in a project that would take up half a day a week. The junior's boss took Giuseppe aside and excoriated him for stealing his resource and invading his patch. It was true he had not followed the right protocols and the colleague was probably right, technically, but he massively overreacted.

In another situation, Giuseppe had offered to help on something very trivial involving another department's work. Its head of six years started sending tetchy emails about how Giuseppe was trespassing on his domain and with a wounded, hissy, yah-boo tone said that since he was looking to give up this particular role, he could have it anyway. Giuseppe replied, 'No, I don't want it' but the colleague had already had a conversation with their boss. It was rampaging paranoia, a case of 'hit him before he hits me'.

Giuseppe may be right in his generalisation about this. It is an interesting fact that the most frequent comment preceding a city centre violent crime in England is 'What are you looking at?' In the vast majority of cases, the person who subsequently gets assaulted was not 'looking' at the assailant at all, or certainly not with a look that was hostile or humiliating or taunting. Most physical violence is the consequence of imagined threats and it may be the same with aggressive reactions in offices.

However, it is vital to realise that you may sometimes be suffering from the shortcomings or irrationality that your astuteness has led you to believe is common around you, that you are projecting attributes or emotions of your own on to someone else*. This is the same mechanism (called projection) that clouded Jill when she believed Geraldine perceived her as a rival – Jill projected her own rivalry on to Geraldine and based her response on that false assumption.

When the new female head of an adjacent department to Giuseppe's arrived, Giuseppe sent her a copy of some plans he had, purely for information in case they had implications for her, and out of courtesy. He had seen her CV and assumed they would work well together. She replied with a detailed rewording of the document, far exceeding what he had expected, as if she were editing his work. He found himself getting 'prickly and huffy'. Okay, his university degree had been in engineering and he had concentrated on science subjects at secondary school, but he felt she was implying he lacked the capacity to express himself clearly.

Only after he had calmed down and realised this was paranoia did he deal with the matter. He was projecting his insecurities on to her and then relating to her as if she was accusing him of being inadequate. Rather than send an email, he rang her up and said 'I just want to establish the ground rules.' All he wanted to convey was that she did not need to spend two hours of her weekend rewriting his strategy documents. He did realise this response could be seen otherwise, so he was very nervous about it. He didn't want to 'seem like a jerk', particularly to someone who was new.

Astuteness about how others may perceive your actions is, of course, tremendously important.

An interesting detail of this story is his use of the phone. He believes that for almost anything important you should not use email because it is liable to seem either too aggressive or defensive. If you use a phone call or a face-to-face meeting, it is more possible to regulate the emotions, monitoring if the other person has got your message, and if necessary, to have a dialogue so an amicable feeling of a 'win-win' solution can be reached.

Giuseppe's astuteness is fully evolved; Jill's is evolving. For most of us it is a learnt ability that increases with experience. But a few people start out astute. On day one of their first job, their automatic astuteness is fine-tuned and although experience refines their deliberate astuteness, it is already at a high level.

When Sofia left her comprehensive school in south-east England, she had just turned eighteen. Because her father was from Germany, she had a fascination with European politics and a strong drive to explore it in her year off before university. She was a focused individual with a robust work ethic. 'People at school said they were going to find themselves in a bag of coke in Peru. My wish was to work in the parliament of the European Union.' Many of her friends went straight on to university but she wanted a break from education, albeit not in search of hedonism. 'From September, when they started at university, everyone was posting pictures on Facebook showing just how drunk they were getting in their freshers' week. I wanted a proper job.'

Her clarity about what interested her and how she wanted to pursue it meant Sofia had the basic building block of astuteness. You need to know what you really want in order to get it. Based on her awareness of where she was trying to get to, she was able to work out who could help her along the way.

A lucky break got her a meeting with Tim, the chief of staff of a Euro MP who needed an intern. A mutual acquaintance put in a word for her as someone who would rub along well with others in the office. Obviously that would not be enough to get the job, she needed to prove herself. To this end, she read up on the policy areas of particular concern to the MEP. However, that would not have been enough either. There were innumerable other applicants, most of them with degrees and many five or more years older.

Sofia says the interview went well because, 'It turns out Tim is possibly one of the nicest people I have ever met in my life, which put me at my ease. It also turns out the EU is brimming with intelligent people who are just frighteningly clever, which made me insecure, so I tried to come across as intelligent as possible. I have to say I used a lot of long words.' Now aged nineteen, some of Sofia's use of language has the commonplace imprecisions of a person of that age. Her extreme adjectives – one of the 'nicest' people, 'frighteningly' clever – are examples. But even her inaccuracy in the use of these words reveals a kind of astuteness. She holds back from the indiscriminate superlatives of her generation, only rarely and discerningly wheeling out the odd 'awesome' or 'brilliant'.

Throughout her time at the EU, she did her best to wrap her relationships in the cloak of friendship. She frequently uses the word 'friend' when she means colleague or acquaintance (a generational misuse, possibly promoted by the misleading use of the word 'friend' by Facebook when it refers to someone who has simply become a contact). But Sofia was well aware of the distinction: she has deliberately adopted a friendly strategy of encouraging everyone to like her, and of trying to be likeable in work contexts.

Likewise, although frequently speaking of the impressiveness and niceness of people whom she often adopted into her inclusive family of 'friends', it turns out her awareness of their shortcomings and potential hostility was not blunted. The important ingredient of her success was that she could identify precisely in what way each person was 'nice' or 'intelligent' and then adjust herself to that. There is good evidence that the astute are adroit chameleons*, good at reading who others want them to be, and being that person. Such expediency does not necessarily mean they lose sight of who they are and what they want.

Being acutely conscious of what she ultimately wanted to achieve – to become a Euro MP herself – meant Sofia was much better placed to be calculating in her use of the opportunity of an internship at the EU parliament. As we shall see, by the time she set off to university, she had established a solid position. But she is harshly realistic about what will happen when she seeks to return in three years' time. She suspects she will have to start again as an intern, then work her way up to researcher, then on to the position she occupied by the end of her time at the EU, effectively, the chief of staff for one of the MEPs.

Since she had only one year before she would be off to university, Sofia needed to establish firm connections that would allow her re-entry once she has finished her degree. As she puts it, 'You've got to pick the people who you know will want to get behind you.' To this end she has established two political mentors, both of them reliable personal relationships. Both these men have told her, 'If you just do everything I say, then in ten, twelve years' time you will be an MEP in a safe seat.'

The first is Tim, the chief of staff who gave her her first job, with whom she has remained 'really good' friends. I suspect that when Sofia denotes someone in that category, she means they are someone who would be a true friend, even if they could not help her in her career. But she also admires him, and a rare rash of superlatives are accorded: 'He's an amazing person ... he is going to go far, you can tell. So intelligent, so brilliant, so on the ball, but also so determined and ambitious, and he has this amazing quality of being so nice and kind and genuine. It's very rare to meet one of those.' Her automatic astuteness indicated to her his likely career trajectory, so as soon as she met him she realised she had to stay on his radar as much as possible. Although, as we shall see, she stopped working with him soon after arriving at the EU, she has been careful to meet up with him regularly. He is thirty-four and there are no romantic complications, which is not true of all her associates from the EU, as we shall also see. She has astutely divined why not.

By a remarkable coincidence, before Tim worked in the EU, he had been a doctor and, it so happened, had known a number of girls of Sofia's age who are friends of hers, because they lived in the same part of the country. This means that she exists in his mind as a child, as someone who is associated with women he would never think of in a romantic context, sort of 'out of bounds'. As Sofia puts it, she believes he would just feel it was 'too weird' for him if he thought of her like that. The relationship with her other mentor is also platonic.

He is a Euro MP that just finds Sofia 'Very interesting – we talk about so many different things.' They have a shared passion for modern American literature and ballet. She finds his ideas fascinating and she thinks he feels the same about hers. When I asked whether she thought he had any amorous intentions towards her she observed that, 'I think he is still in love with his ex-girlfriend, he talks about her all the time. Which I find so much easier. If someone else is in their lives, I don't have to make any effort in that direction, either to attract them or fend them off.' Dealing with the advances of men is an area in which she displays considerable astuteness.

Having gained her foothold in the EU, Sofia was quick to begin her climb from the intern foothills. In the first week she remained 'glued to' Tim and one lunchtime in a Brussels parliament restaurant, a golden opportunity arose. She is aware that, as an attractive eighteen-year-old, it is a good idea to present herself in an earnest, rather than flirtatious way if she wants people to support her professionally, rather than seek to exploit her or view her rise with scepticism. At the same time, she is comfortable with the fact that she is good-looking, happy to wear a tight skirt or more demure attire, depending on the circumstances, and aware of the effect this has on others, so when John, a Euro MP and old friend of Tim's, joined them at their lunch table, she felt no unease that John clearly was showing an interest. Sofia was going to be in need of another job when her short period of work experience with Tim came to an end and that very evening, John told Tim she could come and work in his office. Meeting up the next morning, he stressed that he did not even need to see her curriculum vitae. Tim explained what John liked about her was 'Nothing very subtle: John likes to be around pretty things.' There was no surprise that John did not ask about her political knowledge or what skills she had. She simply happened to be wearing a tight skirt that day.

This was not her normal attire. For the interview with Tim it had been a black jacket and roomy skirt. She recalls that, 'I didn't think a short skirt or being dolled up would be appropriate, nor that it would be likely to work. I am already so conscious that people will judge me just by what I look like. Maybe it's an advantage because people remember who I am. Even now, long afterwards, people still come up to John and say "How's your 'fit' researcher, how's she doing?" That does not bother me in itself. He also quite likes them asking that, it gives him prestige. I know that is shallow but because it's how I got in. I had to prove myself to him even more through intelligence and usefulness. Instead of staying nine to five, I would get in at eight thirty and stay till seven, effectively indicating that I'm not here just because of what I look like, it's my actual ability and conscientiousness.' Interestingly, studies show that, along with chameleonism, conscientiousness* also tends to go with astuteness.

Managing John's desire for her and converting it into friendship has been about astuteness. Sofia has an unclouded perception of the situation she was in at the EU. She points out that this is an environment in which there are not many attractive young women and a great many testosterone-fuelled men away from their families. For someone like her, she says, sleeping with them would be 'like shooting fish in a barrel'. Hardly a week went by without her being propositioned. Personally and professionally she had to use good judgement and, since she likes sex and is agnostic regarding older men, her boundaries were put to the test. What she never did was sleep with anyone for career reasons. Anyway, it was easy to say no to sex with a lot of the men because she did not find them attractive. She was also careful not to drink much alcohol, usually having cranberry juice, which people assumed had vodka in it. The trickiest relationship was with her boss, John.

He has a fiancée whom she believes he will marry. Nonetheless, during the first two weeks of being there he jokingly asked to marry her two or three times. Every time she did something right he would say 'Oh God, why don't we just get married?' This was ostensibly humorous and was never accompanied by actual sexual advances. However, she was all too aware that the situation could easily become awkward, that he was grooming her for an actual declaration of love or sexual encounter. There was also the possibility that an implicit blackmail could emerge: 'sleep with me or you lose your job'.

By the time John did get around to doing something that could not be ignored, when both of them knew for sure that he was unambiguously seeking sex for real rather than flirting, she knew him well enough to work out how to put him off. For one thing, by then she was sleeping with several different men. Whilst John did not know for sure about any of these, she had ensured that he had a pretty good idea that she was already spoken for. After work, they had taken to going together to the bars around Brussels where much of the politicking goes on. He had witnessed numerous men making passes at her, so he had picked up on the fact that she got a lot of attention.

More than this, she worked out that if he thought she was spoken for, he was the kind of man who would accept that as a reason. So she told a story to a friend of his which she was sure would get back to him. She had had two dates on Valentine's Day and they had both turned up at the same time. It was a harmless yarn but he picked up on it, recognising she had a sex life and joking about her profligacy. Lots of his friends suggested to him that she had boyfriends as well. This implicitly put him out of the reckoning without making him feel inferior because he was the kind of man who felt his status was increased by having a highly desired assistant.

To avoid a reputation as a 'slag' and as someone who was sleeping her way to power, she carefully controlled how much information anyone had about what she actually did, shrouding herself in mystery to a certain extent. She realised it would be useful to her if it was known that she was not a nun, that men would think they had a chance with her and that this would advance her career. But she controlled the information, which she would let slip in such a way that it seemed everything said about her was based on assumption. No one ever quite knew what was really going on. She did not tell anyone actual names or numbers. She had also worked out that, on the whole, unless you are wildly and publicly promiscuous, as a woman today you are allowed to behave like a man. Men are not stigmatised if they have multiple partners, so long as they do not treat the women badly. Indeed, being Jack the Lad is seen by some as admirable. Something similar is now the case for young women.

By the time John made his move, Sofia had already proved herself to be professionally capable, far beyond her years and had become indispensable to the working of his office. He also realised she was a valuable social asset. Many of the most interesting things happened after work, that was where vital information was acquired about what was really going on, who had what ideas, who was ambitious, who was getting out of line. Because she stayed sober, Sofia would be able to recall what had been said the next morning. She was also useful to him as an ice-breaker – 'Hi, meet my shiny new toy' – and as someone who could provide anecdotes, had opinions of her own, was not just something to look at. In short, John is a compulsive socialiser who had found a useful companion in Sofia, as well as a highly efficient office administrator, speech-writer and adviser. She was in a position where he would not want to do anything that would mean he lost her.

As an attractive woman, she had had plenty of experience of letting men down gently before she arrived at the EU, of subtly saying 'Thanks for the compliment but I really don't want to sleep with you.' She usually used humour, 'Oh very funny', it's a bit of a joke, but it's not going anywhere. On the evening he tried to sleep with her, she joked that she would break his heart, saying 'You don't want this, trust me.' Then she used the, 'Oh what a laugh this is, what an amusing proposal that could be', before quickly changing the subject, 'Have you done that speech yet?' He was happy to be let off the hook, with 'Oh damn, yeah, got to do that'.

Of course, that did not completely extinguish his desire for her but she was able to find other methods for reinforcing her message. Colleagues in John's constituency office had started having an affair, which ended acrimoniously. They were now getting on so badly that it was causing havoc. Sofia found herself having to do much of their work and she was careful to have seemingly friendly chats with John about what a bad idea office affairs are. He still sometimes joked that 'Sleeping with the boss will get you everywhere.' But she had thought this through in every way. She did not find him attractive but even if she had done so, she would never have allowed anything to happen. A lot of her political friends asked her about it but she would have regarded it as a dangerous mistake, something that could do her no good.

Interestingly, she did have a steady relationship for some time with John's best friend, another MEP whom she found attractive, if a little dull. When I raised the possibility that this might lead John to feel very envious if he found out, she seemed to have considered all the angles. If her boyfriend got drunk and revealed something, there was a good chance he would not be taken seriously. If necessary, she could plausibly deny it and laugh it off, or if forced to do so, retreat behind an elusive mask. But it was unlikely the MEP would want anyone to know, it might damage his career for it to emerge that a thirty-five-year-old was sleeping with a nineteen-year-old.

*

Sofia's story illustrates well the scientific evidence regarding astuteness*. People who are good at it are also liable to be chameleons and conscientious. If you are both conscientious and astute, you are also very likely to be politically skilled. As we saw to varying degrees, both these traits were also evident in the stories of Jill and Giuseppe.

What should be apparent by now is that astuteness is an essential prerequisite for political skill. Jill could not have become Ahmed's assistant and made that work without being astute. Giuseppe could not have juggled suppliers and employers, and played his boss, without astuteness. Likewise, if she had not been astute, Sofia could not have both fended off her boss and become an indispensable figure in his life.

However, it is one thing to be astute, it is quite another to be able to execute plans. To do so you must identify the right tactics and employ them effectively. This brings us to the nuts and bolts of office political activity: tactics.

Chapter 9

Ingratiation

Ingratiation works*…durr! It's obvious: if you need something from some-one and you can get them to like you by making them feel good, they are more likely to give you what you want. Not so durr is that you must read the other person right and execute your ingratiatory attempt well, easier said than done. First, you need to identify what will make the target person feel good. Second, you need to find the right way to achieve that in a way experienced by the target as sincere.

Ingratiation can be done using a number of different techniques, alone or in combination. I shall focus on three main ones: chameleonism, flattery and favour-rendering.

Chameleonism

Chameleonism is the mirroring of another's mannerisms* or speech pattern back to them, and in most cases, whatever ingratiatory tactic is employed, be it flattery, charm or some kind of inducement (professional or personal), a measure of chameleonism is usually essential. It is a rare instance of a trait that has been thoroughly, scientifically and skilfully researched.

Constant chameleons strategically cultivate public appearances by paying close attention to their social surroundings and endlessly adapt-ing to fit in with them. Known technically as 'high self-monitors', they are social pragmatists. They construct and project images with the goal of impressing others, seeking enhanced status. It is virtually impossible to rise to the top of a corporation without employing some chameleonism. Even the brassiest and most brutal of non-corporate entrepreneurs know how to do it, although in their cases, they tend to use it rarely with their employees, reserving it for rivals or negotiations.

To a certain extent, nearly everyone does it automatically when in the presence of a person from whom they want something. If someone else reflects your own views back to you or seems like you (because they are using your terminology, gestures, emotional tone), you feel better disposed towards them. The propensity to mirror has its origins in infancy, when our parents unthinkingly smile and wave back at us in response to our smile or wave, or use 'goo-goo, ga-ga' noises that precisely mimic the tone and volume of our noises. From those early beginnings come basic intimacy and the capacity to get on to another person's wavelength. Being mirrored early on enables us to become mirrors ourselves.

In later life, at school with friends or when observing role models on television, we pick up on their signature behavioural patterns and incorporate them, just as our parents did with us. Once in the office, we quickly latch on to cultural and behavioural norms, and to greater or lesser degrees, adopt them in order to fit in. Ingratiatory subordinates particularly imitate bosses, often unwittingly adopting their favourite words or gestures when in their company.

You can work out how much of a chameleon you are from the following test. Read each of the following statements about your behaviour at work, grading your response to each one according to the scale below. Then add up your total score.

1. Never
2. Rarely
3. Occasionally
4. Quite often
5. Frequently

1. I am a different character at home than I am at work.
2. I find I have less and less in common with my old friends.
3. I tend to follow workplace fads and fashions.
4. I can justify behaviour I would have disapproved of in the past.
5. I find myself using the office jargon without realising it.
6. I believe that to 'get on' I need to be seen to fit in.
7. I behave in ways that I think others (or my boss) want me to.
8. I feel embarrassed about some of my attitudes or hobbies and hide them from colleagues.
9. I always do the 'social thing' in the office even when I don't want to.
10. I find myself judging others for not fitting in.
11. There are some changes in myself since being in my present job that I do not like.
12. I do things I don't agree with without challenging myself.
13. I find I agree with many of the attitudes and opinions expressed at work.

If you score under 26, you are non-chameleon. A score of 24–39 is medium. Over 40, and the nearer you are to the maximum possible of 65, the closer you are to being a constant chameleon.

People who score high on this test of self-monitoring – what I call constant chameleons – are much more deliberate about these processes than non-chameleons. They carefully squirrel away facts and behavioural patterns of others, choosing the right moment to play them back to targets whom they wish to impress or gain favours from. For example, using precisely the same phrases or individual words can be highly effective. When I was working as a documentary television producer in the early 1990s, there was an executive who started using the expression 'up to speed' as a trendy way of conveying the idea that a person was on the ball and well informed. A junior colleague with whom I was working was sarcastic about this behind the executive's back but when speaking with him, managed to find a way to use those exact words, winning the executive's approbation. The executive had no idea he had just been the victim of chameleonism. Similarly, working in television during that period, the senior figures in the organisation took to wearing sharp designer suits (this was before the era of women executives in that industry). Aspirant executives started doing the same.

Charlie, the consummate actor from Chapter 7, is the most skilled constant chameleon I have encountered. From his initial interview for his job at the broking company onwards, he identified precisely what would please others and then impersonated it flawlessly. But as we saw, he was such an extreme case that it proved unsustainable for him personally and, as we shall see, constant chameleons can penalise the organisation they work for, as well as themselves, by this trait.

In contrast to constant chameleons, non-chameleons attempt actively to convey to others that they present no false images, itself a form of image management. They are less willing and less able to project impressions that are different from their privately experienced self. They do care about their impressions but only to the extent that it is a genuine reflection of self. As such, they use impression management as a principled strategy of representing their 'true self' to others. For this there is often a price to be paid, in terms of career progression. Put crudely, telling the truth at all times limits your success. Hence, both constant chameleonism and non-chameleonism carry penalties.

Studies of constant chameleons* suggest ten main findings about them compared with occasional or non-chameleons.

1. They use impression management tactics more often and especially proficiently.
2. They are slightly more likely to be successful in their careers, though they see themselves as more so than they really are. They exaggerate their seniority, pay and so forth compared with objective measures, but it is true that there is some career premium.

3. They tend to be seen as more leader-like in the eyes of others, possibly because they manage impressions so that their public image matches critical features that others expect in leaders, like being dynamic and assertive. However, there is no evidence that they are actually more effective leaders. There is, in short, a measure of charlatanism regarding their perception of their success and they do not make more effective leaders than a non-chameleon.

4. They are slightly more likely to have better educational records and to gain higher scores on problem solving and IQ tests.

5. They are more likely to report higher levels of job involvement. They claim to be more invested in their roles than people who emphasise their 'true self'.

6. However, despite their claim to be more invested in their work, they actually have less commitment to their organisation, and are quicker to move company if it suits them, making them disloyal employees. They are also prone to lack of commitment in personal relationships (including a tendency towards sexual infidelity), which are consequently less stable.

7. They are more likely to experience (or report) greater role stress, because they are constantly struggling to get a good fit between who they are supposed to be and who they really are.

8. Although presenting themselves as being more involved in their jobs, the greater role stress and lack of commitment to their organisations makes them less satisfied by their work.

9. We become less chameleon-like as we get older.

10. Men used to be more chameleon than women at work, although this finding is based on studies from over ten years ago and may not still be true.

Overall, unless you do not care at all about your career progression, it is essential to be capable of chameleonism sometimes*. If you do not make your bosses and peers feel you are like them to some degree, you will pay a career price for seeming like an outsider. However, there is a strong case for suggesting that it should be a strategy that you adopt sparingly if you want to feel satisfied in your work.

For instance, Georgina is an accountant in a global firm who used chameleonism to achieve a higher appraisal rating than would otherwise have been the case. Her boss, Samuel, had known her work from early on in her career at the company and she realised he was destined to rise high. She carefully cultivated their relationship, doing her best to make it personal and friendly through shared interests. He was keen on French Provençal cooking, so was she. Unlike others in that office, both also liked discussing culture, history and politics. Both were graduates of Cambridge University, and since he was a bit of an academic snob, that worked in her favour. Given this common ground, it was not hard for her to make him feel that they were fellow travellers. Mostly she did not have to pretend, she genuinely enjoyed his company, but she had to be slightly manipulative in other respects.

She could see that he was lonely and did not have a girlfriend, staying late in the office almost every night. She was in her early thirties, he was forty and she could tell that he found her physically attractive. He would make disparaging comments about the appearance of other women and she worked out that her somewhat graceful, neat self-presentation appealed. However, she was careful not to lead him on. She had a boyfriend, whom she married during this period, and although Samuel mildly flirted with her, she never allowed it to seem more than a joke with perhaps just a tiny hint of promise. She had to fake intimacy at other times as well. At the end of the working day he would come in for a chat. She would think 'Oh shit, it's Samuel', knowing it might make her late for evening social engagements, but she would pretend to enjoy his company for as long as suited him. He was prone to telling long-winded stories, and she would go to some lengths to make him feel that they personally related to her experience, acting like a mirror. Above all, his jokes were not at all to her taste and in an ordinary social situation she would have made it obvious she was not amused. Instead, she let him think she shared his sense of humour. Whilst this did cost her a measure of emotional labour – a conflict between true feelings and expressed emotion – she used her insight that she was doing this deliberately to minimise the stress.

Within her highly competitive world, these relatively minor acts of chameleonism paid off handsomely. When he was promoted, he became the ultimate arbiter of her bonus. When the pot was shared out, she usually got more than her fair share simply because he felt she was a like-minded person. Georgina's skill at her work was part of the reason for the bonuses and there was no question of imagining that the bonuses would give him romantic or sexual opportunities. But she estimated that the chameleonism probably added 20 per cent to what she got. It was a simple case of effective chameleonism for some of the time in that particular working relationship, a healthy exercise in office politics.

Equally, healthy chameleonism can be used on subordinates to great effect. Jan, a harassed junior management consultant in a top company described how she went to great lengths to cultivate personal assistants. Because the PAs had little financial incentive to do more than the minimum, if you were a junior executive you could only get their cooperation through personal relationships. If she had a spare moment she would call in the PA and ask about her children or social life, taking care to find matching stories to make the PA feel they were on the same level, human beings just trying to get by. She also did this with the PAs of senior figures in her department, knowing that the bosses sometimes used their PAs to take the temperature and that it was possible if Jan's name came up, that they would speak approvingly of her.

This kind of occasional chameleonism is harder for a boss or subordinate to spot and consequently, can be more effective. However, constant

chameleons are a mixed blessing*. Their lack of commitment to the organisation* and tendency to feel stress in their roles is balanced out by
the fact that they are keen to fit in (making them pliable), to get ahead
and to do whatever it takes to be liked. There is evidence that chameleonism is more common among senior managers* than less powerful
employees, although it is unclear whether this is because it becomes
increasingly necessary as you rise, or whether those with the attribute ascend because of it. There is certainly a question mark over whether they
truly contribute more to the organisation. There are studies showing*
that those who want to be true to themselves but also have more to offer
are less likely to be promoted than relatively untalented chameleons.
This suggests strongly that chameleonism undermines meritocracy, that
it is a major means by which the relatively untalented progress.

Chameleons are also more prone to move between organisations*.
This is a key predictor of career success but from an employer's standpoint,
if someone measures high on this trait, it points to a lack of loyalty.

From an employer's perspective*, there is another reason to question
promoting chameleons into leadership roles: who or what provides the
rudder for a ship that is captained by someone who looks to others for cues
as to what to think and who to be? Their wish to fit in with surroundings
contributes to their ascent into senior management. Yet for them to do a
good job, they need a potent strategic plan and to provide some measure
of ethical guidance. Whilst non-chameleons may rub along less well with
their peers, they may be more likely to have this strong sense of strategy.

Constant chameleons will pretty much do whatever it takes to
enhance their social appearance in a given situation, making them eth-
ically pragmatic, looking to others to determine what to believe and how
to act. As such, they are susceptible to unethical influences. It is true that
they would also be likely to conform to ethical behaviour if that were the
prevailing social norm in their organisation. But in the ambiguous organisational and wider political cultures which are now so common, their

ethics could go astray. If they are the sort of chameleon whose guiding principle is to win at all costs, it would likely lead to taking advantage of others on a regular basis. It is very likely that executive chameleonism was a contributory factor to the failure of high-flying companies such as Enron, WorldCom, Northern Rock and Lehman Brothers. Non-chameleons are better able to cope with role and organisational ambiguity because they know who they are, relying on their own internalised values. Senior managers who have identified constant chameleonism in an employee who is being considered for promotion should beware of over-promoting them. They are skilled at giving the impression of having more leadership qualities than is actually the case, because they are good actors.

Flattery

Flattery is the manipulation of another by making them feel enhanced and is a tool for self-advancement. Flattery is strategic praise, praise with a purpose. It may be inflated and exaggerated, or it may be accurate and truthful, but it is praise that seeks a result, whether preferential treatment or an office with a window.

It certainly can be remarkably effective. I was surprised when a hugely powerful man of exceptional integrity and little vanity, someone I had known from my earliest years, told me that if he had one piece of advice to pass on, it was that 'flattery works'. I could not begin to imagine how he could be flattered, this was a man with a bloodhound's nose for inauthenticity. If you went to the theatre with him and made a pretentious observation about the show when driving home, he had a way of subtly letting you know that you had just said something self-aggrandising, however clever your observation. Yet even someone as astute as him was a sucker for flattery. 'I fell for it more often than I care to remember,' he told me.

The danger with flattery is if it is noticed*. That only has to happen once and it could change the way the target perceives you for ever. Okay, there are the occasional safe bets. As described by Charlie, the master thespian from Chapter 7, the head honcho in his company was guaranteed to respond well to a request to describe the moment he bid successfully for a very rare picture by a famous Impressionist painter. Equally, there are colleagues in every organisation whose vanity and self-love know no bounds. Such a person will not notice even crude flattery. But these are exceptions. Normally, deliberate flattery should not be undertaken lightly. If detected, it can make you seem generally smarmy and untrustworthy, or it can point up a clash of values.

A senior executive described to me how one of his subordinates got it wrong. The subordinate was known to be a ladies' man. During a social occasion, the executive commented on the attractiveness of a female colleague, as he believed she was using this attribute to advance herself, but that was not clear from what he said. The subordinate misread the comment, assuming it meant the executive was also leery.

A few days later the executive took his female PA out for lunch. On their return, the subordinate sought to flatter the executive by saying 'Nice one, boss, you obviously know what you are doing', giving him a 'nudge nudge, wink wink' look to indicate a manly collusion regarding sexual affairs. Just this single comment caused considerable harm. Not only was the executive not a ladies' man, he was deeply offended by the idea. The subordinate's progress within the company suffered grievously.

Flattery works best if you keep it as close as possible to the truth of what you really feel. If you can find something about the other person that you genuinely admire, it's more likely to sound true. That can turn into a general habit of simply being positive to colleagues about their performance. If they have done something well, tell them. This does not need to be a bland 'have a nice day' automated friendliness. You can be someone who is relied upon to give credit when it is due.

That kind of praise is subtly different from deliberate and calculated exercises in dishonest ego massage. Sofia, the nineteen-year-old intern in the European Union parliament from the last chapter, knew how to flatter deliberately. When surrounded for much of the time by lascivious, often tipsy, middle-aged men, this was not difficult. If necessary, she simply would lie, saying 'I heard the question you put to that committee the other day – you really nailed them', and the man would start purring. But on other occasions she had to be more adept.

John, the MEP for whom she worked, had a speechwriter who spent one day a week in their office. This was a twenty-six-year-old woman, named Helga. At first she was markedly standoffish to Sofia, cold and pointedly ignoring the 'new girl', refusing to even speak to her, continually trying to put the junior in her place. Helga never asked Sofia to do anything for her, research or other help with the speeches, although Sofia made it apparent that she was available to assist in any way.

Sofia thought carefully about what might be motivating this attitude and how to change it. Her automatic astuteness radar told her that it could partly be a matter of female sabre rattling. Her own more youthful and glamorous looks could mean Helga felt threatened in this domain, since Helga might be used to being the only object of desire in this sexist, male-dominated environment for most of the time and might not like competition. Sofia evaluated Helga as 'All right looking: nice body, nice face but nothing special.' So her first tactic was to be friendly to her regardless of how unfriendly the response, trying to give off the impression that she posed no threat as a female rival whatever. When Helga arrived she would welcome her by saying 'Hi, Helga, how are you? You look so nice today.' By pointedly and repeatedly referring to Helga's pleasant appearance, she hoped to relegate her own.

At the same time, she bent over backwards to convey that she respected Helga's greater experience and capability, encouraging her to feel that she did not regard herself as any sort of match in those respects. She wanted to show that she was not trying to take over her job in any way, steal the speechwriting role or the attention of John. A key way of doing this was to pointedly defer to her in front of him, when they were all together. If John asked her to do something, Sofia would suggest that it might be better if Helga did it and that she would only be suitable if Helga was too busy, for Helga was the one who would know best. This technique is known as 'supplication', in which you strategically present yourself as weak or insufficiently qualified to perform a task. It is most often used as a way to get out of doing something you do not want to do, perhaps because you see the task as a poisoned chalice or simply because you cannot be bothered. But in this case, Sofia used it as a form of flattery and quite quickly, Helga began to regard her as less of a threat and to sometimes say to John 'I'm too busy, let Sofia do it.'

It turned out that Helga had far too much work and was only too happy to pass on some to Sofia, once she ceased to see her as a personal and professional threat. Sure enough, by the time she set off for university, Sofia had established herself as one of John's main speechwriters. She and Helga became firm friends, eventually sharing an apartment.

Sofia makes the point that had Helga been a man, different tactics, with some of the same elements but differently executed, would have been required. But whether dealing with men or women, the same principles of flattery apply. Some of it can be done as part of a general tactic – as was very much Sofia's approach – of being positive about others' successes, for which no falseness is required. With other people and in specific situations, a well-acted deliberate lie is effective: telling the MEPs how wonderful their performances were or telling Helga how nice she looked.

Favour-rendering

Another simple and fundamental ingratiation method is to do favours for colleagues, actions that help them which are not required as part of your role ('favour-rendering'). This was the main tactic Sofia used to deal with Miguel, the principal rival in the office where she worked.

When she started there as an intern she quickly realised Miguel was someone she would find it hard to like. She recalls that he was 'Possibly the most miserable, difficult person in the world.' A friendly greeting on a Monday morning would be returned with, at best, a grunt. Even when dealing with senior political figures, he only just managed to avoid being actively rude by his manner. He had no social life, and Sofia quickly realised that he resented her arrival.

Pursuing her friendly philosophy, she set about winning Miguel over by persistently offering to do anything he did not want to do. For example, the nearest shop where milk could be purchased for the coffee was a ten-minute walk away. If there was none she would run and get some because he liked a lot of milk in his coffee. She stayed late in the office to make sure everything had been done. Since he was both inefficient and idle, he appreciated that she was saving his skin.

Very gradually, she converted the favour-rendering into a way of displacing him and, insofar as he was capable of it, making him amicable towards her. It was Miguel's job to do the press releases for John. One day, John suggested that Sofia take a look at one. Since Miguel was 'As humourless as a cornflake', she inserted a joke, which John appreciated. As a result, she was given the releases to read through after Miguel had done them and before they went to John. She would correct the many spelling and grammatical errors, at first, then she started inserting useful changes to the wording. When Miguel showed them to John, they were considerably improved. Sofia was well aware that he took credit for her changes but did not complain about this. Eventually, Miguel came to trust her to such an extent that he made the mistake of suggesting that she do one all by herself. When she showed it to John, he was full of praise and although Miguel did not like that, there was nothing he could do about it. From then on there was a change in the office dynamics. Within two months she was responsible for the releases and became increasingly indispensable. John would make jokes, saying 'Miguel, why do we have you here?' First thing in the morning John would ask her what was on. When he had a practical problem to solve, like what shareholdings to declare, he would turn to her.

Like Sofia, Giuseppe the pharmaceuticals executive from the last chapter, also found favour-rendering very helpful. For example, he fostered a good relationship with a headhunter – who subsequently played a crucial role in his career – by sending her the names of colleagues who might be useful candidates for jobs she was trying to fill. Giuseppe is strongly of the view that 'what goes round comes around' and what is more, that there is a price to pay for not rendering favours, for being, essentially, selfish.

It was for this reason that he disliked one colleague whom he had known for twenty years. She had never lasted more than two years in any organisation, criss-crossing her way between a variety of different functions. She believed you get on by doing your own thing very well and ignoring everyone else.

One day, Giuseppe sent her a CV of a friend in case the guy might be useful to her. The man was looking to get back to the UK and had worked in pharmaceuticals before. He seemed potentially right for her department and she replied that they were looking for someone like that. However, Giuseppe never heard anything again about it, despite following it up several times.

On another occasion he sent her a potentially very useful connection she could use to advance her part of the business. Again, he never heard back.

Giuseppe concluded, 'I will never do anything for her now. I pushed two things her way and she wasn't prepared to spend even five minutes thinking about it. I know her, have done so for twenty years. If she treats me with that disdain, and we are equals in the business, pretty much, how does she treat other people? It's just so stupid.'

At the very least, if others attempt favour-rendering with you, it is important to appear responsive and grateful, even if you are not. More generally, it is true that what goes round does indeed come around. People who favour-render tend to prosper*. Obviously, the lower down you are in an organisation, the more user-friendly you should be. As you rise further up, Giuseppe's benign approach is often advantageous but that does not mean becoming a dustbin for all the jobs no one wants. Favours should be offered strategically, and ultimately with some view to self-advantage, not on the basis of promiscuous altruism. If you are the kind of person who everyone knows is a soft touch for unwanted tasks, doing them because you are desperate to be liked and lack self-esteem, you have to recognise the pattern and put a stop to it.

Put simply, ingratiation is the least line of resistance in most situations. It will rarely do you any harm and is likely to help in creating a good vibe for you in your professional network, a good reputation. However, it is not as proactive as the tactics we come to next, ones which are more direct in pursuing a goal.

Chapter 10

Go-getting

A cluster of tactics can be used when you are hoping to get your way through forceful action: assertiveness, self-promotion, feedback-seeking, negotiations, networking and reputation-building. None of them necessarily require you to be devious or aggressive. They are building blocks from which any career is actively assembled.

Assertiveness

This entails actions like making demands, setting deadlines and checking up on others. An assertive person is not expressing anger or hostility, they are calmly insisting on their view. Insofar as they impose it, they do so by reasoning, a firm manner and, if necessary, the threat of legitimate sanctions or adverse consequences. Being assertive indicates that you are not prepared to back down and that you understand alternative views, but are not swayed by them. This is not bullying, it is not actual coercion, although implicit or explicit indications are made of the costs of non-compliance.

It is sometimes mistakenly assumed that assertive people are conspicuous extroverts. This is not necessarily the case. One middle-ranking woman manager whom I interviewed is quiet, with a fringe behind which you cannot always see her eyes, and speaks with a mild voice. Popular with colleagues, nothing seems to faze her. Whereas such 'nice' people can run the risk of having work dumped on them which no one else wants, ending up working long hours for little recognition or reward, she is highly skilled at saying 'no' to requests she does not wish to take on. She knows what is best for her, as well as being a team player.

Ironically, when I interviewed her, beguiled by her mild manner I was concerned that she might lack assertiveness and found myself trying to persuade her to go on an assertiveness training course. Many courses in political skills are of doubtful value but these ones are often highly effective. With great deftness she rejected the idea, making it clear that she was confident she had no need of that help. I had misread her badly because I persisted. She gave me a stern look and in a flat, emotionless voice asserted that 'No, thank you, I don't think I will be doing one of those courses', then changed the subject.

The astute are better able to read with whom to be assertive, when and where*. For example, Stanley worked in a commercial law firm and found himself in an awkward position when a senior partner sent round an email to all juniors stating that they would be considered for an unattractive secondment to a foreign country unless they came to him and explained why they shouldn't be. The boss's PA was immediately inundated with requests for meetings with him by juniors hoping to make the case against it being them, so career-limiting was the role. Stanley carefully avoided being first in this queue and quizzed his peers as to what arguments had held water. His initial plan was to argue that, having only recently become engaged to his fiancée, it would be inappropriate. However, one of his peers had tried that unsuccessfully. The boss was a top lawyer and a supremely skilled advocate, highly aggressive and domineering. He would only be swayed by powerful arguments backed by evidence. Armed with them, Stanley went in, stood his ground and after forty-five minutes of cross-questioning, his case was accepted.

Most of the risk attached to assertiveness is when it is attempted with superiors. Insisting on your position with a boss is unwise if it is clear that, however wrong they may be, they have decided on the course they are going to take. Whilst it may be strategically sensible in the long run to have registered your opposition to a plan, so that if it goes wrong there is a record that you showed your disagreement, that is all assertiveness may be able to achieve.

For example, Sofia, the MEP's intern, was smart enough to realise that her boss was compromising her when involving her in an expenses claim. There were several items that she pointed out to him were not strictly within the rules, which he admitted. She firmly insisted that she did not want to be associated with this claim and that she intended to take the position that she knew nothing about it. He was fine with this. She had astutely anticipated that this was a problem which could come back to bite her. If she achieved her longer-term goal of becoming an MEP herself and if he became the subject of an investigation, she wanted to be able to honestly protest that she had played no role in the claims.

Self-promotion

Self-promotion entails appearing to be competent and showing your colleagues your competence. Drawing attention to your talents and achievements is difficult to pull off. It runs the risk of seeming like boastfulness. There is a danger of inciting envy, competitiveness and enmity. Done badly, you come across as artificial and conceited. Done well, you come across as impressive.

Skilfully executed, self-promotion produces admiration and higher valuation by bosses. What is more, there are risks attached to not doing it: your worth may be underestimated because it is unnoticed.

You need to start with an unvarnished, astute reading of your true talents and contribution. You also need to be insightful about your current levels of political skill. Finally, you need to put the two together to work out how much to big yourself up, to whom, when.

A vital consideration is the culture of the organisation and country in which you are working. As Charlie illustrated so fully in Chapter 7, if you are in a dog-eat-dog financial services corporation, the careers of those who do no self-promotion are liable to suffer. At the opposite extreme, if you are working for a charity concerned with the welfare of the disadvantaged or disabled, where all employees are assumed to be motivated by looking after their clients, rather than self-advancement, self-promotion has to be done by stealth.

In general, self-promotion is expected in the nations* where there are insecure employment conditions, like the English-speaking ones and particularly America. This has even become true in the British civil service, where once just a whiff of it would have been frowned upon.

It has to be done much more cautiously in most Asian countries, like China and Japan, where modesty is highly valued. There, it is vital to be seen to be advancing the group, not the individual. Self-promotion is mainly achieved by subtly indicating one's contribution to the greater good of your work team and wider organisation.

Feedback-seeking

Quite a few workers today find themselves in a feedback vacuum, working from home or largely communicating by phone or email with peers, employees or supervisors. The lack of objective measures of productivity for the average office worker also makes it hard to evaluate whether or not they are doing things correctly.

There are some solid research findings regarding feedback-seeking*. Three basic motives have been identified. The **instrumental motive** aims to achieve a practical goal, like getting a pay rise, or to learn how to perform better. The **ego-based motive** is to achieve an emotional goal: to defend or enhance a fragile ego. The **image-based motive** protects or enhances impressions that others hold of you.

Regarding the instrumental motive, the studies show that people eager to improve their performance seek feedback more, and the higher the value they place on the task, the more they do it. Likewise, in a new job, people look for more information about how they are doing to work out how to improve. The tougher the tasks, the more they do so in new jobs.

The more credible the feedback source, the more likely they are to be consulted. Superiors are the most likely targets for this reason, but also are likely to be approached because their appraisal determines your pay and promotion.

Seeking feedback becomes less frequent the higher a manager's position. As your position in the hierarchy goes up, the extent and richness of feedback received spontaneously from others declines. People fear giving honest appraisals to those above them and senior managers have to be cunning to get it from subordinates.

Since success at work depends partly on understanding where you have gone wrong and how to do better, instrumental feedback-seeking is a good tactic. However, for reasons which will become apparent, we are often reluctant to seek it, either for fear of our ego being hurt or to protect our status.

In general, people strongly prefer positive feedback that bolsters self-esteem. Negative feedback can damage your pride and feeling of self-worth, especially if your identity is heavily vested in work. People with low self-esteem employ a variety of ways to avoid or distort information that hurts. If criticised they may impugn the critic's motives or simply misrepresent the criticism to themselves as not negative, then ignore it. Truly self-confident people who believe they are effective seek feedback more and are better able to cope with negative responses.

The studies also show that the extent of a person's defensiveness can be influenced by the basic beliefs they hold about the causes of their capacities. If they see themselves as fixed, genetically determined, they tend to be more defensive. If they believe they are malleable, able to improve performance through hard work and learning, they tend to be less so. Even after poor performance, the ones with the malleable self-model are more likely to seek both positive and negative feedback in the hope of finding out how to do better. The fixed kind are much more scared of negative feed-back since their logic implies they are doomed to fail, as they are unable to change their genes.

Another risk of feedback is that it might show you up in front of oth-ers, reducing your status. People enquire less about their performance if they fear it will make them seem bad. The longer someone has been at a company, the less they seek feedback. They fear that others will think they should already know how they are doing whereas newcomers are less con-cerned about loss of face – its understandable that they might not yet know what is needed or if they are matching up. If feedback results are known in advance to be going to be made public, people who fear negative appraisal are less willing to seek it.

Feedback seekers can be scared that simply to appear to need feed-back, craving a pat on the head, can harm them. They may also fear that encouraging a peer or supervisor to say their faults out loud rather than on paper will make them seem worse. Equally, others may encourage hear-ing them if they think it will be positive so that their bosses hear themselves giving those messages. Indeed, there is evidence for both these ideas: experiments show that supervisors' perceptions truly can be changed just by speaking their view out loud – both good and bad feedback – rather than merely thinking or writing it.

Interestingly, more frequent seeking of negative feedback is associ-ated with higher effectiveness ratings by colleagues. Managers and junior employees who seek it are regarded as open and responsive, likewise junior employees. Exposing yourself as someone craving positive feedback, by contrast, tends to result in lower appraisals of effectiveness.

For those who work in a different culture from their original one, it is worth noting that feedback-seeking is much less common where loss of face is a major issue, as is the case in Asian countries. In such collectivist cultures, individuals seek more feedback about group rather than individ-ual performance and will not do so via a direct enquiry, as that would bring

too much individual attention to the performer. Performers in individualistic cultures where the goal is to stand out, as is the case in America,
express a stronger desire for feedback on successes. In collectivist cultures, where the goal is to fit in, they want information on failures. These
patterns are linked to different underlying theories of the self. In individualistic cultures the self is often thought of as a set of relatively fixed inner
attributes, leading to a strong motive to see oneself in a positive light. In
collectivistic cultures, on the other hand, the self is seen as more mutable,
leading to an emphasis on hard work and self-improvement. Individual-
ists working in a collectivist culture, or vice versa, need to be aware of this.

For example, consider an individualistic American fishing for complimentary positive feedback from collectivist Asian colleagues. Both parties
could find the transaction frustrating. To the Asians, the feedback-seeking
may be viewed as selfish and rude. What is more, the provider of positive
feedback may fear they will be viewed as weak for doing so. The failure to
receive positive feedback is likely to frustrate or upset the American, especially if they have low self-esteem. Conversely, a group of Americans may
develop doubts about the competence and engagement level of an Asian
who seldom seeks or provides feedback, seeing them as a 'loser'.

Ideally, it's best to be self-confident enough to seek both positive and
negative feedback, with a view to improving performance. Defensive
reactions to negative feedback, whether because of a fragile self-esteem or
fearing humiliation in front of peers, should be avoided. Equally, fishing
for positive feedback to boost esteem or to big yourself up is unwise.

Pay and promotion negotiations

You should start with a clear picture of your real worth, of how your boss
perceives that and how far you want to push it. In this regard it is interesting
how Giuseppe, the pharmaceuticals executive from Chapter 8, regarded
his reward packages.

He points out that the further down the system, the more your pay is based on measurable performance expressed in an annual cash salary. As you rise further up, a bonus and some kind of share-based incentive scheme are introduced. If you have a group function, as he now does, heading a department, the ultimate sums are based on the financial performance of the group, calculated through the total shareholder return: share price plus dividends relative to a basket of comparable stocks in the sector. Within this broad picture, personal performance is assessed relative to the five or six objectives he is set at the beginning of the year, although finding measurable metrics in his line of work is very hard, so ultimately, he says, it comes down to 'Does your boss think you were doing a good job?'

Throughout his career, bosses have used scales to assess performance, such as one ranging from 'poor' to 'improvement needed' to 'good' to 'exceptional'. Nearly always, he scores around the good mark, hardly ever exceptional. He believes that is because he is not prepared 'to invent work'. He likes to come home at a reasonable hour. He has never played the 'jacket on the back of the chair' game, or pointedly been the last person to leave the office. He regards that as a total waste of time. He despises people who work for him who play those tricks. He is conscientious but he is not willing to pretend to be more so than is really the case.

At the beginning of his career, he admits he could have improved his score by such manoeuvres. But as soon as he rose higher, he decided what mattered most was the kind of pay grade he was on, the result of promotions. Even if he did exceptionally well on a lower pay grade, he would still get less than if doing reasonably on a higher pay grade. His focus, therefore, was always more on gaining promotion than on maximising his reward package. The multiples of basic salary that are awarded once you get to the top, he says, 'are absolutely phenomenal'. He has yet to get there but is satisfied by the amounts he obtains as a senior manager, which are huge compared with the national average wage.

Giuseppe feels passionately that it is a terrible mistake to concern yourself with what your peers are paid. He knew a man with a senior position like his own who was generally a decent, likeable person, as well as being intelligent and interesting. His best friend in the office, they spent a lot of time chatting together. The great blight in this man's life was his relative pay: who got what and what options scheme they were on. Giuseppe was cagey about the details of his reward package, without wanting to be dishonest, whereas this man was always very open about his. Being paid more, Giuseppe was careful not to tell him the details. This man was still relatively young and had no children. With no family-related outgoings like school fees to pay, he was on a massive income, able to indulge in unlimited fine dining, first-class air travel and fast cars. Yet he was consumed with envy when he eventually worked out exactly what Giuseppe was on and there was non-stop whining about other people in the business whom he felt he outperformed. He did a good job but Giuseppe commented that he was, 'Fucking well paid, let's not beat around the bush. And if he hadn't known what anyone else was paid, he would have been happy. Because he knew, it ate him up.'

If he ever becomes a CEO, Giuseppe says he will make it a disciplinary offence to reveal even your basic salary to any of your colleagues. He says, 'The only reason anyone tells how much they earn is if they are disgruntled or to show off. Frankly, I am paid lots of money and I don't want to know what anyone else around me is paid. It could make me unhappy. I am happy, why would I want to be unhappy?'

Regarding the actual meeting to discuss pay with bosses, Giuseppe also has a useful tip. 'When people negotiate over pay, they always do it when their boss is sitting across from them with the letter telling them what they are going to be paid. That's too late. The time when you negotiate is halfway through the year, when you say, "Things have been going pretty well but obviously I will be looking for a decent pay rise this year because I haven't had x, y and z for the last three, and I know what Bloggins is paid, down the road."' This is a simple but effective approach. By the time you are in the annual meeting to decide your pay, the boss has more or less made a decision. You need to have done the spadework long before that meeting.

An important factor is your reading of the overall state of the organisation you are in, astuteness about its past and future, and about the gap between the official rhetoric and the reality. Samuel, a junior manager, was told that he should expect to be paid about half of what he brought into the company, the other half represented as paying for the support functions of his role – IT, secretarial and so on. This was the rationale, but it did not work like that in practice. Believing it, he went out and found about £100,000 of business for the company. At that point he was paid £35,000. When it came to the annual pay negotiation he pointed this out and asked for a concomitant bonus. He was only offered 10 per cent of his salary, whereas having brought in £100,000, it should have been half that figure if the rules were being followed. At first he argued strongly about this, but it was a good example of how neither rationality nor conscientiousness are enough to win an office argument. Eventually he worked out that the company had originally intended this system to be implemented but that because it was failing and moribund, it was incapable of doing so.

Realising that the official account of the system and the reality were quite different, he did not make the same mistake the following year. He went out and obtained an offer of a better job and immediately he got the pay rise he sought. One of the few really reliable pieces of evidence regarding both pay and promotion is that those who move company frequently do better.

What was more, he had prepared the ground by making big efforts to convince his boss that he was working hard, even though, relative to the efforts of the previous year, he had been slacking. His conclusion was that 'What you get is based on how much they like you, big time. In theory it's how hard you have worked too, but creating a perception of working hard is more important than the reality. It's also important how likely they think you are to leave.'

Another factor to be borne in mind in the run-up to pay negotiations is sabotage, as was discussed in Chapter 7. Whilst you may not engage in it, there is always the possibility that others do. One autumn, Samuel was puzzled when a rival sent round an email complaining that he had not done a particular piece of work. There was no substance to the claim and he was able to rebut it. The purpose was clearly to diminish his success so that a bigger slice of the pot would go to the rival.

The key to pay negotiations, therefore, is to have prepared your ground well before you go into the decisive meeting. You need to be well thought of by your boss, personally and professionally, and they need to be fully apprised of what you have contributed (or the perception of you as a hard-working and substantial contributor to the pot needs to be there, whatever the reality). You need to make sure they are aware you could be head-hunted if they do not meet your demands. Alas, above all, you need your boss to like you and enjoy pleasing you*.

Networking

Networking means forging links with useful people within your organisation and related ones. Beyond the peers, subordinates, bosses and outsiders that your tasks bring you into contact with, you need to have relationships with people who may have no immediate practical purpose but who may do so in the future. Exchanging information with them and establishing your readiness to consider future possibilities is a vital component of most successful careers. Networkers build strong alliances and coalitions*, resulting in social capital that can be called upon, as required.

Chameleons and extroverts are especially likely to be good at this* but almost anyone is capable of it. The convivial, humorous and affable* find it easier than people without these characteristics, who can, nonetheless, train themselves up to do it.

Those who are thinking ahead, beyond their current role, have in mind a narrative of possible career scenarios. They can picture how others who currently are of no practical advantage to them, perhaps in a department which is unrelated to their present one, or perhaps working in another company altogether, how these people may be useful in a future situation. Part of these relationships entails establishing who is good at their job – for example, you might need such a person to work for you in the future – and who you feel comfortable with. Equally, through networking you learn who to avoid.

It starts within the organisation where you work. Alongside its official hierarchy, there are always social ones which more or less affect career advancement. For instance, Samuel, the junior manager, found himself on the edge of a sociable group who looked after each other. If you wronged one of them it was as if you had wronged all of them, very like at school. This applied even to people high up the organisation, their life could be made hard if they wronged someone in that group. If someone had been upset in the group, like a girlfriend of one of the members, they could make people feel uncomfortable. Others who wanted to be in the gang would also shun the supposed criminal.

The group started organising formal social events, which impressed the senior management. There was a charity for people working in this profession. The group would arrange enormous bashes with famous bands singing and auctions for expensive holidays. The CEO would be there bidding £30,000 for a new set of tables or a week on a West Indian island for £20,000.

Being in the group led to contact with these senior people, in itself an important advantage. Some of the group were deliberately doing this for career advancement, others would initially see it as like a school or university friendship gang, just wanting to be in the in-crowd. At the events they would meet the head of this or that department from America or Asia, and after that they would realise the usefulness of that event. The personal and professional got blurred.

Forming these kinds of groups, whether social or professional, is known as coalition building. Networkers do it all the time. Coalition tactics entail using peer or subordinate support of a position taken or resources requested, counting on a 'strength in numbers' approach. Even senior figures may be affected by the pressure from sheer weight of numbers.

Networking can be made easier by prior advantages due to family contacts. Giuseppe, the pharmaceuticals executive, is an expert networker and has benefitted in that way. He has been careful to cultivate a wide circle of contacts, including some very powerful ones. He accepts that advancement is partly a matter of who you know, not just what you know or how good you are at your job. For example, after starting at a new company he sensed that one of the senior managers was a bit prickly. However, a couple of weeks later the manager came up and said 'I just had lunch with Mr X. He was speaking highly of you.' This was a highly esteemed and powerful figure with whom Giuseppe had both personal and professional links. Ever since then the prickly manager and Giuseppe have got on like a house on fire. Because Giuseppe comes from a well-to-do family, and went to privileged schools and universities, he has a network of relationships stretching back a long way. Whilst none of these have led to actual nepotism, they have helped to oil the wheels of his career.

For instance, Mr X played a significant role in Giuseppe's most important job to date. He offered a reference, which gave Giuseppe a gravitas and impression of having clout that other candidates without such friends in high places would have lacked. What is more, if you have good network connections with senior figures within your organisation, it is possible sometimes to make 'upward appeals', in which you go behind your peers' back and persuade a patron or well-disposed senior executive to advance your schemes rather than those of your rivals.

For workers today in many professions, headhunters are a vital group to network: the more obscure your area of expertise, the more important they can be. Giuseppe maintains that you must be quite tough and cautious with them, beneath the schmoozing. He warns that, 'Every interaction you have with them gets written down. All the big headhunting companies have good customer relations management systems, analysing their clients and customers. They have a "spooky" knowledge of you and the things you might have said. They are very good at getting stuff out of you about your colleagues. They do that thing of saying "Oh yes, your marketing director, what's her name?" and suddenly you find yourself spouting lots of stuff about her. It's classic spy stuff, basically. If you are conscious that you can play the game, you are giving them a bit of information, it makes you a useful person for them to network with. If you are not actually talented it won't make any difference to whether they get you jobs but it's a way to give them a reason to stay in touch.'

Giuseppe found that when they tapped him up he was careful to keep the connection going. He makes sure he attends industry events or drinks organised by them. He does not go to many work-related events but for them, he makes the time.

Once they engage with him about a possible job, he believes in pressurising them to be forthcoming about what is happening, being assertive. For example, one firm put him forward for a post which he did not get. They gave the reason that he could not have started immediately, whereas the successful candidate could. However, Giuseppe did not feel it was completely clear what had happened as they gave him contradictory feedback. After the interview with them he had been told it had gone well, yet a few weeks later the message was less positive. He was unable to get a clear picture of what had gone wrong but because he had made such an effort with the headhunting profession, another supplied the inside story. This was a man he had known for many years and sent a couple of people who had turned out very well. A seed planted through networking now bore fruit. His pal was able to find out that Giuseppe had not been put forward for the job at all, even though he had the best CV for it, the right track record. Subsequently, it was this same headhunter pal who got him the job he had always wanted.

In the end, if you are not ambitious you will not bother with networking. In the vast majority of professions, for those who want to reach senior posts, it is indispensable. Alas, if you loathe small talk or find socialising dull, you will find it tiresome. It is one of those areas where, if you really are ambitious, you will have to change yourself. Some kind of short-term therapist should be able to help you with improving your skills in doing it, and enable you to find aspects of networking that are enjoyable and help you to overcome any blocks you may have. This is worth doing if you are ambitious and it is holding you back.

Reputation-building

Professional reputation is defined as the positive and negative beliefs that are held by your peers regarding your abilities, personality and future behaviour. Your reputation is mainly the product of first-hand experiences that others have of you, be they at meetings or working together, but also when gossiping by the coffee machine or in the pub or at other informal events. Networking is therefore critical in building reputation. It is significantly affected by what your peers say to each other about you. This may or may not be based on one of the peers' first-hand experiences. In the case of chief executives of large companies, for example, many of the employees will never have met them and much of the reputation is based on hearsay.

Both within your organisation and within the wider field* in which you work, reputation strongly affects promotion prospects, new job offers outside your company and the amount you get paid. People with favourable reputations are regarded as more legitimate, competent and trustworthy. They are accorded more status and regarded as more effective. As a result, they accumulate more power and influence, and win more professional autonomy and latitude regarding their decisions.

Reputation has a benign effect on your career in several ways. For example, the behaviour of individuals who are perceived as reputable is more frequently attributed to altruistic motives. It is regarded as benefitting the unit or organisation as a whole, which is likely to result in higher than average performance ratings from supervisors and peers. In addition, good reputation reduces uncertainty. It leads others to make assumptions that your future behaviour will be reliable, effective and otherwise admirable. The studies confirm that office politics is the main cause of good reputation*.

Reputation is particularly important if you are in a leadership role*. Three factors have been identified as being critical for what reputation a leader gains.

Impressive educational records are an important signal and their value is greater if from a top-tier institution. The connotations associated with them (selectivity, quality) have reputational benefits for all, but interestingly, this is even more so for women and people from ethnic or other minorities. For leaders from these groups, it seems to act as the strongest validation. Second comes your networking ability, so that leaders who have networked well have better reputations. Third comes your style, the manner in which behaviour is expressed rather than the behaviour itself. Affability, perceptiveness, self-control and proactivity contribute most to political effectiveness, in turn making for a winning style.

Being a go-getter, it may be seen, does not require you to come across as a hungry and ambitious person. The key is to override any tendency to be passive whilst at the same time, being astute and effective in using go-getting tactics. If alert and up for it, go-getting will greatly improve your career prospects.

Chapter 11

Virtuosity

It should be clear by now that it is not enough to be a dutiful, talented and nice person in order to succeed in your career. Having said that, virtuous traits – conscientiousness, honesty and rationality – used effectively can obviously benefit you. To some extent, whether you are truly virtuous in these ways is less important than whether you are perceived to have these traits. From an office political standpoint, virtue has to be analysed as a form of impression management. Strictly speaking, even authenticity can be regarded as a strategy.

Conscientiousness

There is solid evidence that, on the whole, people who work hard* are more likely to earn more and rise higher than those who do not. However, we all know plenty of hard workers who seem to achieve less than their diligence might lead one to expect, because they lack political skills. There are also people who work too hard, the obsessive workaholics who get too close to the job, have no life and become ineffectual because they cannot see the wood for the trees. Over-conscientiousness is bad for your physical and mental health*.

It is important to ask whose interests your conscience is serving. If you are feeling you must do everything in your power to serve the organisation, to give them a fair day's work for the pay you receive, fine. But you must also be aware of your duty to yourself as a whole person who needs work to be a sustainable part of a rich life*.

As with everything else, political skill is important. Being dutiful in your service to the company will not be rewarded if your boss does not notice it. For instance, a middle-ranking manager in a clearing bank started his career with the idea that all he had to do to succeed was to work hard. He quickly learnt it was not that simple. His job today entails periods of intense activity followed by relatively little work. He has developed a policy of pointedly telling everyone when he is working really hard. He would never have done that when he started but nowadays, if he is working past ten in the evening he will let everyone know about it in advance and, afterwards, be sure to let drop that he has done so.

He believes that, as a junior, you have someone above you who has someone above them who has someone above them who decides everyone's wages. If you don't tell anyone you are working hard, your manager will probably know, but none of the others will. If you tell everyone you work hard, the chance of the person at the top hearing about it is greater.

He has also noticed that the timing of when you work hard is important, dating back to his schooldays. If you worked hard for the first two weeks of term, preferably scoring 20 out of 20 on tests, getting homework in early and asked intelligent questions, it can take the teachers the rest of the year to work out you have been slacking. So in his present job, he always works really hard from January to April, the months in Britain with inclement weather. When it gets to the bonus appraisal time in the autumn, he believes his bosses still assume he is working hard, even though he has eased off during the summer. Towards Christmas, he says, 'I do bugger all.'

It is advantageous to be perceived* as not purely conscientious when it suits your interests, to be seen as someone willing to also work hard in the interests of colleagues and the organisation: someone willing to get involved in whip-rounds for leaving presents and other activities that are *pro bonum publicum*. A selfish concern with your own interests can result in being classified as only out for yourself, no matter how diligent you are. If your boss and peers find you reluctant to do anything that will not benefit you personally, word gets around. Whilst you may be a stellar performer and that may result in some extra rewards, your adverse reputation can damage longer-term promotion prospects.

Honesty

To some extent, everyone struggles with the tension between what they truly feel and the face they must present to the world. In nearly all situations, life is a compromise. In professional life, one of the happiest resolutions to this can be to adopt the posture of being honest and authentic. The extent to which the actor admits to themselves it is a posture will vary and it becomes unsustainable if it is downright fraudulent, in which you are presenting yourself as an Honest Joe, when engaging in deceit (allegedly so, for example, in the case of Tony 'I think people know I'm an honest kinda guy' Blair). But to aim to be honest and to see oneself in that way with some justice is a comfortable emotional place from which to start the day and it can prove fruitful as a political strategy.

Giuseppe, the pharmaceuticals executive, is an example. He claims that he has always been 'amazingly up front with my bosses'. What is interesting is the way in which he represents this to himself because he genuinely does not believe he engages in deception, although inevitably he sometimes does so, apparently unaware that it is the case.

For example, he felt genuine affection for and loyalty to his patron, Carlo. However, after being at that company for several years, it was his greatest wish to obtain a similar position in a larger company that was a competitor, one that Carlo loathed. When that job came up, he sneaked off to be interviewed by a headhunter. As chance would have it, during this meeting his phone kept buzzing so persistently that he felt he had no choice but to answer it. Excusing himself, he took the call. It was Carlo on the line, who said 'Well, that wasn't very nice, was it?' Fortunately, this was not a reference to the fact that Giuseppe had been caught red-handed flirting with a competitor, Carlo was referring to an international incident that had affected the company's share price. Giuseppe had to terminate the interview and withdraw himself from consideration.

In telling me this story, Giuseppe reported no unease about disloyalty to Carlo. A couple of days later when the crisis had died down, he went into Carlo's office and said, 'Oh, by the way, this is where I was, this is what I was doing, and I have withdrawn myself.' Apparently, Carlo was 'totally fine' with that.

Explaining this use of honesty as a strategy, Giuseppe's first point was simply that he wanted Carlo to know he had not been asleep on the job, to explain why he had not immediately answered the phone during the crisis. But he also did it to plant the seed that he would be leaving in around a year's time. He commented that, 'You have to always let your boss know where you are.' Apparently Carlo's reaction was 'I totally understand, it will be a great opportunity'. Giuseppe felt it was also helpful to be honest in that Carlo would believe him when he now said he was going to stay, would trust him. In effect, Giuseppe was saying it was not odd that he was leaving after so long when tempted by this fantastic opportunity but that he was being loyal.

Of course, in relating this sequence of events to me Giuseppe had lost track of the fact that he had been disloyal. What if the headhunter had put him forward for the job and he had taken it? In his retelling of the story, to himself as much as to me, he saw himself as having been Honest Joe, but the reality had been he was deceiving his patron. When pushed about this he maintained that he had always had an honesty policy in his dealings with all colleagues. He could think of almost nothing he would not be open about. Okay, he would lie if asked to betray a confidence and he was of the view that it was best for everyone if people did not reveal their salaries, to prevent discontent. But apart from that, it was honesty all the way. When I pointed out that he did not tell Carlo he was going to see the headhunter or tell him where he was when the phone call came through, he told me that he regarded omission as different from dishonesty.

What I interpreted Giuseppe to be really saying was that he avoids barefaced black lies and cannot imagine a situation where his political skills would fail him so badly that he found himself being forced to tell one. In this sense, possibly, he actually is as honest as he believes. However, it is hard to conceive of how he could survive without telling plenty of white lies and lies of omission, and in this sense, is probably guilty of frequent daily dishonesty.

What works well for him, though, is that he does have a moral map and sticks to it. Unlike a constant chameleon, he is able to stay true to himself, though he must have to bend with the wind sometimes. This strategy probably feeds his career success. Despite the fact that his ambiguous role in quoting prices to his chief executive and to the suppliers of commodities means he is constantly having to mislead two different parties, he manages to feel he stays honest and, within the rules he has set himself, I daresay he does. If he feels honest, that subtly is conveyed to his colleagues, so they trust him, which is particularly vital in his role.

The ingratiatory tactics of flattery, favour-rendering and chameleonism all carry with them the risk of dishonesty and inauthenticity. In the long term, these can come back to bite you* if you get found out, and harm your career. And – at least as important – continuously betraying your true self is hard to sustain, as star actor Charlie discovered. Whilst honesty can work as a soft tactic, making you seem credible, if it is being feigned too much or there is too much self-deception, it will end in tears. Staying true to yourself as much as possible not only seems a good idea personally, ultimately it is a good plan, professionally.

Rationality

Rationality entails making a good case* that is well argued and based on sound information. Alas, by no means does the rational case always win the day in the workplace. Nonetheless, there is some evidence that when pursued astutely, it can swing things.

It would be lovely to imagine that it would always be that way but as everyone knows, many factors other than the rational affect such everyday matters as which products get sold, how they should be promoted or who is going to get a pay rise. Given that so much depends on the relative organisational power of the various decision makers, it is vital not to become overly attached to rationality.

I have never forgotten being told by a New Labour cabinet minister how shocked he had been by the degree to which personal and office political issues influenced outcomes on major matters. He told me that ridiculous factors could affect it, like if the prime minister happened to be in a bad mood or the random absence through illness of a key civil servant from the decisive meeting. He was amazed at how frequently the most rational case for the public good did not prevail.

You might imagine that in the world of business it would be different, that the costs and benefits would usually triumph. Alas, it is not so. Turf wars between departmental heads, patronage from senior executives, personal enmities, a whole host of more or less irrational factors often influence the final decision about a particular business decision.

When it comes to rationality, you should always remember that although you may win the battle through your superior ideas and evidence, that does not mean you will win the war. On all occasions in the workplace, before you make your rational case in an important situation, you should ask yourself what precisely you are hoping to achieve. Just because you are right about something does not mean it is the correct thing to say.

For example, a health service administrator was in a meeting with a senior doctor who was making the case for extra funding for his speciality. The administrator had already presented graphs, circulating books of appendices as additional support, showing that there were several other specialities in much greater need of the money in question. On a rational basis, the public and the hospital itself would be far better served by doing as the administrator suggested. However, it was also abundantly clear from the way the other people in the meeting were reacting that, for their own complex office political reasons, they were going to back the doctor. The administrator realised that on this occasion, persisting with rationality was not going to achieve anything. Having ensured that the issue was properly minuted for future reference, the administrator chose to remain silent. This showed political skill.

If you are someone who is conscientious, honest and rational*, and who regards office politics as antithetical to these traits, think again. Assuming you want to get your way in the workplace, you may be betraying yourself if you do not use astuteness and appropriate tactics to advance your cause. Whether you are a dinner lady, a primary school teacher or an aspirant executive, you will not be betraying your moral code by following the advice in this book – becoming more aware of yourself and others, and using that information to further your interests.

Chapter 12

Dirty Tricks

Anyone who has ever worked in an organisation – in other words, nearly all of us – knows that dirty tactics are common and can make a big difference to how successful you are, for good or ill. As you will see, they can be ethical and highly beneficial to the organisation, as well as to your individual career. Executed incompetently, they are liable to backfire loudly and harmfully. Done malevolently or unscrupulously, there can be penalties too.

I outlined the dirty trick of sabotage in Chapter 7, illustrated through Charlie's story. Other tactics that amount to dirty tricks include blackmail, defamation and deception. Most of us feel uneasy about doing any of them and leave it to the triadic individual to engage in them. At the very least, though, you need to understand that even if you do not use them, others may do so. You need to be able to suss that out when it happens. What is more, dirty tricks are not necessarily as black and white as you may think. There are circumstances in which they are morally justifiable. To be clear then, there may be occasions on which you should use dirty tricks, rare those these may be. Also, it's vital you allow yourself to attribute them to others, without becoming paranoid! Unless you realise that sometimes people will engage in these manoeuvres, you can leave yourself open to them, and, defenceless, be destroyed by them.

Blackmail

This is almost the diametrical opposite of favour-rendering. As opposed to offering to help someone else in the hope that this favour will ultimately be returned, blackmail aims to coerce the target person to do as you wish by threatening them with harm. Although rare, there are circumstances under which it is both legitimate and effective*. It is also important to consider how you would deal with it were you to be threatened in that way.

Sofia, the young intern to the MEP described in Chapter 8, had some chilling blackmail tales to tell. In particular, she described how Friedrich, a German lobbyist and speechwriter, has managed to use blackmail to become selected as a future candidate for a safe MEP seat. He also recently obtained a lucrative and powerful lobbying post, making him responsible for the publicising of a major policy initiative, by the same means.

Although she is careful to say that she does not regard him as a friend, she believes she knows him well, having taken care to cultivate and get on well with him. People in the EU parliament pay close attention to what he says. He is often to be found in attendance at crucial meetings to which outsiders would not normally have access. He is a mine of information about delicate policy matters and the personal lives of those who work at the EU.

Sofia regards him as deeply objectionable: a lecherous, crass, malicious man, 'an arsehole'. Almost without fail, when she goes for a drink with him, he will make lewdly suggestive remarks, which she deflects. If she is trying to find something out, for example, he will say 'I will tell you that if you let me put my hand up your skirt.' She does not regard him as very professional in other ways either, often turning up late for meetings and quite sloppy in his thinking. He is neither especially quick-witted nor at all intellectually gifted. He is a poor chameleon, doing little to adapt his persona according to the company he is in. Yet he has an excellent memory and he is a sponge for information, which he constantly gathers and retains. Widely reviled, he has nonetheless succeeded and is likely to continue doing so. The main, perhaps sole, reason for this is his constant use of blackmail.

His contacts with the press and with political Internet websites are so extensive that there is no one in the EU who does not fear him. He has made himself invaluable to the media. However much they may dislike him personally, too many of their scoops and too much of their reliable inside information comes from him. He is able to do this because the politicians and their support staffs provide him with advantageous access to information. They do that because they need his inside knowledge and use him to pass damaging information about adversaries to journalists. But they also do it because, at other times, he threatens them with dangerous revelations unless they tell him what he wants or act as he wishes. He is a lethal middleman.

As a result, socially he knows who is sleeping with whom, and politically, he knows who has betrayed whom, and who is plotting to do so in the future. This web of gossip and facts has been woven over a good many years.

The prime example of how he used blackmail to advance himself was in obtaining his role as lobbyist on a major policy initiative. There were several people responsible for deciding who should have that role. One of them had been having an affair that he did not want his wife or constituents to know about. Another did not want it revealed that he had leaked a damaging story about his leader. Friedrich was not especially subtle in conveying to them that he wanted the job. Without going quite as far as directly threatening to reveal the information, he intimated that, in both cases, these things were known to him and that it would be such a pity if they became public. Friedrich exulted in telling Sofia all this, perhaps hoping that his bragging would make him attractive to her.

Whilst this example might seem very extreme and rare to the average reader, it is not so uncommon in some domains of work. In the space between party politics, corporations, the media and the police, there are many examples from all over the world of powerful figures using blackmail or being the object thereof. Although they do not often become common knowledge, they occur more frequently than you might think.

There is also a grey area in between blackmail and favour-rendering* that many readers will be more aware of. At its simplest, this can be a 'you scratch my back, I'll scratch yours' arrangement. When benign, this could simply be that two managers make a private deal to help each other in some way which is not advantageous to their organisation. On other occasions, colleagues may make deals with each other, in which they both agree to overlook something that might harm the other. It might be that one person implicitly agrees to keep quiet about a lost contract, in return for which, the other omits to highlight something similar when next meeting with their mutual boss. An unspoken element of entering into such arrangements is that the arrangement itself becomes a bargaining chip. If its existence came to light, damage would be done.

A simple example is an understanding which was arrived at between a manager and one of his juniors. The manager is well known in his field as the author of a highly specialised book about the marketing of engineering products. Considerable esteem has accrued to him from it. That it was largely devised and written by the subordinate is not known. The subordinate has agreed to allow this misapprehension to continue, in return for unmerited advancement and silence about a bad mistake he made earlier in his career, known only to the manager.

If ever there as an area in which astuteness is vital, it is this. Anyone going down this road has got to be extremely good at predicting how others will behave and reading their motives. The potential for these kinds of manoeuvres to blow up their instigators is considerable.

The ethical case for blackmail* arises in situations where the blackmailer is serving a greater good. Sofia, for example, can foresee circumstances in which she might be willing to use certain information against certain people where she is sure that it would be a means of protecting the public good. For instance, she knows of one scheme that is being hatched in the EU which would divert a great deal of money into a project that is largely worthless, but which would enrich the supporters of a leading politician. Under certain circumstances, she would feel no compunction in using damaging information about that politician to stop them from pursuing this scheme. Through her relationship with Friedrich, she believes she could even pull it off without her fingerprints being detected.

Defamation

As an impression management tactic*, defamation (distinct from its legal meaning) means harming another person's reputation. It can be done in a variety of ways. In the dirty world of politics, Sofia has been sent on several missions by her boss to meet with Friedrich and provide harmful information about rivals that has subsequently appeared in the media. More commonly, it is done by word of mouth within or between organisations, informally.

Hardly a day goes by in which colleagues are not explicitly or implicitly asked for opinions about the personality and competence of each other. The politically astute and effective person does not find it hard to manipulate these opportunities to their advantage. If you want to go down this road, it can be done by planting seeds of doubt or asking questions. Creating doubts about a colleague in the mind of a peer is best achieved if the peer arrives at the idea themselves. If you are asked about a rival's competence, try to start by presenting yourself as positive about them in general. Then when the chance arises, a question about their suitability for a role or task can be asked. As we saw in the case of Charlie, the star actor in Chapter 7, he was able to take advantage of cosy chats during flights with his boss to do down his rivals through subtle planting of doubts.

Defamation of competitors outside organisations is also common*. For example, a simple and effective method for dealing with a widespread medical problem was developed by a doctor. Mainly because it was so successful, it received considerable publicity. The trouble was that several drug companies had been making large profits from selling medicines that were supposed to treat the same problem, although they were actually largely ineffectual. The drug companies dealt with the threat by going to the largest charity working in that field. Because of the close links between the charity and the drug companies, it was happy to spread all manner of rumours about the doctor's personal and professional reliability. When that did not kill the method (because it worked), they created a more structural solution, getting the method declared unethical and harmful by an industry body. Since the doctor was an individual, lacking the funds for a legal battle, there was nothing she could do to prevent this.

As with blackmail, defamation carries considerable risks. Non-chameleons who regard truth telling as part of their persona are especially at risk of harming themselves by being undiplomatically blunt about the shortcomings of colleagues. Whether speaking to the person's face or to a third party, making negative comments about their personality or performance is unwise unless it is likely to serve a purpose. There is much to be said for asking yourself what will be achieved by saying (or writing) anything negative before doing so. If you hope to improve the performance of a subordinate, certainly, a frank account of the ways in which they are failing may be useful. But it is rarely the case that either peers or bosses will thank you for such feedback, and if you speak ill of them to third parties, you should always consider what the person would feel if they heard you saying these things. There is a high likelihood that such negative commentary will find its way back to the other person, creating an enemy, and to what end?

Deception

Lying has been extensively researched*. It is extremely common. On average, when white lies are included*, people lie in one out of every five of
their daily exchanges with other people. They do it less with intimates, so
it happens more at work than at home. Mostly, these are white lies, ones of
omission or where details are changed to alter the impression given. This
is often to avoid unnecessary or unwanted conflict, or to protect the lis-
tener from a hurtful truth, sugaring the pill.

Ironically, the consequences of detected deception tend to be similar
to the very ones the deceiver intended to avoid, such as loss of credibility,
loss of trust and damage to personal relationships. In general, we tend to
look upon self-advantaging lies less favourably than ones for the benefit
of others. White lies are viewed as more acceptable than deception that is
patently manipulative of others. Usually, liars report that there seems to be
no viable truthful alternative when they do it.

Sofia, the MEP intern, summarised well the attitude of many workers
to white lies. 'I haven't had to tell any actual black lies to anyone, which is
great because it goes against my moral code. I don't mind not telling the
entire truth and consciously letting other people assume certain things, so
that if the situation rebounds back to me I can honestly say "Oh no, I really
didn't say that." I didn't, they just kind of assumed it. Maybe I should have
a problem about that. But I have not had to expressly lie. Or maybe I just
choose my words very carefully.' For example, once she had assumed a
central role in the running of her MEP's office, it was frequently assumed
by outsiders that she was in fact the office manager, since Miguel, the
official occupant of the post, was so invisible and ineffectual. She would
simply not correct their misapprehension, knowing that she was deliberately encouraging them to believe something that was false, a classic
white lie.

Sofia also says that she sometimes tells lies for no rational purpose,
something that puzzles her. This is commoner than you might think:

completely random and irrational lying. For example, on some occasions she would say she was aged twenty-five even though she knew that this could easily be shown to be untrue. She has no idea why she did that. In evaluating others, you need to bear in mind that some lies are just inexplicable and seemingly motiveless (in fact, if a psychoanalyst were let loose on these incidents, there would always be a plausible unconscious reason – human beings are not rational to a large degree and unconscious motives constantly pepper our behaviour and experience).

Black lies in organisations* come in many forms, ranging from minor acts, such as exaggerating work experience on a CV, to much bigger ones, up to and including criminal fraudulence, like concealing negative financial information to deter questioning about accounting practices. They inevitably carry a much greater risk. If you have told colleagues something that is actually untrue, the real situation may emerge and unless you are able to plausibly and successfully deny having told the lie, you may well be sacked.

Tim, a skilled politician, illustrates the effective telling of a black lie. He used it to get a colleague, Julie, a powerful post. She was an outsider who had not even considered applying until he persuaded her to go for it. Tim got the headhunter to put her on the list, then had himself invited to a barbecue that a director of the company was going to, whom Tim knew well and who did not know of his role in the matter. The director ran through the candidates, and how he was going to back a colleague of his. Tim pointed out a number of ways in which this would not be advantageous to him. For example, from now on when there was a major success, whose photograph would be in the trade press? Would it be him or the colleague, who is famous for his skills in this area? When things go wrong, who will get the blame? The last thing the director wanted was an expert colleague taking all the credit, none of the blame. The director saw his point and asked who else there was, weren't the other candidates all idiots? Tim remained silent until the director mentioned that there's a woman he had never heard of. Tim said 'Tell me about her', and after listening said 'Isn't she perfect? Who on that list will depend on you most?' The director saw the virtue of this but asked Tim if he knew her or anything about her. Tim replied, 'no', a black lie. The director realised Julie would suit him, went to the chairman and they switched from his friend to Julie.

Crucially, Tim had worked out that he could square his lie with Julie. In asking her never to reveal her relationship with him to the director, he could be taking a risk. But he knew her well enough to be sure she would not let him down and after all, she was heavily in his debt.

At its most extreme, deception entails deliberately seeking to place a colleague in an indefensible position. Samantha, a day nursery worker, had become the target of victimisation from its head. This was a highly Machiavellian woman who would stop at nothing to best a colleague.

Occasionally, it was accepted practice for the workers to bring their own children to the nursery if their child minder or other carer was unable to look after them. One day, Samantha brought in her son but forgot to get the permission of the head, a standard practice that was more a matter of politeness than anything. In an extremely devious act, the head chose this as the day to do the annual fire practice. Sure enough, when all the children were counted in the playground, Samantha's son was identified. Affecting shock and outrage, the head was able to get her sacked on the basis of this infraction. That staff were normally given prior warning of alarm practices proved that the head had chosen that day knowing it would show up Samantha. Needless to say, the head denied any such intention.

Organisations vary considerably in how deceitful they are, depending to some degree on the example set by the leaders. Deceitful leaders breed cultures in which deceit is rife*. However, this is moderated by the reasons for it. The studies show that if leaders are broadly altruistic*, and are believed by their followers to be ultimately motivated by the general good, they will tolerate deceit much more than if the leader is perceived to be self-interested. Where there are cliques of senior managers who are perceived to be self-interested, the impact is even worse. On the whole, employees in deceitful organisations* have much less commitment to them. They also express much greater dissatisfaction with their work lives. Many studies have shown a direct connection between selfishly motivated leader deceitfulness and lack of trust among employees. That is expressed in poor performance, high turnover rates and an unethical organisational climate.

National structural factors are also important*. Nations with insecure employment conditions, where there is maximum outsourcing of tasks to cheaper external companies, short contracts and low pay, tend to have lower levels of trust. Leaders are more at risk of being under pressure to be egotistically deceitful, employees have strong incentives to mistrust them and each other. This is true of conditions in English-speaking nations and in some emerging economies, especially Russia. It is also found in some Asian ones, such as India and Singapore, much less so in north-western European nations and Japan.

It is a common phenomenon for both the business and political leaders of companies and nations with insecure employment conditions to present themselves as altruistically motivated. Business schools encourage such self-presentation and that altruistic presentation is indispensible for politicians. However, the very fact that the business leaders' reward packages are hundreds of times greater than the average employees' is liable to be regarded as giving the lie to this gloss. Likewise, for all the politicians' protestations, when they leave office and earn millions of pounds for apparently minimal exertion (for example, the £12 million earned by Tony Blair's companies in 2011), the electorates often draw the conclusion that they have been the victims of deceit. Since these processes have become endemic over several decades, widespread cynicism greets the pronouncements of both business and political leaders in English-speaking nations.

If nothing else, you need to be savvy in spotting the dirty tricks of those around you and protecting yourself from them. Moral outrage is not going to be enough, you need to be shrewd and, if necessary, fight fire with fire. However, a final issue now arises: how can you know where to draw the line? The answer is emotionally healthy office politics.

Conclusion

Emotionally Healthy Office Politics

What I have tried to suggest in this book is that office politics are essential if you want to have an enjoyable, successful working life. If you pretend to yourself that you never engage in them, you are almost certainly deceiving yourself. Some degree of ingratiation or go-getting or virtuous impression management are inevitable, perhaps even some dirty tricks. Non-Machiavels and non-chameleons are kidding themselves that they are as pure as they would like to think. To some degree all of us have to put our interests before others and must engage in some deceit.

At the same time, I am certainly not advocating that you become a ruthless, self-obsessed manipulator. I have spent half of the book describing the evils of triadic psychology, the harm it does to colleagues, organisations and even whole nations, not forgetting the harm done to the triadics themselves.

Both triadic office politics and their converse, i.e., the pretence that it is possible to live altogether free from artifice and self-advancement, are unsatisfactory. In their stead, I have suggested ways to improve your astuteness, acting, networking and tactics: office political skills. What remains is to spell out in more detail precisely what I mean by emotionally healthy office politics. In order to do that, first of all, I need to explain what I mean by emotional health itself. I have tried to develop this concept as an alternative to the normal ones which are offered as psychological aspirations. What I do not mean is 'mentally healthy', which is merely the absence of mental illness. Nor do I mean happy, which is an ill-defined and unattainable goal that means little more than pleasure and is at best a temporary state. Also, I am averse to the words 'life satisfaction', which tend just to mean materially well off. Finally, I do not mean well-being, a nebulous idea at best.

In a forthcoming book on the subject* entitled *How to Improve Your Emotional Health*, I have put forward an alternative, the idea of emotional health, characterising it as follows:

> Emotional health is the sense that what is happening, is happening now. It is first-hand, immediate … You are, as the sports commentators put it, 'in the zone'.
>
> You feel real rather than false … You know what you are thinking and feeling …
>
> You have your own consistent ethical code which enables you to distinguish right from wrong … You have the capacity for insight into your own actions …
>
> In your moment-to-moment dealings with other people, you are a good judge of what they are feeling and thinking … You are adaptable, but without losing yourself … Your real self is as close as possible to the one you are presenting to others, depending on what is feasible. If a lie is necessary, you lie …
>
> You are spontaneous and always searching for the playful way to handle things … You are not bogged down in needy, childish, greedy, game-playing manipulation.
>
> You may suffer depressions, rages, phobias, all manner of problems from time to time. You make mistakes. But because of your emotional health, you are far better at living in the present and

finding the value in your existence, whatever is going on, making you resilient.

When people leave your company, they often feel better able to function, more vivacious and playful. Your emotional wellness rubs off on them. You are no martyr but you are widely regarded as a valuable contributor to your social and professional circles.

Of course, no one is actually like this all the time, what I am describing is an ideal to which we can only aspire. I estimate that perhaps only 5 to 10 per cent of people manage to achieve being like this, and even then, only in part for some of the time. The rest of us must settle for trying to get closer to them, without expecting the full monty. In terms of this book, the crucial point is that office politics have a part to play in nurturing emotional health, and vice versa.

If we take each of the components of emotional health, we can see that they contribute to office political skills and at the same time, that these skills are a part of being emotionally healthy.

Living in the present is a prerequisite for automatic astuteness. If you cast your mind back to Sofia, the MEP's intern, she was able to think on her feet because she was alert to what was going on around her from moment to moment. She instantly apprehended that her colleague Miguel, the office manager, was a lonely, humourless workaholic, enabling her to outwit him. She dealt with the almost daily advances of John, her MEP boss, by knowing instantly what she and he were feeling, and using that to keep him at bay. Because she lived in the present, she could manage the complicated dilemmas that daily presented themselves. At the same time, she needed the skill of astuteness in order to achieve her goals. Emotional health and that skill went hand in hand.

Incapacity to live in the present has also emerged as a major office political handicap. If you think back to Gerald, the vet from Chapter 2, it was only possible for the psychopathic Jan to deceive him for so long because he was so oblivious to what was immediately happening in the here and now. Again and again she would betray him, but because he was so away with the fairies, he could not see it. The same was true of Tom the primary schoolteacher. In both cases, they had ideals of what they were trying to achieve in their particular workplaces. These blinded them to what was happening before their eyes: psychopathic Jan was stealing Gerald's ideas, rubbishing him to key people he had introduced her to and manipulating them to suit her ends; Machiavellian Sheila, the head teacher, was implementing a devious plan to destroy both Tom and his school in order to emerge as an educational heroine. Had both of these victims of triadic colleagues been living more in the present, and less in a dream of what ought to be, they would have been better placed to achieve their goals. They also needed office political skills, which they lacked, if they were to do so, ultimately benefitting their emotional health and the greater goods that were driving them.

Insight into oneself, or the lack of it, has recurred as critical for the characters in this book. Giuseppe, the pharmaceuticals executive, displayed impressive self-awareness when responding to his colleague's rewriting of his business plan. You will recall that he had sent it to her for information; she returned it with excessively detailed commentary. His initial reaction was that she was putting him down, feeling that because he had an engineering degree she might be suggesting he lacked literary skills. Once he had realised his reaction was due to his insecurities, he was able to make an effective and appropriate response. His emotional health avoided an office political problem; his office political skill increased his chance of being emotionally healthy.

Equally, there have been numerous examples of lack of insight causing problems. A prime instance was Jill, the thirty-three-year-old in Chapter 8 who worked for the organisation arranging faith events. Whilst she was capable of self-reflection, she failed to see that her initial perception of her colleague Geraldine was incorrect because she lacked insight: Jill is someone who's childhood history (competition with her sisters) makes her liable to perceive attractive and highly educated women as rivals. Even more startlingly, Terry, the hapless therapist turned TV producer, was hopelessly unaware that his own sexual repression was driving his wish to 'liberate' others from that problem.

Fluid, two-way communication usually makes for more effective office politics. Whilst there may be specific occasions where it is tactically effective to assert yourself, this is exceptional. On others, you are best off shutting up shop and letting others dominate, such as when you have tried to use rationality to win the day but realise nothing will be achieved by persisting. But for the vast majority of the time, being open to what others are saying and determined to make yourself heard is the best place to be. Political skill will enable you to know which is the appropriate communicative mode, so your emotional health will benefit from it as well as promoting better skills. It's win-win.

Playfulness is a cardinal virtue in offices. Not only does it enable you to enjoy your daily life, it will enliven that of colleagues. As the evidence shows, people with good political skills are far more likely to emerge from stressful organisational environments with a sense of well-being. Where there is a threat of job cuts or a tyrannical boss, possessing playfulness will enable you to survive better, and remember that life is to be enjoyed, not endured. The playful (as opposed to purely game-playing) are also more able to enjoy the pretences that are sometimes demanded if you are to be tactically effective. If you have to use humour or artifice to get your way, doing so playfully will almost certainly mean your performance is better. Skill and this aspect of emotional health go hand in hand.

Vivacity is similarly helpful in being effective. At the simplest level, if you are conscientious then bringing vivacity to your efforts will make them enthusiastic and fun, rather than earnest and pedantic. This infects your colleagues, creating an atmosphere of enjoyment in meeting challenges.

It is all too easy to feel downtrodden by long hours or tedious tasks. Possessing this aspect of emotional health protects against that, which translates into more effective politics: your dynamism will help to carry you through when attempting tactical manoeuvres.

Authenticity is at the heart of emotionally healthy office politics and the nub of this book's argument. Whereas the scientific literature proposes that you must have at least the appearance of sincerity in order to function effectively, I maintain that authenticity is a much more useful idea. Sincerity is feeling something passionately, believing it is right; authenticity means you have a core sense of who you are, and what is true, real and ethical. These are not the same as sincere passion. The great advantage of authenticity is that it provides a powerful anchor for your psychology. From that safe anchorage, you can afford to adopt personae, if necessary. You will be better able to listen to other points of view and where you find your own lacking, to change. Whilst you may need to conceal your authentic thoughts and feelings from others if it is expedient, you will be more consistently yourself across differing situations. This stability radiates to colleagues, helping your reputation. It also protects you from losing your bearings, as happened to thespian Charlie from Chapter 7.

Authenticity is, perhaps, the defining feature of great leaders. They know how to dissemble, to compromise, to fight their corner. They can do this because they have a rock-solid sense of who they are and what really matters. This conveys itself to colleagues and beyond, often through subtle signals in the way they communicate.

Above all, whether a leader or not, the authentic know where the lines are between what they are prepared to do in the name of success and what they are not. During the chapters on tactics, readers may have been struggling with where these lines are. For example, neither constant chameleonism nor non-chameleonism are desirable. You may agree, but when it comes to deliberately faking a sense of communality with a colleague, how do you decide what is too much or too little? If you are authentic, you will know. The same goes for dirty tricks, go-getting and the rest of the tactics. Authenticity is the ultimate emotionally healthy assistant to office politics because it arbitrates what is real and true for you.

The conflict I have returned to repeatedly in these pages is between being true to yourself and the face you must present to your colleagues. Through the stories of the people I interviewed, I have done my best to illustrate that this is a subtle, delicate matter, most notably, the tale of Charlie, the actor from Chapter 7. Being totally false may have enabled him to achieve a certain success but in the long run, it was not emotionally healthy for him, and ultimately meant he had to give up his job. Equally, I have provided several stories of the opposite extreme, people whose lack of a sufficiently sophisticated persona prevented them from succeeding. Tom the primary school teacher in Chapter 6 had to give up his job too, albeit for very different reasons from Charlie. Gerald, the naive vet who was exploited by the triadic psychopath Jan in Chapter 2, was prevented from achieving his goals by his emotional immaturity.

What I hope you have gained from reading this book is the idea that emotionally healthy office politics can enable you to reduce the burden of emotional labour you carry during your working life. Whilst it will never be perfect, all of us can find a better fit between who we truly are and the person we present ourselves as being. If that means developing personae for different situations, so be it. There is no shame in that. There is no existential falsehood in it. Oscar Wilde was right: sometimes we are more real through artifice. Whether using a carapace to smile at an obnoxious customer at the checkout or to lie to a colleague who is trying to destroy your career, you are being true to yourself. By being more self-aware and deliberate in your office politics, you can be of greater benefit to colleagues and your organisation. And you can also vastly improve the enjoyment and fulfilment of your occupation.

Endnotes
and References

Introduction

3   **They are four times commoner**: Babiak, P. et al., 2010, 'Corporate psychopathy: taking the walk', *Behavioral Science and the Law*, 28, 1–20; see also Mullins-Sweat, S.N. et al., 2010, 'The search for the successful Psychopath', *J of Research in Personality*, 44, 554–8.

3   **People at or near the top**: e.g. Rayburn, J.M. et al., 1996, 'Relationship between machiavellianism and Type A personality and ethical orientation', *J of Business Ethics*, 15, 1209–19. For evidence that Machiavellianism peaks during junior management but declines as you get higher up, see DuPont, A.M. et al. 1996, 'Does management experience change the ethical perceptions of retail professionals: a comparison of the ethical perceptions of current graduates with those of recent graduates', *J of Business Ethics*, 15, 815–26.

4   **Senior managers are more likely**: Board, B.J. et al., 2005, 'Disordered personalities at work', *Psychology, Crime and Law*, 11, 17–32.

4   **the number of such triadic people has greatly increased**: for narcissism see Twenge, J.M. et al., 2008, 'Egos inflating over time: a
cross-temporal meta-analysis of the narcissistic personality inventory', *J of Personality*, 76, 875–901.

For Machiavellianism see Jakobwitz, S. et al., 2006, 'The dark
triad and normal personality traits Sharon', *Personality and Individual Differences*, 40, 331–9; see also Webster, R.L. et al., 2002,
'Comparing levels of machiavellianism of today's college students
with college students of the 1960s', *Teaching Business Ethics*, 6,
435–45.

For psychopathy see Twenge, J.M. et al., 2010, 'Birth cohort
increases in psychopathology among young Americans, 1938–
2007: A cross-temporal meta-analysis of the MMPI', *Clinical
Psychology Review*, 30, 145–54.

For evidence of variations between nations, see Huang, Y. et al.,
2009, 'DSM-IV personality disorders in the WHO world mental
health surveys', *British Journal of Psychiatry*, 195, 46–53; for the
range of narcissism in different nations, see Foster, J.D. et al. 2003,
'Individual difference in narcissism: inflated self-views across the
lifespan and around the world', *J of Research in Personality*, 37,
469–86.

6   **Small wonder, then, that studies show that those social skills
that make you likeable**: Margo, J. et al., 2006, *Freedom's Orphans:
Raising youth in a changing world*, London: Institute of Public Policy Research.

6   **Studies of crude measures of personality**: for this assertion and the
one that measures intelligence and similar general mental ability
(GMA) tests are less important than office politics, here is a brief
summary of the evidence:

GMA, Personality and Office Politics

It is widely assumed that being 'bright' causes success. Equally, it is presumed that certain personality traits contribute significantly. There exists a large industry measuring both these attributes for employers, on the assumption that test results can be used to help pick the right people for initial employment and subsequent promotion. Yet, despite thousands of studies into the matter, however measured, neither general mental ability (GMA) nor personality are very reliable predictors of who will succeed. As a key meta-analysis of the evidence shows, although ultimate career success is helped by hard work, it is also heavily dependent on your skills in making bosses like you (Thomas et al., 2005).

Although opinions differ as to its precise definition, intelligence can be defined as a general mental capability that includes the ability to reason, plan, solve problems, think abstractly, comprehend complex ideas, learn quickly and learn from experience. All tests of this cognitive ability are surprisingly bad at predicting who will succeed. At best, they only account for approximately 25–50 per cent of the variance in job performance (Mayer et al., 2000; see also Goldstein et al., 2002). In other words, when seeking to explain why one person is more or less successful than another, their scores on tests of GMA do not explain three-quarters to half of the difference between them.

It is true that GMA is a predictor of success in exams and, subsequently, of job performance (Kuncel et al., 2004). But the amount it is able to explain is remarkably little compared with what many people might assume. Interestingly, a meta-analysis of 109 studies showed the great importance of feelings of self-efficacy and being motivated to do well in explaining university performance (Robbins et al., 2004). Being good at reasoning or thinking abstractly or learning quickly, you might suppose, would explain a great deal of why some people do better than others. It is not so, whether you are looking at low-level employees, like shopping-till assistants, or near the top, like senior executives – the fact that one executive scores higher than another does not predict who will be best or who will go even higher.

Obviously, specialist mental abilities have to be up to a certain standard in order for a person to be accepted as a doctor or engineer or linguist. But once beyond the level required to qualify, higher scores do not measure who will be paid the most or have the most senior positions in subsequent careers.

If GMA is only a weak or moderate predictor of success, you might suppose personality would explain a good deal of what is still unexplained. Decades of research have led to the conclusion that there are five main personality traits, known as The Big 5: emotional stability, extroversion, openness to experience, agreeableness and conscientiousness (Judge et al., 2005). Emotional stability entails positive emotional adjustment and seldom experiencing negatives like anxiety, insecurity and hostility. Extroversion is the tendency to be sociable, assertive and active and to experience positive emotions, such as energy and zeal. Openness to experience is the disposition to be imaginative, nonconforming, unconventional and autonomous. Agreeableness is the tendency to be trusting, compliant, caring and gentle. Conscientiousness comprises two related facets, achievement and dependability.

Insofar as it affects success, personality leads individuals to be interested in certain jobs, as well as leading organisations to select certain individuals for them. Personality also influences individual performance on the job in a way that will lead to higher compensation, new job responsibilities and promotions into higher organisational ranks. Finally, personality influences the ways in which individuals engage in social interactions at work. Social interactions can lead to any number of outcomes, ranging from improved knowledge of the job and role to more visibility in the organisation.

Despite these reasons for supposing personality would influence success, these traits have little effect, either in combination or alone (Blinkhorn et al., 1990; Johnson et al., 2011). Even when success is divided into two different kinds, this is so. Intrinsic success entails the person's feeling that they enjoy their work and find it fulfilling. Extrinsic success is measured by levels of pay and organisational elevation. Big 5 personality traits are a poor predictor in both kinds.

In the cases of conscientiousness, emotional stability and extroversion, the evidence is inconsistent – some studies find positive effects on both kinds of success, others do not. Overall, there is a slight impact of possessing these traits on success, but it is marginal. In the case of openness to experience there is no proven consistent effect and, as regards agreeableness, it seems to reduce the likelihood (interestingly, emotional intelligence has similar effects – e.g. see Song et al. (2010) – suggesting that Mr Nice Guy does not prosper in the mostly American samples studied). Overall, conscientiousness and extroversion may be associated with slightly higher levels of both extrinsic and intrinsic career success, and neuroticism and agreeableness associated with slightly lower levels of career success.

Interestingly, there is no correlation between GMA scores and personality traits – extroverts or neurotics or whatever are not more likely to have higher or lower intelligence. The two sets of measures would appear to exist independently of each other.

It is possible that the small effects of GMA and personality merely reflect inadequate measurement of these variables. However, a great deal of money and time have been expended (and is spent by corporations) seeking to perfect the testing. More likely is that there are other factors that determine success.

An obvious one is how motivated a person is. The measures of motivation are remarkably crude but, for example, the degree to which a person is achievement-minded has been shown to have an influence (e.g. Freund et al., 2011). Likewise, emotional intelligence (EI) has been shown to predict job performance to some extent (Van Rooy et al., 2004). Given how important social skills are in a largely service-based economy, in which the large turbulence of takeovers and restructuring is a commonplace, it would make sense if EI affected success – being good at understanding how you and others feel would be an advantage, especially in times of stress. But most likely to be critical is office political skill (of which EI could be regarded as a sub-category). This has been shown to exist independently of GMA – how good you are at politics is unconnected with the scores you get on GMA tests (Ferris et al., 2001; Ferris et al., 2005). That is important: political skill is definitely not just something that bright people are better at. Lots of bright people are bad at politics, and plenty of people who do not score highly on GMA tests are good at politics. It has also been shown to have a significant effect on the evaluations that bosses give their juniors (Ferris et al., 2005). To some extent, there is an overlap between some Big 5 traits and political skills. It may be the mix of political skill with personality and a basic level of GMA that ultimately determines success, combined, of course, with the kind and extent of motivation to achieve. But of these, political skill may be the most important.

Blinkhorn, S. et al., 1990, 'The insignificance of personality testing', *Nature*, 348, 671–2.

Ferris, G.R. et al., 2001, 'Interaction of social skill and general mental ability on job performance and salary', *J of Applied Psychology*, 86, 1075–82.

Endnotes and References

Ferris, G.R. et al., 2005, 'Development and validation of the political skill inventory', *J of Management*, 31, 126–51.

Freund, P.A. et al., 2011, 'Who wants to take an intelligence test? Personality and achievement motivation in the context of ability testing', *Personality and Individual Differences*, 50, 723–8.

Goldstein, H.W. et al., 2002, 'g: Is this your final answer', *Human Performance*, 15, 123–42.

Johnson, C.E. et al., 2011, 'Spuriouser and spuriouser: the use of ipsative personality tests', *J of Occupational and Organizational Psychology*, 61, 153–63.

Judge, T.A. et al., 2007, 'Personality and career success', in Gunz, H.P. et al., *Handbook of Career Studies*, New York: Sage.

Kuncel, N.R. et al., 2004, 'Academic Performance, Career Potential, Creativity, and Job Performance: Can One Construct Predict Them All?', *J of Personality and Social Psychology*, 86, 148–61.

Mayer, J. et al., 2000, 'Models of emotional intelligence', in Sternberg, R. (ed.), *Handbook of Intelligence*, pp. 396–420, Cambridge, England: Cambridge University Press.

Robbins, S.B. et al., 2004, 'Do psychosocial and study skill factors predict college outcomes? A meta-analysis', *Psychological Bulletin*, 130, 261–88.

Song, L.J. et al., 2010, 'The differential effects of general mental ability and emotional intelligence on academic performance and social interactions', *Intelligence*, 38, 137–43.

Thomas, W.H. et al., 2005, 'Predictors of objective and subjective career success: a meta-analysis', *Personnel Psychology*, 58, 367–408.

Van Rooy, D.L. et al., 2004, 'Emotional intelligence: A meta-analytic investigation of predictive validity and nomological net', *Journal of Vocational Behavior*, 65, 71–95.

8 **Studies show that Americans who are aggressive and rude**: Judge, T.A. et al., 2012, 'Do Nice Guys – and Gals – Really Finish Last? The joint effect of sex and agreeableness on income', *J of Personality and Social Psychology*, 102, 390–407; there is also evidence that affluent Americans are less empathic than low-income ones: Kraus, M.W. et al., 2010, 'Social class, contextualism and empathic accuracy', *Psychological Science*, 21, 1716–23.

Part One

Chapter 1

14 **there has been some good-quality research**: Jonason, P.K. et al., 2010, 'The Dirty Dozen: A Concise Measure of the Dark Triad', *Psychological Assessment*, 22, 420–32.

15 **a study in 1998**: McHoskey, J.W. et al., 1998, 'Machiavellianism and psychopathy', *J of Personality and Social Psychology*, 74, 192–210.

16 **In a series of further studies**: McHoskey, J.W. et al., 1998, 'Machiavellianism and psychopathy', *J of Personality and Social Psychology*, 74, 192–210.

16 **In 2002, narcissism was added to the mix**: Paulus, D.L. et al., 2002, Machiavellianism, and psychopathy', *J of Research in Personality*, 36, 556–63. It should be noted, however, that the link between narcissism and Machiavellianism was already established: McHoskey, J.W., 1995, 'Narcissism and machiavellianism', *Psychological Reports*, 77, 755–9.

17   **This finding was repeated in 2006**: Jakobwitz, S. et al., 2006, 'The dark triad and normal personality traits Sharon', *Personality and Individual Differences*, 40, 331–9.

17   **A further study explored the issue**: Jonason, P.K. et al., 2010, 'Who is James Bond?: The Dark Triad as an Agentic Social Style', *J Individual Differences Research*, 8, 111–20.

17   **They are more likely to poach**: Jonason, P.K. et al., 2010, 'The costs and benefits of the Dark Triad: Implications for mate poaching and mate retention tactics', *Personality and Individual Differences*, 48, 373–8.

17   **They are less likely to feel intimate connection with lovers**: Ali, F. et al., 2010, 'The dark side of love and life satisfaction: Associations with intimate relationships, psychopathy and machiavellianism', *Personality and Individual Differences*, 48, 228–33.

17   **Detailed examination of their romantic style**: Jonason, P.K. et al., 2010, 'The dark side of love: Love styles and the Dark Triad', *Personality and Individual Differences*, 49, 606–10.

18   **Their impatience and need for immediate gratification**: Jonason, P.K. et al., 2010, 'Living a Fast Life: The Dark Triad and Life History Theory', *Human Nature*, 21, 428–42.

18   **Humour can be one of their weapons**: Veselka, L. et al., 2010, 'Relations between humour styles and the dark triad traits of personality', *Personality and Individual Differences*, 48, 772–4.

Chapter 2

21   **Whilst not necessarily getting to the top**: e.g. Bablak, P., 2007, *Snakes in Suits: When Psychopaths Go to Work*, New York: Harper-Collins; Stout, M., 2007, *The Sociopath Next Door*, New York: Broadway Books; Ronson, J., 2012, *The Psychopath Test*, London: Picador.

26   **A key study**: Babiak, P. et al., 2010, 'Corporate psychopathy: taking the walk', *Behavioral Science and the Law*, 28, 1–20; see also Mullins-Sweat, S.N. et al., 2010, 'The search for the successful Psychopath', *J of Research in Personality*, 44, 554–8.

Chapter 3

39   **The classic Machiavel**: Nelson, G. et al., 1991, 'Machiavellianism revisited', *J of Business Ethics*, 10, 633–9; Fehr, B. et al., 1992, 'The construct of machiavellianism: twenty years later', in Spielberger, C.D. et al., *Advances in Personality Assessment*, Volume 9, Hillsdale, NJ: Erlbaum; for the original studies, see Christie, R. et al., 1970, *Studies in Machiavellianism*, New York: Academic Press.

Chapter 4

47   **American psychologist Jean Twenge**: Twenge, J.M. et al., 2008, 'Egos inflating over time: a cross-temporal meta-analysis of the narcissistic personality inventory', *J of Personality*, 76, 875–901; see also Twenge, J.M., 2010, *The Narcissism Epidemic: living in the age of entitlement*, New York: Free Press.

47   **people don't come much more narcissistic than that**: Young, S.M. et al., 2006, 'Narcissism and celebrity', *J of Research in Personality*, 40, 463–71.

48   **Arguable plusses**: for evidence of the assertions on this page, see Twenge, J.M., 2010, *The Narcissism Epidemic: living in the age of entitlement*, New York: Free Press.

48   **National differences are the most profound**: Foster, J.D. et al., 2003, 'Individual difference in narcissism: inflated self-views across the lifespan and around the world', *J of Research in Personality*, 37, 469–86; see also Huang, Y. et al., 2009, 'DSM-IV personality disorders in the WHO world mental health surveys', *British Journal of Psychiatry*, 195, 46–53.

Chapter 5

55   **they are very liable to feel like impostors**: for a fine account of the range of imposturousness, see Gediman, H., 1985, 'Imposture, inauthenticity and feeling fraudulent', *J of the American Psychoanalytic Society*, 33, 911–36.

59   **imposture is a close relative of emotional health**: for discussion of this see chapter 10 of my book, James, O. W., 2007, *Affluenza: How to be successful and stay sane*, London: Vermilion; see also chapter 6 of James, O.W., 2002, *They F*** You Up: How to survive family life*, London: Bloomsbury.

Chapter 6

61   **Over the last thirty years**: for narcissism see Twenge, J.M. et al., 2008, 'Egos inflating over time: a cross-temporal meta-analysis of the narcissistic personality inventory', *J of Personality*, 76, 875–901.

       For Machiavellianism see Jakobwitz, S. et al., 2006, 'The dark triad and normal personality traits Sharon', *Personality and Individual Differences* 40, 331–9; see also Webster, R.L. et al., 2002, 'Comparing levels of machiavellianism of today's college students with college students of the 1960s', *Teaching Business Ethics*, 6, 435–45.

For psychopathy see Twenge, J.M. et al.2010, 'Birth cohort increases in psychopathology among young Americans, 1938–2007: A cross- temporal meta-analysis of the MMPI', *Clinical Psychology Review*, 30, 145–54.

61   **my suspicion is that triadic functioning**: see my book, James, O.W., 2007, *Affluenza: How to be successful and stay sane*, London: Vermilion; see also James, O.W. 2008, *The Selfish Capitalist*, London: Vermilion.

74   **a survey I did**: published in the *Mail On Sunday* business section, 1992.

83   **the New York psychoanalyst Brenda Berger**: Berger, B., 2000, 'Prisoners of liberation: a psychoanalytic perspective on disenchantment and burnout among career women lawyers', *J of Clinical Psychology*, 56, 665–73.

84   **and has accelerated**: for narcissism see Twenge, J.M. et al., 2008, 'Egos inflating over time: a cross-temporal meta-analysis of the narcissistic personality inventory', *J of Personality*, 76, 875–901.

For Machiavellianism see Jakobwitz, S. et al., 2006, 'The dark triad and normal personality traits Sharon', *Personality and Individual Differences* 40, 331–9; see also Webster, R.L. et al., 2002, 'Comparing levels of machiavellianism of today's college students with college students of the 1960s', *Teaching Business Ethics*, 6, 435–45.

For psychopathy see Twenge, J.M, et al., 2010, 'Birth cohort increases in psychopathology among young Americans,

1938–2007: A cross- temporal meta-analysis of the MMPI', *Clinical Psychology Review*, 30, 145–54.

88   **triadic individuals have prospered**: Boddy, C.R.P., 2010, 'Corporate psychopaths and organizational type', *J of Public Affairs*, 10, 300–10.

89   **more triadic in the last thirty years**: for narcissism see Twenge, J.M. et al., 2008, 'Egos inflating over time: a cross-temporal meta-analysis of the narcissistic personality inventory', *J of Personality*, 76, 875–901.

     For Machiavellianism see Jakobwitz, S. et al., 2006, 'The dark triad and normal personality traits Sharon', *Personality and Individual Differences* 40, 331–9; see also Webster, R.L. et al., 2002, 'Comparing levels of machiavellianism of today's college students with college students of the 1960s', *Teaching Business Ethics*, 6, 435–45.

     For psychopathy see Twenge, J.M. et al., 2010, 'Birth cohort increases in psychopathology among young Americans, 1938–2007: A cross- temporal meta-analysis of the MMPI', *Clinical Psychology Review*, 30, 145–54.

90   **factors that determine how triadic a nation is**: Foster, J.D. et al., 2003, 'Individual difference in narcissism: inflated self-views across the lifespan and around the world', *J of Research in Personality*, 37, 469–86; see also Huang, Y. et al., 2009, 'DSM-IV personality disorders in the WHO world mental health surveys', *British Journal of Psychiatry*, 195, 46–53.

91   **The form of political economy**: James, O.W., 2008, *The Selfish Capitalist*, London: Vermilion.

91   **Americans are the most narcissistic people on earth**: Foster, J.D. et al., 2003, 'Individual difference in narcissism: inflated self-views across the lifespan and around the world', *J of Research in Personality*, 37, 469–86.

91   **They have high rates**: Foster, J.D. et al., 2003, 'Individual difference in narcissism: inflated self-views across the lifespan and around the world', *J of Research in Personality*, 37, 469–86; Huang, Y. et al., 2009, 'DSM-IV personality disorders in the WHO world mental health surveys', *British Journal of Psychiatry*, 195, 46–53.

91   **through their universities and business schools**: Harvey, D., 2007, *A Brief History of Neoliberalism*, Oxford: Oxford University Press.

92   **what I call Unselfish Capitalism**: for an unselfish capitalist manifesto see chapter 12, James, O.W., 2007, *Affluenza: How to be successful and stay sane*, London: Vermilion; see also James, O.W., 2008, *The Selfish Capitalist*, London: Vermilion.

Part Two
Introduction

97   **Scientific studies have not identified one single**: For a review of different impression management techniques and their effectiveness, see Bolino, M.C. et al., 2008, 'A Multi-Level Review of Impression Management Motives and Behaviors', *J of Management*, 34, 1080–1109.

97   **Political skill is crucial**: Ferris, G.R. et al., 2005, 'Development and validation of the political skill inventory', *J of Management*, 31, 126–51; Ferris, G.R. et al., 2005, *Political Skill at Work: Impact*

on work effectiveness, Palo Alto, CA: Davies-Black; Ng, T.W.H. et al., 2005, 'Predictors of objective and subjective career success: a meta-analysis', *Personnel Psychology*, 58, 367–408; Todd, S.Y. et al., 2009, 'Career success implications of political skill', *J of Social Psychology*, 149, 179–204.

97   **One study measured the personalities of car salesmen**: Blickle, G. et al., 2010, 'Political skill as moderator of personality-job performance relationships in socioanalytic theory: test of the getting ahead motive in automobile sales', *J of Vocational Behavior*, 76, 326–35.

98   **There are at least thirty-four Impression Management strategies**: Higgins, C.A. et al., 2003, 'Influence tactics and work outcomes: a meta-analysis', *J of Organizational Behavior*, 24, 89–106.

98   **Two soft tactics**: Falbe, C.M. et al., 1992, 'Consequences for managers of using single influence tactics and combinations of tactics', *Academy of Management Journal*, 35, 638–52.

98   **people in America who act tough**: Judge, T.A. et al., 2012, 'Do Nice Guys – and Gals – Really Finish Last? The joint effect of sex and agreeableness on income', *J of Personality and Social Psychology*, 102, 390–407.

98   **Tactics also vary in their efficacy**: Higgins, C.A. et al., 2003, 'Influence tactics and work outcomes: a meta-analysis', *J of Organizational Behavior*, 24, 89–106.

98   **if you use self-promotion**: Harris, K.J. et al., 2008, 'The Impact of Political Skill on Impression Management Effectiveness', *J of Applied Psychology*, 92, 278–85.

99   **In every study**: Ferris, G.R. et al., 2005, 'Development and validation of the political skill inventory', *J of Management*, 31, 126–51;
Ferris, G.R. et al., 2007, 'Political Skill in organizations', *J of Management*, 33, 290–320.

Chapter 7

101   **To succeed in office politics you have got to be able to act**: for
an analysis of the guiles of leaders, see Gardner, W.L. et al., 1998,
'The charismatic relationship: a dramaturgical perspective', *Academy of Management Review*, 23, 32–58. See also Goffman, E.,
1959, *The Presentation of Self in Everyday Life*, London: Penguin.

103   **The scientific evidence for what tactics work in interviews**:
Giacalone, R.A. et al., 1990, *Impression Management in the
Organization*, Hillside, NJ: Erlbaum; Higgins, C.A. et al., 2003,
'Influence tactics and work outcomes: a meta-analysis', *J of Orga-
nizational Behavior*, 24, 89–106.

103   **Whilst on the whole, as you might expect, the studies show**: e.g.
Kristof-Brown, A. et al., 2002, 'Applicant Impression Management', *J of Management*, 28, 27–46.

116   **it is a fact that, overall, neither tests of ability nor tests of personality**: see review above, note p. 237, 'GMA, Personality and Office
Politics'.

116   **Contrary to what you might expect**: Ferris, G.R. et al., 2005,
'Development and validation of the political skill inventory', *J of
Management*, 31, 126–51; Ferris, G.R. et al., 2005, *Political Skill
at Work: Impact on work effectiveness*, Palo Alto, CA: Davies-Black;

Todd, S.Y. et al., 2009, 'Career success implications of political skill', *J of Social Psychology*, 149, 179–204.

117 **there is a correlation between level of education and income**: Judge, T.A. et al., 1995, 'An empirical investigation of the predictors of executive career success', *Personnel Psychology*, 48, 485–519.

117 **a great deal of this reflects family background**: Sutton Trust, 2011, see http://www.suttontrust.com/research/summary-what-prospects-for-mobility-in-the-uk

118 **Scientifically speaking, the predictive power of these tests**: see review above, note p. 237, 'GMA, Personality and Office Politics'.

124 **you have to make sure the boss does not realise**: Turnley, W.H. et al., 2001, 'Achieving Desired Images While Avoiding Undesired Images: Exploring the Role of Self-Monitoring in Impression Management', *J of Applied Psychology*, 86, 351–60.

124 **tournament payment systems**: Carpenter, J. et al., 2007, *Tournaments and Office Politics: Evidence from a Real Effort Experiment*, Discussion Paper No. 2972, Bonn: Institute for the Study of Labor (IZA).

128 **There are some interesting studies**: e.g. Harbring, C. et al., 2003, 'An experimental study on tournament design', *Labour Economics*, 10, 443–64; Harbring, C. et al., 2008, 'How many winners are good to have? On tournaments with sabotage', *J of Economic Behavior & Organization*, 65, 682–702.

128   **In one experiment**: Carpenter, J. et al., 2007, *Tournaments and Office Politics: Evidence from a Real Effort Experiment*, Discussion Paper No. 2972, Bonn: Institute for the Study of Labor (IZA).

132   **Students of business suggest that cooperation**: e.g. Chen, K-P, 2003, 'Sabotage in promotion tournaments', *J of Law, Economics and Organization*, 19, 119–40.

133   **The gap between wages received by employees**: Harbring, C. et al., 2004, 'Incentives in tournaments with endogenous prize selection', Paper No. 1340, Bonn: Institute for the Study of Labor (IZA).

133   **One analysis reveals that the larger the spread**: Harbring, C. et al., 2008, 'How many winners are good to have? On tournaments with sabotage', *J of Economic Behavior & Organization*, 65, 682–702.

133   **For instance, a study showed how the creation of the British football Premier League**: Garicano, L. et al., 2005, *Sabotage in Tournaments: Making the Beautiful Game a Bit Less Beautiful*, Chicago: Center for Economic Policy Research, CEPR Discussion Paper 5231.

136   **The evidence shows that high-flyers**: e.g. Seibert, S.E. et al., 2001, 'A social capital theory of career success', *Academy of Management Journal*, 44, 219–37.

136   **Studies show that high-flyers**: Thomas, W.H. et al., 2005, 'Predictors of objective and subjective career success: a meta-analysis', *Personnel Psychology*, 58, 367–408; see also Inkson, K. et al., 2001, 'How to be a successful career capitalist', *Organizational Dynamics*, 30, 48–61.

140   **In a study of 105 managers**: Perrewe, P.L. et al., 2000, 'Political skill: an antidote for workplace stressors', *The Academy of Management Executive*, 14, 115–23.

140   **Another study was of two large samples**: Hochwarter, W.A. et al., 2006, 'The interaction of social skill and organizational support on job performance', *J of Applied Psychology*, 91, 482–9.

140   **In a sample of financial services workers**: Hochwarter, W.A. et al., 2007, 'Political skill as neutralizer of felt accountability – job tension effects on job performance ratings: A longitudinal investigation', *Organizational Behavior and Human Decision Processes*, 102, 226–39.

141   **Perhaps the most sophisticated study in this field**: Treadway, D.C. et al., 2005, 'Political will, political skill, and political behavior', *J of Organizational Behavior*, 26, 229–45.

143   **A further body of evidence**: for a plethora of studies supporting this contention where the scientific papers are mostly available as downloads, go to http://www.selfdeterminationtheory.org

Chapter 8

146   **You need to be astute in three respects**: for the explanation of astuteness as a political skill and its correlates, see Ferris, G.R. et al., 2005, 'Development and validation of the political skill inventory', *J of Management*, 31, 126–51; Ferris, G.R. et al., 2005, *Political Skill at Work: Impact on work effectiveness*, Palo Alto, CA:

Davies-Black; Ferris, G.R. et al., 2007, 'Political skill in organiza-tions', *J of Management*, 33, 290–320.

147   **You can achieve astuteness by two psychological processes**: for a
       popular account of this phenomenon, see Kahneman, D., 2012,
       Thinking Fast and Slow, London: Penguin.

149   **With training, they can be taught to use their conscious minds**:
       Dawson, G., 2008, 'Early behavioral intervention, brain plasticity
       and the prevention of autism spectrum disorder', *Development and
       Psychopathology*, 20, 775–803.

150   **About 40 per cent of people**: Bakermans-Kranenburg, M.J. et al.,
       2009, 'The first 10,000 adult attachment interviews: distribution
       of adult attachment representations in clinical and non-clinical
       groups', *Attachment and Human Development*, 11, 223–63.

150   **it triggers a false self**: for a vivid account of such 'schizoid' func-
       tioning, see Storr, A., 1970, *Human Aggression*, London: Penguin.

150   **Depending on our childhood histories**: see my book, James,
       O.W., 2002, *They F*** You Up: How to survive family life*, Lon-
       don: Bloomsbury.

154   **Research shows that when we are asked to make judgements**:
       Chen, S. et al., 1999, 'Relationships from the past in the present',
       in Zanna, M.P., *Advances in Experimental Psychology*, 31, 123–90.

154   **If a group of strangers are put in a room together**: this can be
       inferred from Andersen, S.M. et al., 1996, 'Responding to signif-
       icant others when they are not there', in Sorrentino, S.M. et al.,

Handbook of Motivation and Cognition, 3, 262–321; Hinkley, K. et al., 1996, 'Activating transference without consciousness', *J of Personality and Social Psychology*, 71, 1279–95; Berk, M.S. et al., 2000, 'The impact of past relationships on interpersonal behaviour', *J of Personality and Social Psychology*, 79, 546–62.

165   **projecting attributes or emotions of your own on to someone else**: Andersen, S.M. et al., 2000, 'Transference', *The Psychologist*, 12, 608–9; Berk, M.S. et al., 2000, 'The impact of past relationships on interpersonal behaviour', *J of Personality and Social Psychology*, 79, 546–62.

168–9 **There is good evidence that the astute are adroit chameleons**: Ambady, N. et al., 1995, 'On judging and being judged accurately in zero-acquaintance situations', *J of Personality and Social Psychology*, 69, 518–29.

170   **studies show that, along with chameleonism, conscientiousness**: Ferris, G.R. et al., 2005, 'Development and validation of the political skill inventory', *J of Management*, 31, 126–51; Ferris, G.R. et al., 2005, *Political Skill at Work: Impact on work effectiveness*, Palo Alto, CA: Davies-Black; Ferris, G.R. et al., 2007, 'Political skill in organizations', *J of Management*, 33, 290–320.

174   **the scientific evidence regarding astuteness**: Ferris, G.R. et al., 2005, 'Development and validation of the political skill inventory', *J of Management*, 31, 126–51; Ferris, G.R. et al., 2005, *Political Skill at Work: Impact on work effectiveness*, Palo Alto, CA: Davies-Black; Ferris, G.R. et al., 2007, 'Political skill in organizations', *J of Management*, 33, 290–320.

Chapter 9

175 **Ingratiation works**: see Higgins, C.A. et al., 2003, 'Influence tactics and work outcomes: a meta-analysis', *J of Organizational Behavior*, 24, 89–106. See also Judge, T.A. et al., 1994, 'Political influence behavior and career success', *J of Management*, 20, 43–63.

175 **Chameleonism is the mirroring of another's mannerisms**: for summaries of the evidence on chameleons, see Day, D.V. et al., 2002, 'Self-monitoring personality at work: a meta-analytic investigation of construct validity', *J of Applied Psychology*, 87, 390–401; Day, D.V. et al., 2006, 'Self-monitoring at work: a motive-based perspective', *J of Personality*, 74, 685–714.

178 **Studies of constant chameleons**: Day, D.V. et al., 2002, 'Self-monitoring personality at work: a meta-analytic investigation of construct validity', *J of Applied Psychology*, 87, 390–401.

179 **it is essential to be capable of chameleonism sometimes**: evidence that they are more successful is found in Day, D.V. et al., 2002, 'Self-monitoring personality at work: a meta-analytic investigation of construct validity', *J of Applied Psychology*, 87, 390–401; Day, D.V. et al., 2006, 'Self-monitoring at work: a motive-based perspective', *J of Personality*, 74, 685–714; evidence that they make better networkers, making them more successful, is in Metha, A. et al., 2001, 'The social networks of high and low self-monitors: implications for workplace performance', *Administrative Science Quarterly*, 46, 121–46.

182–3 **However, constant chameleons are a mixed blessing**: there are a number of interesting findings – some fairly incidental, others less so – about chameleons which might give reason to suppose they are a mixed blessing:

1. As consumers, they are more materialistic: Browne, B.A. et al., 1997, 'Conceptualizing self-monitoring: links to materialism and product involvement', *J of Consumer Marketing*, 14, 31–44. They are more easily swayed by brands: Aaker, J.L., 1999, 'The Malleable Self', *J of Marketing Research*, 36, 1, 1–12.

2. They are more liable to be addicted to using their mobile phones: Takao, M. et al., 2009, 'Addictive Personality and Problematic Mobile Phone Use', *Cyberpsychology and Behavior*, 12, 501–7.

3. They are more liable to look upon lying as an acceptable tactic, especially when concerned with trying to create an image in the eyes of others: McLeod, B.A., 2008, 'Predicting the acceptability and likelihood of lying: The interaction of personality with type of lie', *Personality and Individual Differences*, 45, 591–6. They are better liars: independent observers are less able to detect it when chameleons are lying: Miller, G.R., 1983, 'Self-monitoring, rehearsal and deceptive communication', *Human Communication Research*, 10, 97–117.

4. Pupils perceive them to be better teachers: Larkin, J.E., 1987, 'Are Good Teachers Perceived as High Self-Monitors?', *Personality and Social Psychology Bulletin*, 13, 64–72.

5. They are better at three key impression management tactics: ingratiation, self-promotion and exemplification: Turnley, W.H. et al., 2001, 'Achieved desired images', *J of Applied Psychology*, 86, 351–60.

6. They get more depressed and anxious if there is a discrepancy between how they see themselves and how others see them: Gonnerman, M.E., 2000, 'The Relationship between Self-Discrepancies and Affective States: The Moderating Roles of Self-Monitoring and Standpoints on the Self', *Personality and Social Psychology Bulletin*, 26, 810–19.

7. As you would expect, they change their behaviour and self-presentation more in different situations: Snyder, M., 1976, 'Behavior and attitude: Some people are more consistent than others', *J of Personality*, 44, 501–17.
8. They rightly perceive themselves as being more humorous: others judge them so in experimental conditions: Turner, R.G., 1980, 'Self-monitoring and humor production', *J of Personality*, 48, 163–70.
9. They make more effort to seem like good organisational citizens, even though their commitment to their organisation is less: Blakely, G.L. et al., 2003, 'Are Chameleons Good Citizens? A Longitudinal Study of the Relationship between Self-Monitoring and Organizational Citizenship Behavior', *J of Business and Psychology*, 18, 131–44.
10. They are more popular with friends and with parents: Howells, G.N. et al., 1993, 'Self-monitoring and personality: Would the real high self-monitor please stand up?' *J of Social Behavior & Personality*, 8, 59–72.
11. They are more fickle in romantic relationships: Norris, S.L., et al., 1999, 'Self-monitoring, trust and commitment in romantic relationships', *J of Social Psychology*, 139, 215–20.

182 **Their lack of commitment to the organisation**: Jenkins, J.M., 2006, 'Self-monitoring and turnover: the impact of personality on intent to leave', *J of Organizational Behavior*, 14, 83–91.

182 **evidence that chameleonism is more common among senior managers**: Dobbins, G.H. et al., 1990, 'The role of self-monitoring and gender on leader emergence: a laboratory and field study', *J of Management*, 16, 609–18; Kilduff, M. et al., 1994, 'Do chameleons get ahead? The effects of self-monitoring on

managerial careers', *Academy of Management Journal*, 37, 1047–60.

182   **There are studies showing**: Mehra, A. et al., 2001, 'The social networks of high and low self-monitors: implications for workplace performance', *Administrative Science Quarterly*, 46, 121–46; Kilduff, M. et al., 1994, 'Do chameleons get ahead? The effects of self-monitoring on managerial careers', *Academy of Management Journal*, 37, 1047–60.

182   **Chameleons are also more prone to move between organisations**: Kilduff, M. et al., 1994, 'Do chameleons get ahead? The effects of self-monitoring on managerial careers', *Academy of Management Journal*, 37, 1047–60.

182   **From an employer's perspective**: see the conclusion to Day, D.V. et al., 2006, 'Self-monitoring at work: a motive-based perspective', *J of Personality*, 74, 685–714.

183   **The danger with flattery is if it is noticed**: Turnley, W.H. et al., 2001, 'Achieving Desired Images While Avoiding Undesired Images: Exploring the Role of Self-Monitoring in Impression Management', *J of Applied Psychology*, 86, 351–60.

188   **People who favour-render tend to prosper**: Falbe, C.M. et al., 1992, 'Consequences for managers of using single influence tactics and combinations of tactics', *Academy of Management Journal*, 35, 638–52.

Chapter 10

192   **The astute are better able to read with whom to be assertive, when and where**: Harris, K.J. et al., 2008, 'The Impact of Political

Skill on Impression Management Effectiveness', *J of Applied Psychology*, 92, 278–85.

194   **In general, self-promotion is expected in the nations**: Foster, J.D. et al., 2003, 'Individual difference in narcissism: inflated self-views across the lifespan and around the world', *J of Research in Personality*, 37, 469–86; Twenge, J.M., 2010, *The Narcissism Epidemic: living in the age of entitlement*, New York: Free Press.

194   **There are some solid research findings on feedback-seeking**: all the evidence cited in this section is referenced in Ashford, S.J. et al., 2003, 'Reflections on the Looking Glass: A Review of Research on Feedback-Seeking Behavior in Organizations', *J of Management*, 29, 773–99.

201   **Alas, above all, you need your boss to like you and enjoy pleasing you**: the merits of different tactics for achieving this are summarised in the review by Higgins, C.A. et al., 2003, 'Influence tactics and work outcomes: a meta-analysis', *J of Organizational Behavior*, 24, 89–106; for the importance of ingratiation and self-promotion see Ellis, A.P.J. et al., 2002, 'The use of impression management tactics in structured interviews: A function of question type?', *J of Applied Psychology*, 87, 1200–208; for role of office politics, see Harris, K.J. et al., 2008, 'The Impact of Political Skill on Impression Management Effectiveness', *J of Applied Psychology*, 92, 278–85.

201   **Networkers build strong alliances and coalitions**: Eby, L.T. et al., 2003, 'Predictors of success in the era of the boundaryless career', *J of Organizational Behavior*, 24, 689–708.

201   **Chameleons and extroverts are especially likely to be good at this**: Metha, A. et al., 2001, 'The social networks of high and low self-monitors: implications for workplace performance', *Administrative Science Quarterly*, 46, 121–46.

201   **The convivial, humorous and affable**: Ng, T.W.H. et al., 2005, 'Predictors of objective and subjective career success: a meta-analysis', *Personnel Psychology*, 58, 367–408.

205   **Both within your organisation and within the wider field**: Hochwarter, W.A. et al., 2007, 'Reputation as a Moderator of Political Behavior–Work Outcomes Relationships: A Two-Study Investigation with Convergent Results', *J of Applied Psychology*, 92, 567–76.

206   **The studies confirm that office politics is the main cause of good reputation**: Liu, Y. et al., 2007, 'Dispositional antecedents and outcomes of political skill in organizations: A four-study investigation with convergence', *J of Vocational Behavior*, 71, 146–65.

206   **Reputation is particularly important if you are in a leadership role**: Halla, A.T. et al., 2004, 'Leader reputation and accountability in organizations: Implications for dysfunctional leader behavior', *The Leadership Quarterly*, 15, 515–36.

Chapter 11

207   **There is solid evidence that, on the whole, people who work hard**: Dudley, N.M. et al., 2006, 'A meta-analytic investigation of conscientiousness in the prediction of job performance: examining the intercorrelations and the incremental validity of narrow traits', *J of Applied Psychology*, 91, 40–57.

207   **Over-conscientiousness is bad for your physical and mental health**: Van Beek, L. et al., 2011, 'For fun, love or money: what drives workaholic, engaged and burned-out employees at work?', *Applied Psychology*, 61, 30–55.

208   **needs work to be a sustainable part of a rich life**: Van Beek, L. et al., 2011, 'Workaholic and work engaged employees: dead ringers or worlds apart?', *J of Occupational Health Psychology*, 16, 468–82.

208   **It is advantageous to be perceived**: Hochwarter, W.A. et al., 1999, 'Commitment as an antidote to the tension and turnover consequences of organizational politics', *J of Vocational Behavior*, 55, 277–97.

211   **In the long term, these can come back to bite you**: Turnley, W.H. et al., 2001, 'Achieving Desired Images While Avoiding Undesired Images: Exploring the Role of Self-Monitoring in Impression Management', *J of Applied Psychology*, 86, 351–60.

211   **Rationality entails making a good case**: Buckle, G. et al., 2006, 'Some outcomes of pressure, ingratiation and rational persuasion used with peers in the workplace', *J of Applied Psychology*, 33, 648–65.

213   **If you are someone who is conscientious, honest and rational**: Todd, S.Y. et al., 2009, 'Career success implications of political skill', *J of Social Psychology*, 149, 179–204.

Chapter 12

216   **Although rare, there are circumstances under which it is both legitimate and effective**: Buchanan, D.A., 2008, 'You stab my

back, I'll stab yours: management experience and perceptions of organizational political behaviour', *British J of Management*, 19, 49–64; Li, T. et al., 2008, 'Bad apples in bad (business) barrels: the love of money, machiavellianism, risk tolerance and unethical behaviour', *Management Decision*, 46, 243–63.

218   **There is also a grey area in between blackmail and favour-rendering**: Buckle, G. et al., 2006, 'Some outcomes of pressure, ingratiation and rational persuasion used with peers in the workplace', *J of Applied Psychology*, 33, 648–65.

218   **The ethical case for blackmail**: Buchanan, D.A., 2008, 'You stab my back, I'll stab yours: management experience and perceptions of organizational political behaviour', *British J of Management*, 19, 49–64.

219   **As an impression management tactic**: Noon, M. et al., 1993, 'News from behind my hand: gossip in organizations', *Organization Studies*, 14, 23–36.

220   **Defamation of competitors outside organisations is also common**: Mohamed, A.A. et al., 2004, 'An exploratory study of interorganizational defamation: an organizational impression management perspective', *International J of Organizational Analysis*, 12, 129–45.

221   **Lying has been extensively researched**: DePaulo, B.M. et al., 1996, 'Lying in everyday life', *J of Personality and Social Psychology*, 70, 979–95.

221   **On average, when white lies are included**: DePaulo, B.M. et al.,

1996, 'Lying in everyday life', *J of Personality and Social Psychology*, 70, 979–95.

222   **Black lies in organisations**: Zanzi, A. et al., 2002, 'Sanctioned versus non-sanctioned political tactics', *J of Managerial Issues*, 13, 245–63; Fleming, P. et al., 2008, 'The escalation of deception in organizations', *J of Business Ethics*, 81, 837–50.

223   **Deceitful leaders breed cultures in which deceit is rife**: Griffith, J.A. et al., 2011, 'Subordinate Organizational Commitment', *J of Leadership and Organizational Studies*, 18, 508–31.

223   **The studies show that if leaders are broadly altruistic**: Lilius, J.B. et al., 2008, 'The contours and consequences of compassion at work', *J of Organizational Behavior*, 29, 193–218.

224   **employees in deceitful organisations**: De Cremer, D. et al., 2006, 'Self-sacrificial leadership and follower self-esteem: When collective identification matters', *Group Dynamics: Theory, Research, and Practice*, 10, 233–45.

224   **National structural factors are also important**: ILO (International Labour Organization), 2004, *Economic Security for a Better World*, Geneva: ILO.

Conclusion

228   **In a forthcoming book on the subject**: James, O.W. (to be published February 2014), *How to Improve Your Emotional Health*, London: Macmillan.

Acknowledgements

First and foremost, thanks to all the people who gave of their time and emotional resources to be interviewed for the book. In most cases, it entailed digging deep to identify the specific examples of their office political doings. I learnt a great deal from them: thank you on every level.

Thanks also to my friends, who helped me find the interviewees. They must remain nameless if the anonymity of the interviewees is to be maintained but busting a gut to help me find them can hardly have been at the top of their list of priorities, it was invaluable.

Thanks to Neil Philip and Emma Bradford for their neighbourly encouragement.

Thanks to Jemima Biddulph for editing the book at the first stage and then inspiring structural improvements, as usual, a crucial intervention.

Thanks to Andrew Kidd and Gillon Aitken for their considerable support over the long period in which this book bounced about before actually getting written.

The greatest thanks to Fiona MacIntyre at Ebury for insisting I prioritise the book. I confess to having had misgivings that now was the right time to do it; she was right, I was wrong. Thanks too to Susanna Abbott and Louise Francis for their encouragement and work in bringing the book to fruition.

As ever, thanks to my wife Clare for her forbearance but more than this, the very helpful suggestions she made for amendment of the text. Of all my books, this is the one to which she has made the most active and significant contribution: xxx.

Index

Selfish Capitalist 91, 92, 246, 247, 248
service sector:
    metrics in, lack of objective 4–7,
        70, 73–4, 116–25, 198
    prevalence of triadic natures in
        4–5
    shift from manufacturing jobs to
        4–5, 6, 73, 74
sexuality:
    acting and 123
    astuteness and 170–4
    chameleonism and 180–1
    detachment and game playing
        and 17
    equality and 136–9
    flattery and 184
    income and 242, 249
    James Bond and 17
    Machiavellianism and 17, 18, 44
    narcissists and 48
    psychopaths and 16, 22, 23
    television industry and 62–7, 71,
        231
    triadic nature and 17, 18, 22, 23
Sheila (primary school headteacher)
    85–9, 230
short-term thinking 15, 18, 48, 91,
    205
Simon (school teacher) 49–51
sincerity, the appearance of 2, 175,
    232
Singapore 224
Skinner, Frank 57
Sofia (European Union worker)
    166–74, 184–8, 193, 216–17,
    218–19, 221–2, 229
Spain 92
stable environments, seeking 40, 42
Stanley (lawyer) 192
stress:
    acting and 140–1
    chameleonism and 179, 181, 182
    employment conditions and 8
    GMA and 240
    office political skill and 231, 253
    professions and 81, 93

supplication 186
Sweden 90, 91

taking credit for what is not yours 6,
    29–34, 52, 70, 90, 119, 184,
    187, 222
television production 5–7, 28, 62–76
    awareness of triadic tendencies
        in 70–3
    chameleonism in 177–8
    dependent on skill in
        manipulating other people
        69–70
    identifying achievement in 5, 70,
        73–4
    lack of training and expertise
        within 69
    love/sex lives within 62–76
    ruthlessness and cunning in
        67–8
    six stages of 5
    triadic people in 28, 61–76
Terry (property tycoon) 42–4
Terry (TV producer) 62–3, 64–5, 66,
    231
Tim (politician) 222–3
Tom (primary school teacher) 85–9,
    230
tournament payment systems 119,
    124–5, 129–31, 132, 133,
    251–2
transactional analyst 111
triadic characteristics/people 4, 7–9,
    13–93, 227
    a vicious combination 13–19
    increase in number of triadic
        people in recent years 4, 17,
        47–8, 61, 92–3, 236, 246,
        247
triadic characteristics/people
    Machiavellianism
        see Machiavels
    narcissism see narcissism
    nations where most prevalent see
        nations and under individual
        nation name

There is currently an epidemic of 'affluenza' throughout the world – an obsessive, envious, keeping-up-with-the-Joneses – that has resulted in huge increases in depression and anxiety among millions.

Over a nine-month period, bestselling author Oliver James travelled around the world to try to find out why. He discovered how, despite very different cultures and levels of wealth, affluenza is spreading. He asks: why do so many more people want what they haven't got and want to be someone they're not, despite being richer and freer from traditional restraints? And, in so doing, he uncovers the answer to how to reconnect with what really matters and learn to value what you've already got. In other words, how to be successful and stay sane.

The Selfish Capitalist

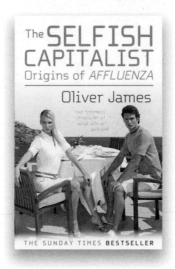

In the bestselling *Affluenza*, world-renowned psychologist Oliver James introduced us to a modern-day virus sweeping through the English-speaking world. Now *The Selfish Capitalist* provides more detailed substantiation for the claims made in Affluenza. It looks deeper into the origins of the virus and outlines the political, economic and social climate in which it has grown. James points out that, since the seventies, the rich have got much, much richer, yet the average person's wage has not increased at all.

A rallying cry to the Government to reduce our levels of distress by adopting a form of unselfish capitalism, this hard-hitting and thought-provoking work tells us why our personal well-being must take precedence over the wealth of a tiny minority if we are to cure ourselves of this disease.

£8.99 | ISBN 9780091924164
Order direct from www.randomhouse.co.uk

Contented Dementia

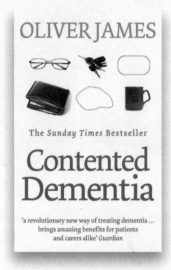

OLIVER JAMES

The *Sunday Times* Bestseller

Contented
Dementia

'a revolutionary new way of treating dementia ...
brings amazing benefits for patients
and carers alike' *Guardian*

Dementia is a little understood and currently incurable illness, but much can be done to maximise the quality of life for people with the condition. *Contented Dementia* outlines a groundbreaking and practical method for managing dementia that will allow both sufferer and carer to maintain the highest possible quality of life, throughout every stage of the illness.

The SPECAL method (Specialized Early Care for Alzheimer's) outlined in this book works by creating links between past memories and the routine activities of daily life in the present. Drawing on real-life examples and user-friendly tried-and-tested methods, Contented Dementia provides essential information and guidance for carers, relatives and professionals.

£12.99 | ISBN 9780091901813
Order direct from www.randomhouse.co.uk